*How to Sell Your
Collectibles,
Antiques,
and Crafts
at a Profit*

How to Sell Your Collectibles, Antiques, and Crafts at a Profit

Marguerite Ashworth Brunner

Rawson Associates Publishers, Inc.
New York

Library of Congress Cataloging in Publication Data

Brunner, Marguerite Ashworth.
  How to sell your collectibles, antiques, and crafts at
a profit.

  1. Selling—Antiques. 2. Selling—Handicraft.
I. Title.
HF5439.A55B78 1977   658.89'7   77-76994
ISBN 0-80256-024-X

Published simultaneously in Canada by
McClelland and Stewart, Ltd.
Manufactured in the United States of America
by The Book Press, Brattleboro, Vermont
First Edition

To Sarah Megan Pfefferle, my beautiful little granddaughter, who brought so much sunshine into my life

Contents

PART I   Every Piece Has a Market

Introduction: Collecting Things Is Profitable as Well
as Fun   3
Chapter 1   Are Your Collectibles Trash or
Treasure?   8
Chapter 2   Nine Ways to Market Your Wares   15

PART II   Turning Collectibles into Cash

Chapter 3   Advertiques   29
Chapter 4   Art   33
Chapter 5   Books, Pamphlets, Maps, Autographs,
and Manuscripts   42
Chapter 6   Bottles, Flasks, and Jars   57
Chapter 7   Clocks, Cameras, Lamps, Telephones,
and Primitives   56
Chapter 8   Old Clothes . . . the Collectible
Ones   63
Chapter 9   Coins and Stamps   67
Chapter 10   Comic Books, Magazines, and
Catalogues   71
Chapter 11   Firearms, Knives, Military Items   74
Chapter 12   Glass and China   78
Chapter 13   Memorabilia   87
Chapter 14   Musical Items   90

Chapter 15   Paper: Postcards, Valentines, Paper
             Dolls, Etc.   94
Chapter 16   Silver, Gold, Pewter, Jewelry, and
             Fountain Pens   99
Chapter 17   Toys   107

PART III   From Your Hands to the Buyer's
Chapter 18   Crafts   113

PART IV   Markets for Your Collectibles and Crafts
Antique Publications and Advertising Rates   123
Dealers and Collectors for Your Collectibles and
    Crafts   127

Index   339

PART I

Every Piece Has a Market

Introduction: Collecting Things Is Profitable as Well as Fun

It is said that we all profit from our mistakes. In this book I hope that you, the reader, may profit from some of mine. Mistakes in buying or selling collectibles can be costly. Ask the dealers you know. If they're honest, they'll admit that it is impossible to know everything about everything.

During my thirty-some years as an antique dealer, I've made many mistakes. I've paid antique prices for reproductions that defied detection by anyone but the experts. I've paid "gold prices" for old pocket watches marked 14 karat that weren't 14 karat at all, simply because I didn't know that early goldsmiths could legally mark their wares any way that pleased them, for there were no laws in this country to protect the consumer in those days.

If it hadn't been for a terrible mistake, I might never have become an antique dealer at all. I dare say that few antique dealers ever went into business with as little knowledge about old things as I had. Back then I couldn't tell one period of furniture from another. The Chippendale-chair "disaster" was the turning point of my career.

During the early 1940s, I worked on one of the major Washington, D.C., newspapers. A bad investment necessitated my moving into smaller living quarters, and, having a lot of surplus furniture, I decided to have a house sale. The furniture I owned was old; much of it had been purchased from the many secondhand shops that used to line M Street in Georgetown. I was astonished at the response from the classified ad I'd placed in a Sunday paper. I never dreamed there was such a market for good secondhand furniture. It was wartime, and good-quality furniture was difficult to find in most furniture stores.

As a result of that first house sale, I began taking phone numbers of late callers, listing what they wanted to buy and what they were willing to pay. This, I thought, would be a terrific way to supplement my weekly income from the paper. I began to scout the secondhand shops on my days off and shop for specific needs of prospective customers. I did very well, too, for I discovered there was a big demand for desks and bookcases and I could never go wrong buying them.

A short time later, I attended a country auction in Virginia. It was a rainy day, and there were few buyers present. The farmer who was conducting the auction was having a difficult time getting bids on any of the household goods. Six old mahogany dining chairs were put up for sale, and although they were very dark and not especially pretty, I bid $2 each and got them for $12. Confident that I could, at the very least, put them with a mahogany table I already had and sell them as a set, I proudly carted them home. To make a long story short, I sold those chairs to an antique dealer for $100, only to find out a week later that she had sold them for $1,000.

When she returned the blankets I'd lent her to wrap around her chairs and casually mentioned that she'd gotten $1,000 for the Chippendale chairs, I was devastated. I'd been boasting to my friend that I'd made more on that one sale than I'd made in a week on the newspaper, and this woman had made $900 and was calm as she could be. Perhaps, I thought, she was accustomed to making big profits—and if this was true of the antique business, I was definitely in the wrong business!

That was the beginning of my education, which has continued to this day. I borrowed or bought every book available on antiques. I visited shops and annoyed the clerks with questions. I visited historical houses and studied the furnishings in each of them.

A Virginia dealer recently told me, "Literally hundreds of thousands of dollars in fakes and misrepresented antiques are sold each year in the United States. It is possible to fool an expert every now and then, but for the average dabbler, it is open season. It's imperative that a collector learn to tell if an item is old and valuable or not."

One dealer has a costly reminder of one of his mistakes, a small table for which he had paid $600. It was the end of a busy "show" day, and when he spied what he believed to be an eighteenth-century oak table, he quickly paid for it and made arrangements to have it delivered to his shop. "I didn't examine it closely enough, and it was my own fault," the dealer said. "When the table arrived at my store, I found it wasn't the eighteenth-century oak piece I thought it was." When he flipped it over, he found a bottom of plywood—hardly a cabinetmaker's conventional material two hundred years ago.

Mrs. L. E. Bush of Richmond, Virginia, who has been a dealer for over thirty-five years and is an expert, was quoted recently as saying, "One of the biggest [areas for] fakes . . . is in Chippendale mirrors. Hundreds of them are coming into this country from England dated in the 1700s that aren't even fifty years old." Other dealers agreed with her and complained that there was much misrepresentation on the market by "marrying" pieces. A "married" piece is one in which parts of two pieces have been joined together in such a way that it can be represented to be a whole piece. The tops of cupboards might come from pieces whose bottoms had been damaged beyond repair, and the bottoms from other pieces whose tops had been damaged or misplaced. The "married" pieces are usually of the same wood and period, and often are hard to detect. But although "married" pieces are often beautiful, they are worth far less than they were in their original state.

One should never feel too silly about making mistakes. The experts make more than they care to admit. How often have you read accounts of museums buying phony "masterpieces"? In our time counterfeiting has extended itself to every form of art, including treasured antiques. The counterfeiters are experts, who use old materials and finishes common to the age they are copying. Many fake antiques are masterpieces in their own right—but they are not the originals they are claimed to be.

Throughout this book prices will be quoted on various items. Prices are ball-park figures, or in some cases figures the items brought recently at auction. It is important to remember that prices vary in different parts of the country. There is no way to tell exactly what a particular item is worth, because chances are it is worth more in one section of America than in another. When I had a shop in Pittsburgh, where glass was plentiful, much of it having been made in Pennsylvania and neighboring states, I found that Southern dealers would travel to Pennsylvania and pay retail prices for fine cut glass for which they were able to get much higher prices in the South. When I had a shop in North Carolina, I found that early primitive pine furniture sold for very little, while marble-topped Victorian pieces brought handsome prices. Those same pine pieces brought much more in Northern and Western states.

6

I have attempted here to bring the buyer and seller together to the advantage of both. There is, I believe, a market for almost anything you have to sell, and there are many ways to sell, some more profitable than others.

I believe the list of dealers and collectors in the back of this book will open many profitable avenues for selling your collectibles. It has been practically impossible in the past for an amateur with collectibles to sell to or even find the dealers and collectors who specialize in the items they have for sale. After an excerpt from my book *Antiques for Amateurs on a Shoestring Budget* appeared in *Woman's Day* in April 1976, there were thousands of letters requesting information on how and where to sell all kinds of things. I discovered, after days of research, that it was most difficult to find the right market for 75-rpm records, old advertising items, and the many other collectibles that the average person has to sell. The results of many months and extensive research have gone into the lists in Part IV of this book. They should make it much easier for you, the reader, to find a market for anything you want to sell.

CHAPTER I

Are Your Collectibles Trash or Treasures?

Collecting things for fun or profit is fast becoming one of the most popular hobbies in our country, and collectors are becoming younger every day. It isn't unusual to find eight- and ten-year-olds bidding competitively with adults at coin, stamp, book, and comic-book auctions and sales. Things children collected in days past (which most of us, as parents, considered junk) have become so valuable in the collecting market that adults are paying fantastic prices for them.

Bubble-gum baseball cards (the rare ones) are bringing outrageous prices. A Homus Wagner baseball card distributed in 1919 by Sweet Caporal Cigarettes sells for $1,500 today. Over 30 million baseball cards were sold in the United States in 1974.

Comic books that we criticized our children for wasting their allowances on are bringing from a few dollars up to hundreds of dollars. Paper dolls are selling today for $10 to $20 and $30. Recently I saw a 10-cent set of Shirley Temple paper dolls bring $12 at auction. The early Campbell Kid paper dolls often bring more.

Phyllis Batelle, in reviewing *Antiques for Amateurs on a Shoestring Budget,* reported in a Baltimore newspaper that her fourteen-year-old son was saving his money to purchase a $150 rare early-Beatles album cover (no record inside). This record cover is a 1966 item, which goes to prove that the valuable collectibles are not necessarily old. She says that one "antique" shop in New York City (in 1976) was selling first-edition Batman comic books for $1,250 each, cereal bowls given away at 1933 movie "bank nights" for $75 each, and tin soldiers (some dented) made around 1926 for $60 a pair.

At an emporium in lower Manhattan called Speakeasy Antiques, Beatles memorabilia is being sold for unbelievable prices. This is where Mrs. Batelle's son found the $150 album cover. Chances are if you owned one of these rare original covers back in 1966, it might have ended up in the trash, for few people stop to think about current items that may well become the collectibles of tomorrow. Newspapers headlined NIXON RESIGNS sold out on the newsstands; a day later, collectors were paying $10 for a copy of yesterday's newspaper.

It just goes to show you that there is a big difference between "junque," as advertised by dealers, and plain "junk." I have come to the conclusion that "junque" means worthless things that take on great value because of their connection or association with famous or special persons, places, or things.

A children's charity expects to raise a considerable amount of money from auctioning off a pair of boxing trunks donated by Muhammad Ali. That same pair of trunks, without the association with the great boxer, would hardly bring more than 50 cents in a thrift shop.

When buying for my shops over the years, I always tried to find out something about the former owners of the merchandise. A good story will sell a piece quicker than a good finish. A dealer I knew in Maryland during the Truman Administration had lots of pieces that he claimed had belonged to Truman Cabinet members. I used to stand aghast as I listened to him tell a prospective customer that this sideboard belonged to Dean Acheson and that table to George Marshall. I couldn't believe that people could be so gullible, but I saw him close many sales after a long dissertation about the former owners.

If you have something that really did belong to a famous person, you should have documentation if you expect to sell it for a lot of money. All buyers are not as gullible as my friend's customers. A letter from the former owner telling how he or she came to own that piece might suffice, although most buyers want more proof.

Remember, too, that because something has great sentimental value to you or your family doesn't mean it is worth anything to anyone else. Family sentiment isn't worth a plugged nickel in the antique market, unless your family happens to be famous.

Patent dates on a piece do not mean that the piece was necessarily *made* on that date. I was appalled to hear an auctioneer recently declare that a fruit jar he offered for sale was over a hundred years old and had the date 1858 right on the glass to prove it. I'm sure he knew that it was a patent date, not a date of making, but someone paid $12 for the jar even though it was very "milky" glass, or what we dealers call "sick glass." Contrary to what the auctioneer told the buyer, that jar could never be cleaned to remove the imperfection.

Imported china is far more valuable than American-made and brings much higher prices in the antique market. Marks are important in determining the age and value of a piece. Factories often changed hands over the years, and the marks on their wares were changed too. It is true that many rare pieces have no marks, having been made before the late 1800s, when it became U.S. law that pieces be marked to indicate country of origin. Antique dealers and china experts can easily distinguish between German,

English, and French pieces. There is a difference that one learns by comparison over the years.

In my early days as an antique dealer, when I knew little about many antiques, I could always recognize Haviland and Limoges china. Perhaps that was because my mother had one of the loveliest sets of Haviland I've ever seen, and as a child I was never allowed to drink from the fragile cups or to wash them after a "company" meal. One of the worst scoldings I received as a child was for using demitasse cups for a tea party with my friends. A single piece of Haviland china can be very valuable today, for there are many dealers who specialize in matching Haviland sets. Several of them will be found in Part IV of this book.

While imported china is more valuable, American glass is most valued. Some of the finest glass makers in the world produced their wares in our East and Midwest.

An important thing to remember in marketing most collectibles is that a sizable collection of almost anything will attract more buyers and be worth a great deal more than a few items sold separately. I saw a large collection of matchbook covers from all over the world bring a substantial price at an auction recently, whereas a few matchbook covers would not even have earned a place in the sale. A substantial collection of wooden kitchen utensils (spoons, forks, paddles) would attract many antique dealers, whereas a few such items would not. If you have a few not-too-valuable collectibles, it would pay for you to build up the collection before attempting to sell. For example, a half dozen postcards would hardly be worth a dealer's time and trouble, but he might even travel some distance to see several hundred, for there is always the possibility that in a sizable collection there may be a few valuable items that would make the trip worthwhile. This principle applies to almost anything.

I suggest the following rules to follow before selling anything:

(1) Study the classified sections of all the antique and craft publications listed in Part IV and in your local newspaper to determine what various items are bringing on the open market. Values change constantly, and it pays to know what others are asking for their collectibles. For instance, if you have a Shirley Temple doll that you would like to sell, check the classified ads for others who have such a doll for sale. If no price is listed in the ad, drop the dealer a note and ask the price of the doll advertised. If you plan to sell to a dealer, you can expect to get about half of what he or she sells the doll for.

(2) Visit the local antique shops in your area and take note of the prices they are getting on the items you have for sale. If you have an item not seen in a shop or advertised elsewhere, take it along and ask the dealer what he or she will give you for it. Most dealers are very cooperative and will gladly tell you about your item, if you're not sure what you have. This is a good way to find out if the items you wish to sell are really old and have any real value, and you're under no obligation to sell to the dealer, although it is wise to let him or her think you might, for dealers do not like to give free appraisals.

(3) Visit your public library and consult one of the many value guides listed in Part IV for the latest values. The prices listed in most of these guidebooks are what the items brought at auction during the year the book was published. Make sure you are looking at the most recent guide.

(4) Are your collectibles worth the price of a classified ad in a newspaper or other publication? Are they worth the postage or transportation charges to sell them by mail? Do you have enough items to warrant a house or garage sale? Would the expenses involved in disposing of them eat up

the profits you might make on them? When a customer of mine discovered there was a market for scrap gold and silver, she neatly boxed a single gold ring and a couple of silver charms and insured the package for $100, sending it first-class mail. She was very annoyed when she discovered that the money she received in return was little more than she had paid in postage. Often you are better off selling locally for less than going through the hassle of packaging and sending a single item (unless, of course, it is a rare one).

(5) Are your items ready to go? Are paper collectibles, coins, stamps, etc., arranged in orderly fashion, displayed to best advantage? Are items clean, inside and out? Remember when you sell something to make sure that nothing of value is stashed away in a drawer or pocket—it happens! A man in Pennsylvania bought a Ben Franklin stove from a charity thrift shop several years ago and discovered, when cleaning out the interior, a can of old silver and gold coins hidden under the ashes. He made no secret of his discovery, and the thrift shop instigated a lawsuit against him for the recovery of the coins; the court ruled that when he bought the stove he also bought its contents and the coins were legally his. It pays to be cautious when selling. Drawers should be removed from furniture and checked out behind as well as inside, and all containers turned upside down to make sure a valuable stamp, receipt, or other paper is not clinging to the sides or bottom.

There are some collectibles of the future, which will be difficult to sell until they have acquired some age. So many worthless items were produced for our nation's two hundredth birthday that bicentennial items are worthless on today's market and will not be valued collectibles for many years. One producer of bicentennial mementos, interviewed during a recent newscast, complained bitterly that King Kong items were outselling his merchandise!

Reproduction glass, which is flooding the market today, will eventually be worth something (especially if Congress gets around to passing the law they've had in committee for several years that would require glass makers to date every piece of glass they produce for sale), but for the time being this glass is too plentiful to be of much value as a collectible. Only the experts can distinguish the reproduction from the old glass, for the same molds are used.

Packaging items, like Mrs. Butterworth's Syrup bottles, found today on market shelves and even in some antique shops, are definitely going to be the collectibles of tomorrow, but are of no value for immediate resale. Once the manufacturer switches to plastic containers, these bottles will immediately become valuable. There are many other items, worth practically nothing for resale today, that are worth keeping for some future date. Glass perfume bottles, medicine bottles, candy and cookie tins are among the collectibles of the future. Any dated item made of glass, tin, or metal will become valuable as it ages. Plastic items are not collectible, for they will hardly survive the years to become antiques.

The old adage "Today's trash is tomorrow's treasure" is true. Even though your collections may not be worth a great deal today, they may well be in the future, and no collector should feel guilty about collecting anything. Collecting should be fun and profitable, even though the profits may be a long way off.

CHAPTER 2

Nine Ways to Market Your Wares

(1) Classified Ads

There are many advantages in selling this way. You can advertise one item or a dozen, set your own hours, and screen your prospective buyers on the telephone.

The classified sections of our nation's newspapers are bursting at the seams with ads for everything from exotic pets (a cobra snake has been waiting for a buyer all week in my town) to the finest and lowliest household items. When you answer a classified ad in your daily paper, you may be surprised at who is holding the sale.

Back in the late fifties, a U.S. Senator's wife (Mrs. Albert Gore of Tennessee) answered a classified ad in one of the Washington, D.C., newspapers to find that another Senator's wife (Jacqueline Kennedy) was having a sale to dispose of some of her unwanted wedding gifts. At one time or another, almost everybody has had an occasion to sell something through classified ads.

To get the best results from an ad, I've found, weekends are the best time to advertise. Weekends around the first of the month are the very best times, for many people get paid then and have money to buy your wares. It pays in the long run to use additional words in the ad to describe your items fully. I always state the price as well. Once I advertised a typewriter for $50 and had a tremendous response. The same day and in the same paper, a friend advertised a similar typewriter and did not state the price she was asking (hers was only $25), and she had only one call. When you note your price in the paper there is no excuse for anyone's calling and declaring he doesn't have enough money or trying to haggle with you to get the price down. State the hours (I use between 10 A.M. and 5 P.M.) so you won't be bothered with phone calls at all hours.

(2) Rummage Sales

Rummage sales are my favorite way of disposing of odds and ends when few things have any great value. My method is to rent a space in a neighborhood parking lot for $10, take card tables and a clothes rack (borrowed from a cleaning establishment), and put pots and pans, odd dishes, and household items in boxes, marking each box with the price of the contents. A box of 25-cent items will sell like hot cakes. When my daughter decided to move to a farm with some other young people, they needed a truck but had no money to buy one, so we had a one-day rummage sale and raised over $500 with a mixture of junk that you wouldn't have believed salable. Most of our items were priced at a dollar or less, and we were kept busy all day.

An empty store is an ideal place for a rummage sale and often can be rented for only a few dollars. The back of the local firehouse or police station is another. Look around your town and find the most suitable place (in a busy section of town with street traffic) and get permission to post a large sign there in advance of the sale. Small signs placed in store and restaurant windows help, too. The most important thing to remember about these sales is that the word "rummage" implies "junk," so you should keep your prices low.

(3) Garage and Yard Sales

Drive along almost any street or highway in America today and you're apt to see handwritten signs posted on trees and fences announcing garage and yard sales in the vicinity. Such a sale of discards has become respectable business—so much so that many city newspapers reserve certain sections of their classified pages for just such sales, and in many areas county and city governments are taking a grim look at the frequency of sales by individuals and threatening to require licenses for individuals who have more than two sales a year. There are reports, too, that the Internal Revenue Service is beginning to take a second look into the garage-sale business.

The advantages of having a garage or yard sale are many. They offer more time for getting your things together and an opportunity to display them to the best advantage. You can sell big items that would cost too much to move to another spot. Above all, if there are leftovers (which there nearly always are), you can keep them in your garage and add to them over the weeks until you have enough to hold another sale. There is no packing up and taking the leftover stuff home at the end of a tiring day. As at the rummage sale, you can sell anything and everything, but I will tell you that customers expect to find more bargains at these sales than they do at rummage sales.

I strongly advise you to place a price on *every* item in a garage or yard sale, so that during the early rush customers do not have to seek you out to ask the price of merchandise. I've often seen customers walking around with merchandise in hand (which keeps someone else from buying it), only to put it down on learning the price. It was after many misfortunes (not being ready when the rush started, having no bags) that I learned to be ready a good two hours before the time mentioned in the paper or on the tree sign;

17

to have all the old grocery bags I could beg from my neighbors; to mark all the merchandise with small pieces of masking tape; and to stay put at a card table (with plenty of change) and have a stapling gun handy to seal the bags as people paid. That way, I avoided a lot of theft and people felt free to look and handle the merchandise as much as they liked. Finally, I never put out valuable or rare pieces in such a sale. You're asking for trouble if you do. If you have fine pieces, they belong in an entirely different kind of sale. In a sale of this sort you can dispose of heavy furniture, household goods, and personal effects, including clothing.

(4) On Consignment

Many people hate dealing with the public and like placing their salable things in a shop on consignment. This way, the shop handles everything from advertising to closing the sale, for a percentage of the final price. There are no overhead expenses in selling this way, and you can be assured that your items are being seen by more potential buyers than if you tried to sell them yourself. In most consignment shops you are allowed to set your own price.

If there are no consignment shops listed in the Yellow Pages or classified section of your telephone book—look under "Clothing Bought and Sold" (they usually sell bric-a-brac, too), "Furniture—Used," and "Antiques"—then contact the antique or secondhand shops in your area and ask if they would take your items on consignment. Most shops will.

(5) Auctions

The policies of auction houses vary greatly. At the ordinary weekly auction, your goods are sold to the highest bidder and you have no control over what they may bring. You are not allowed to bid on your own merchandise, even though you might want to buy it back rather than have it go at an unsatisfactory price. You may even be required to sign a release from responsibility when putting your things up for auction, for few auction houses accept responsibility for theft or loss of merchandise.

If an auction house is well established, you can be fairly certain that your goods will be handled efficiently and that you will be paid promptly (about a week after the sale). If the house is new, you might want to check it out with the Better Business Bureau in your town.

Catalogue sales of antiques differ, however. These sales are usually held once or twice a year by major auction houses, and you may be allowed to submit the lowest price you will consider on your merchandise; the bidding will start at that figure. Make sure that you find out what the rules of the house are before you place your items on the auction block. There are advantages in selling through the regular weekly auctions in your community. Most auction houses will pick up your items and deduct the drayage (moving charge) from the final sale money you are to receive. If you are moving, for instance, and want to sell unwanted items, it is more convenient to have the auction house send movers into your house and remove all the furnishings left there, place them up for sale the next sale day, and mail you a check for the final settlement. This is the easiest way to dispose of your unwanted household goods, even though it may not bring you as much as a private sale might have.

Auction houses that conduct several catalogue sales a year are reputable dealers in antiques, and special care is extended to every item submitted for such a sale. For the ordinary weekly auction house, however, it pays to submit your own list with delivered items and have it signed by an official as confirmation of receipt. When many items are submitted for sale, identifying tags can be lost, and you need proof that such unmarked items are yours.

(6) Flea Markets

Flea markets have sprung up all over the country, and most likely there is one in your area. This differs from other sales in that you rent a table or small space from the flea market and conduct your sale along with dozens of others who have rented similar spaces. In many states, fairgrounds are used in non-fair months for flea markets. The average rental for a single space is about $10, and you can be assured that many people will see your wares, for the attraction of many private sellers and the advertising done by the flea market usually bring a substantial crowd. At such sales you will do well to take better merchandise than you would to a rummage, garage, or yard sale.

(7) Antique and Craft Shows

Antique and craft shows are usually sponsored by a civic or charity organization to raise money for some worthy cause. They are often held in the finest hotels and motels, and dealers and collectors who show their wares pay a fee for the privilege. Fees vary. I have paid as little as $10 for a booth, and as much as $50. If you have valuable merchandise, this is the most profitable way to sell, for collectors and prospective buyers who visit the shows come prepared to buy. You can expect to receive much higher prices here than you would in a shop. Naturally, you take your most prized collections to these shows, for they are attended by collectors and experts from all around the country. One of my friends used to participate in every show within five hundred miles of Pittsburgh, and I'm sure there were buyers who traveled as far to shop.

Antique and craft shows are widely advertised in the antique and crafts publications, as well as newspapers in the areas where they are held. Many are written about in newsletters sent out by the sponsoring organizations, and some antique associations keep mailing lists for such events, but since each show is handled differently, depending on who sponsors it, it would be impossible for me to tell you how to go about renting a booth in the next show in your area, except to say, keep abreast of the news in the publications mentioned in Part IV, and write or call the organizations sponsoring the shows you are interested in and ask for an application. These shows are advertised months in advance, allowing you plenty of time to participate. Once a show is in the planning stage, most dealers are notified immediately, so you might ask a dealer friend to keep you posted on upcoming shows.

(8) Selling Directly to Local Dealers

Selling directly to dealers is generally the least profitable but the quickest way to turn your collectibles into cash. You can expect to get about half the retail price from a dealer, who must resell and make a profit after covering the expenses of maintaining a shop. However, this is an excellent way to raise quick money when you need it, for a dealer will pay you immediately for any items she or he wishes to purchase. When visiting antique shops for any reason, find out what the dealers are looking for. Frequently you will come across an item in one shop that another dealer is looking for desperately, and you may pick up some spare change, or add to your own collection, by bringing the two dealers together.

(9) Selling via Mail Order

An item sold to someone specializing in collecting or selling a particular item will bring you many times over what you might get from an ordinary antique dealer who handles anything and everything old. When I was a dealer, I learned early in the game that it was more profitable for me to sell special finds, those rare and collectible items, to people who collected them or to dealers who specialized in their sale than to sell in a random way. Beautiful pieces of jade often went to a jade dealer for far more than I could have gotten in my own shop, or were traded for many other items that were easier for me to sell at a good price. Unlike many antique dealers, we made a living from our business; we depended on sales for the mortgage payment and expenses of raising our family, so it was important that our stock move quickly and be replaced often.

For many years I kept files on my collectors. The president of one of the large steel companies collected sterling-silver matchboxes; a Pittsburgh customer collected miniature doll furniture, and another fancy fans. None of these items would have brought a third or fourth as much in my shop as I was able to get from my collectors.

There are several important rules to follow if you decide to sell by mail. Never, under any circumstances, send out your items without writing a query letter to the market first. When you write, describe your article, frankly and honestly. If it has flaws or damaged places, say so. Give details: what it is made of, shape, measurements, and marks. Very likely the serious prospective buyer will require a photograph of the item. A self-developing (Polaroid-type) camera is a must for those who sell by mail. Some of these cameras are less than twenty dollars; it is a good investment if you expect to sell to collectors and dealers out of your area. It is advisable to take all your pictures in color, too.

In your correspondence with dealers and collectors, ask their advice about shipping the articles they are contemplating buying from you. We are all aware that shipping fragile things may be risking loss. Parcel post or even first-class-mail packages are handled carelessly these days, even though marked FRAGILE. I was told quite candidly by a postal clerk that insuring a package in no way insured that it wouldn't go astray or get lost altogether.

Shipping goods across country or from one town to another has become a problem for most of us, but some have put their ingenuity to work. A Camden, New Jersey, soup company wanted to send a rare soup tureen, shaped like a rabbit, to a museum across the country. They carefully wrapped it in foam rubber and packed it into a steel-reinforced shipping crate, bought a child's ticket on an airplane, took the crate aboard, and fastened it to the seat with the safety straps. The crate arrived safely at its destination.

I knew a man once who made his living as a "picker" for antique shops. One of his best customers was a shop several hundred miles away. When their business relationship began, with the customer's first order, he bought a metal footlocker (the kind used by servicemen during World War II) and packed the antiques in it. Then he went to the bus station and bought a round-trip ticket on a bus going from his town to the city where his customer was located. At the baggage area, he presented the ticket and checked the footlocker through to the customer's city. Then he mailed the claim check and return half of the ticket to his customer, who claimed the footlocker and returned it, empty, on the other part of the ticket, mailing back the new claim check. The ticket was still good, since neither of them ever boarded the bus. He claimed the baggage was handled more carefully than by mail, and that by using this procedure he was able to continue sending packages over a long period of time on that one ticket. I'm not sure his method was ethical, but it worked!

If you decide to sell by mail, there are many ways to ship your things. Aside from the regular mail service, there is United Parcel, which I have found most reliable. In large cities they will pick up as well as deliver, and special care is taken in handling. In Washington, D.C., you are required to weigh and measure your package and give this information to the clerk who takes your call. You must call a day ahead of pickup and have exact change for paying express charges. In smaller towns you must take your package to their nearest office, as you would to the post office.

You will find the freight-moving companies, including air freight, listed in the Yellow Pages of your telephone book, under the heading "Freight Forwarding." Some pick up and some do not. At your train station, package express is available to you. At the interstate bus stations the package-express service is a convenient way to send things quickly; no special handling is needed, since the recipient must claim the package at its destination.

Here are some special tips on packaging that have come from experts in the field:

There are three types of loads (a term used by the post office and express companies) for shipping. *Easy load* describes one of moderate density which completely fills the container and is not easily damaged by dropping, shock, or puncture of package. It will not shift inside its container. An *average load* is a package of moderate density that completely fills the container through the addition of partitions or supports to fill space. Average loads can be prepackaged by wrapping or positioning in partitions or paperboard boxes or by other means that provide some support to the faces of the package. A *difficult load* is a package that requires a high degree of protection to prevent

24

puncture, shock, or distortion either to the mail handlers or the package. These include fragile items, delicate instruments, high-density, small-bulk items, etc., which do not support the mailing container and are not acceptable in paperboard or fiberboard boxes or bags or wraps of any kind.

An official of an air-express company says that any package shipped by air should be able to survive a three-foot drop. When I told him that this would exclude glass items, he agreed, so we can infer that it would not be practical or advisable to ship fine glass by air—unless, of course, you use the procedure used by the soup company to ship the rabbit tureen.

Recently I had lunch with an official of the National Gallery of Art, in Washington, and he told me that the museum often used this method for shipping small items of great value. He said their paintings are always shipped *in the frames,* which came as a surprise to me, for I know from experience how fragile gold-leafed frames can be. He said the mistake that most people make is in not securing the canvases in the frames; few of them are as secure as they could be. Actually, the frame protects the painting, when it is secure in the frame. The post office issues an illustrated packaging bulletin, which shows how to pack various items. For mirrors and paintings they suggest you use full sections of newspaper rolled tightly across the surface of the article.

Ask the post office for their *Packaging for Mailing,* which is free. For further information, write to Packaging Institute, Inc., 342 Madison Avenue, New York, New York 10017, for their free document *The Glossary of Packaging Terms.*

PART II

Turning Collectibles into Cash

CHAPTER 3

Advertiques

Advertiques, late bloomers in the collecting field, consist of a multitude of items in almost every category. Any item with the name of the firm that gave it away on it is an advertique. Souvenir spoons, tin trays, trade cards, glass advertising paperweights, kitchen utensils with company names on them are just a few of the many items that fall into this category. They can be made of glass, china, wood, plaster, tin or other metals, as well as paper.

Coca-Cola items alone run the gamut from the "Tiffany-type" lamp fixtures, which sell for well over $500, to playing cards. Here's a sample of the Coke collectibles: change trays, serving trays, syrup dispensers and bottles, pocket mirrors, watch fobs, bookmarks, thermometers, periodical advertisements, bottle openers, pon-back buttons, pencil sharpeners, trade tokens, miniature bottles, amber bottles, display bottles, coasters, ash trays, money clips, pocket knives, seltzer bottles, paperweights, snack bowls, glasses, mugs, book covers, key chains, thimbles, toy trucks, commemorative bottles, playing cards, note pads, calendars, posters, matches, clocks, dishes, jewelry, toys, music boxes, dolls, signs, menus, sheet music, blotters, rulers, ice picks, playing cards, checkers, and dominoes, as well as needle cases, cooler boxes, and many, many more.

Early Coca-Cola items are going for premium prices.

A fountain dispenser, circa 1933, in good condition, recently brought $250 at auction. Early display signs (circa 1909) are selling for $50 or more, and a 1934 Coke tray showing Johnny Weissmuller and Maureen O'Sullivan is worth $25 or more.

Many people collect soft-drink items. Sometimes even the company which originally put them out will buy them back for a lot of money. In 1973 the Pepsi-Cola Company ran a full-page advertisement in several women's magazines offering to buy (at your price) any of the old Pepsi trays they had given out at the beginning of their business. A department store in Pittsburgh offered $50 each for plates they had given away at their opening, fifty years before. Just a week before their offer appeared I had sold six of these plates for a dollar each.

Many advertising items used in the eighteenth and nineteenth centuries have continued to be used in the twentieth century. Visit any country church on a hot summer Sunday and you may well find advertising fans on the seats, for the comfort of the congregation. Many of the hymnal books are likewise sponsored by a merchant, whose advertisement adorns the front page or perhaps even the cover. These may well become collectibles of the future. Fans, some fancy, some plain, were used by many companies to sell their wares. Vanity Fair cigarettes gave away attractive accordion-type fans.

Lard, coffee, cigarettes, tobacco, Log Cabin syrup, and many other everyday household staples were housed in tin containers that were often deemed too attractive to throw away. Some were made to be adaptable for other family uses, such as the lard lunch pail and the baking-powder-tin banks.

Pictures of famous people and places decorated many a plate, paperweight, and other advertising matter.

In the late 1800s, companies began issuing advertising

cards, many carrying a slogan about the company's product. Faced with beautiful pictures, they were sometimes signed by the lithographers, which makes dating those cards quite easy. Slogans like "Do you know Uneeda Biscuit" and "Good to the last drop" made their companies famous and have stayed with us down through the years.

Along with the advertising cards, many businesses had giveaways to bring in customers: banks, spoons, measuring cups, buttons, thimbles, pictures of all sorts, some framed and backed by brass or tin. Paper dolls depicting Rose O'Neill's Kewpie and Grace Weiderseim Drayton's Campbell Kids were sought by every household that had small children, and sold many a can of soup or box of Jell-O. These three cherublike figures have never lost their popularity with children and adults alike.

The condition of any advertique is one of the major factors in determining its price. Any antique item bearing the name of a store, business, product, or place is collectible. If the trade name is faded or scarred, the value is greatly reduced.

Advertising buttons are among the most sought after collectibles in this category. For example, a "Drink Moxie" button, multicolored on white background, is worth $7.00 to $10.00; a Montgomery Ward & Co., Inc., button with a scene of their Chicago headquarters is worth $2.25 to $4.00; "Better Buy Buick" buttons, $2.50; "7-Up Likes You," showing red heart on white, is selling for $3.00 and up.

Advertising matchbook covers are coming into their own. There are literally thousands of different ones. The pictorial ones and those picturing famous persons are the most valuable. One showing a picture of Frank Buck is worth $2.50 up; a Jack Dempsey one $2.00 up. An Esso Oil one, picturing the ship *Normandie,* is worth $1.00 or more.

Like the soft-drink advertisers, the beer companies were great for putting their names on things. Tin beer trays bring good prices: A Stegmaier Gold Medal Beer tray with lithograph of the company building is now bringing $25.00 and up; a decorated Budweiser tray $2.50; Ballantine and Schaefer trays $5.00 up.

Trade cards were packaged in many products, but the most collected are those from bubble gum and cigarettes. A Mickey Mouse bubble gum card is worth $2.00, big-league baseball cards (series of 240 cards), $1.50 each, and Indian gum cards about $1.00 each. Arm & Hammer bird cards are selling for about 25 cents each.

Be very cautious before selling any advertising materials that are dated or have pictures of famous persons or events on them (which will also date them), for the prices are skyrocketing all the time. Shirley Temple mugs and pitchers that I sold in my shop ten years ago for 50 cents are bringing anywhere from $10 to $25 on today's market. Many collectors are listed in this book, but it stands to reason that the longer you can hold on to these collectibles, the more they will be worth. There are still many of them available at out-of-the-way country shops and farm auctions, often for very little. For a young person, I think, this category offers the best advantages for a long-term investment. The items take up little storage space and will surely increase in value as the years go by.

CHAPTER 4

Art

John Adams, our second President, had a Puritan's scorn for art. He once remarked, "I would not give a sixpence for a picture of Raphael or a statue of Phidias." The very word "art" covers such a wide field—photography, oils, watercolors, prints, etc.—that in the art field there is almost certainly something to appeal to everyone.

Generally speaking, oil paintings bring higher prices than watercolors, although there are exceptions. It stands to reason that the quality of the work is foremost in placing value on it, and an excellent watercolor would surpass a badly done oil, but for the most part I've had better luck selling oil paintings than I have watercolors.

There seems to be a bit of magic in the very words "oil paintings." Begin an ad for a house sale with these words and watch the people *flock* to your sale—all looking for that old masterpiece for a few dollars. The experience is one you will not soon forget.

Once I had a man call in response to an ad in which I noted, "Oil paintings $10 each," to ask if I had any Van Goghs or Gauguins in the sale. I was so stunned that I couldn't help replying, "Sorry, I don't have a Rembrandt or a da Vinci, either."

Original Currier and Ives prints bring very high prices today, but reproductions do not, although I know a dealer who framed Currier and Ives sets given free one year by a national life insurance company and sold them for $10 to

$25 each. I'm sure many of her customers thought they were buying originals, which can often be distinguished from reproductions by their measurements as well as by marks. For example, if a particular original Currier and Ives is listed as being $28^{1}/_{2}''$ by $14''$, a representation in any other size must be a reproduction. Check *Currier and Ives Prints* by Frederick Cunningham (Crown, 1970).

The nineteenth century gave birth to the development of the first uniquely American art form in the pictorial landscape paintings which depict "how it was or how it looked then." The combination of written journals and primitive paintings has given us a much clearer insight into our early history.

Top-quality folk art from the nineteenth and twentieth centuries is leading the art field in popularity today and bringing fantastic prices. Dealers expect the values on folk paintings (both oils and watercolors) to continue rising. Peter Tillou, a Connecticut dealer-collector, is reported to have paid $40,000 for a pair of nineteenth-century folk portraits in 1976.

George Schoellkopf, a New York dealer, who is considered one of the top experts in folk art, believes that the current popularity of folk art will not level off so long as exciting new discoveries are made, such as a pair of Bartlett portraits found recently by a young couple, which are expected to bring $15,000 the pair at auction. I can remember, not too long ago, when I couldn't sell any kind of portrait in my shops unless they happened to be of pretty women decked out in the finery of the period, like the one I sold in Pittsburgh to a woman who said she would tell her friends it was her grandmother.

If your family has family portraits or other folk art tucked away in attics or barns, you should take a look with new appreciation at those pictures our grandparents treasured. Richard Axtell, a Deposit, New York, dealer who is a specialist in folk art, calls the challenge of discovery a "new frontier in folk art."

Many dealers in folk art caution young collectors to buy what they like and think of investment value as secondary. Here, as in all art, the experts can best determine what is good and valuable.

If you are interested in folk art, you can write to the Museum of American Folk Art, 49 West Fifty-third Street, New York, New York 10019, about joining their membership program.

Any old painting, watercolor, or sketch of a historical time, place, or event may be valuable and should be appraised before marketing.

While the value of the old masterpieces was determined by the stature of the artists, folk and Early American art are not necessarily judged by the same criterion. In many cases the picture itself—how well it was done, who or what it portrayed—carried more weight in determining value than the artist's name or reputation; sometimes the artist was unknown. This is another reason to have your art pieces appraised by reputable dealers and appraisers.

If you have a signed painting but have never heard of the artist, you might call your library and ask them to look in *Who's Who in American Art* or *Who's Who in English Art* to try to identify the artist and the period of time.

Godey's fashion prints have seen a resurgence of popularity in recent years. Many reproductions of these have flooded the market since Depression days in the 1930s and are salable, but antique buffs usually seek the original pages from *Godey's Lady's Book,* published from 1830 to 1878. Reproductions are more colorful, less worn, and are bringing from $3.50 to $12.00 at auctions. Only the serious collector would buy the often yellowed and fraying original prints for from $8.00 to $20.00 or more.

In my years as an antique dealer I saw Wallace Nutting

pictures, reverse paintings on glass, and other forms of art that I sold for very little increase tremendously in value. Nutting's hand-tinted pictures began to be published around 1907, although many were originally published in the late 1800s. They were photographic prints produced by the platinum-print method, individually produced and colored by hand. At one time he had more than a hundred "colorists" working in his shop. The pictures range from New England scenes to the more collectible interior scenes showing people dressed in attire of the period. He signed his pictures in pencil: Wallace Nutting, W. Nutting, or simply W.N. Recently I saw a Nutting picture sell for $75. In the early sixties I sold a copy of the same picture, beautifully framed, for $10.

Wallace Nutting was an extremely versatile man. During the Civil War a Union soldier wrote this inscription in a Bible: "Poolesville, Md. Christmas, 1862. I give this to my baby boy Wallace. May it teach him to follow the great Captain of our salvation." That baby was Wallace Nutting, who was born in Rockbottom, Massachusetts, on November 17, 1861. Wallace began his career as a minister, serving in churches across the nation. From the pulpit, he went into antique-furniture reproductions, restoration of colonial houses, writing books, and photography, which brought him his greatest fame.

Art has long been considered a safe investment, for values go continually up. Back in the thirties, a watercolor, *Boats on the River,* signed with the little butterfly painted in the corner that was the famous "signature" of James McNeill Whistler, sold at C. G. Sloan's Auction House in Washington for $140. In a recent sale at Weschler's Auction House in the same city, a Whistler oil, *Nocturne: Grey and Black* was valued at between $15,000 and $20,000. If *Boats on the River* were put on sale today, it would probably bring in thousands of dollars.

Oil paintings frequently turn up at auction houses and in miscellaneous lots, many not recognized as being valuable. For this reason, if you want to sell a painting at auction it would pay you to consult an auction house that deals *primarily* in art. Many of the art dealers listed in this book also hold auctions. It may pay to place a piece of art on consignment, to be sold at a *catalogue* sale. Frequently this will bring more than a dealer can safely offer you.

Back in 1890, when the seventy-year-old Susan B. Anthony was still in the national spotlight, a Washington artist, Jerome K. Uhl, persuaded her to sit for a portrait, which he hoped to sell to the National American Woman Suffrage Association, founded by Miss Anthony. When the portrait was finished the artist framed it in a beautiful gold-lined shadow-box frame that was ten feet high and five feet wide and presented it to the Association with a price tag of $2,500. The women, few of whom were wealthy, threw up their hands in horror. There was no way they could come up with that much money! The portrait went into storage, and Mr. Uhl died before they could come up with any plan for purchasing the picture.

The picture remained in storage. Finally, in March 1925, Mrs. Anna Hendley, president of the Susan B. Anthony Foundation, was notified by telephone that the portrait was to be auctioned off at Sloan's in exactly two hours to satisfy a $90 storage charge.

Mrs. Hendley pleaded with Sloan's to postpone the sale of the picture for one week, while the ladies tried to raise the storage charge. By the end of the week they had raised $80, and, unable to come up with the full amount, Mrs. Hendley went to the auction to try to buy the painting with what they had. Unfortunately, the bidding went past her, to $85, and Mrs. Hendley stopped the sale with an impassioned plea to the buyers there, telling them how her group had tried to raise the money and had been unable to come up with more than the $80 she carried in her purse.

The sympathetic auctioneer began to make a plea for Mrs. Hendley and the other ladies, and in a few minutes a collection was taken up for the balance of money needed to buy the portrait. Susan B. Anthony would have been very proud of her followers, who went to such great trouble to acquire her portrait for their headquarters.

More and more contemporary artists are finding receptive markets for their work. SoHo, a section of lower Manhattan, where struggling young writers and artists set up housekeeping in lofts, has become the fastest-growing art scene in the country, with perhaps three thousand resident artists and art followers and more than thirty spacious, often luxuriously furnished art galleries. Fortunately for young artists everywhere, the old idea that an artist's work is not appreciated until after he or she is dead and gone is no longer true. No work, whether it be a painting, a sculpture, or whatever, need have a certain number of years on it to be recognized. Works of many young artists are bringing tremendous prices in galleries all over the country, and if you have pieces of art that are good but not old, they are salable and worth querying a market about.

Only twice in its fourteen years of existence has the Woodward Foundation Collection of Contemporary American Art been exhibited in America. The approximately 350 paintings plus a few sculptures in the collection are lent regularly to American ambassadors, to be hung in our embassies all over the world. To date they have hung in forty-one countries, as samples of contemporary American art. The collection includes works by Frank Stella, Andy Warhol, Robert Rauschenberg, Helen Frankenthaler, Claes Oldenburg, Robert Motherwell, Willem de Kooning, Morris Louis, Mark Rothko, Jules Olitski, Kenneth

Noland, Anne Truitt, and many others. Some paintings were purchased for as little as $100, others for as much as $50,000.

To get a collection for an embassy, the ambassador simply visits the headquarters, at 3009 N Street, N.W., Washington, D.C., bringing the floor plans of his new residence. He gets from 10 to 25 paintings. Shipping and insurance are paid by the foundation, and the ambassadors are required to report yearly on the condition of the paintings.

Without a doubt there are more art lovers and more national pride in our own artists than ever before.

In 1974 the St. Louis Mercantile Library announced its intention to put a collection of 112 drawings by the great Missouri artist George Caleb Bingham up for auction. The drawings, the largest known collection of this artist's work, were donated to the library more than a century ago by a former mayor of St. Louis who happened to be a friend of the artist's.

There was such a cry of outrage throughout the state at the news that young Governor Cristopher Bond shamed the library into postponing the auction until June 30, 1976, to give him time to raise the $1.8 million needed to purchase the collection. Bond created a nonprofit organization called Bingham Sketches, Inc., to start the drive. The drawings were circulated over the state and later over other parts of the nation. The Missouri legislature appropriated $500,000 to kick off the drive. Schoolchildren contributed $25,000 in nickels and dimes, and with pledges from art lovers in Missouri and everywhere, the money was raised by the deadline. Bingham's sketches will stay in Missouri, where I'm sure the artist would have wanted them.

Sculpture is an extension of art beyond the ordinary

collector. Collectors of sculpture are experts in their field and need no marketing advice from someone with as little knowledge about the subject as I have.

Modern sculpture has taken its place in museums along with the art of the Old Masters. It is terribly expensive, and pieces are not likely to be found in country auctions or out-of-the-way antique shops. Of the thousands of letters requesting marketing information about various collectibles I received after the excerpt of my book *Antiques for Amateurs* appeared in *Woman's Day* magazine, in April 1976, not one letter asked about sculpture, and for that reason I find it irrelevant in this chapter. Should you (by some miracle) discover a piece, any art dealer listed in the back of this book will be able to appraise and guide you in marketing it.

There are too many famous American artists to list them all, but if you happen to have a work by John Gadsby Chapman (born in Alexandria, Virginia, in 1808), such as *The Baptism of Pocahontas,* which hangs in the Capitol Building in Washington, D.C., or a bird sketch signed by Rex Brasher or a pen-and-ink animal sketch by William Robinson Leigh, you have a valuable collectible.

The art experts say there probably is no field of collecting as hazardous as collecting prints. You need to be an art "detective" to distinguish the difference between reproductions and the original thing.

There were only three methods of printing ever used in producing prints: (1) from a raised surface; (2) from a plane or level surface; (3) from a sunken or intaglio surface.

Sometimes a finished print will combine two of these methods. The value of a print depends on the skill of the artist or print maker and the quality of paper used. Generally, collectible prints are not photographic in origin.

Photography as an art form has finally taken its place in art circles. There were so few really excellent photographers in the early days and the processes of developing and enlarging were so limited that not too many fine photographs are lying around waiting to be discovered in family trunks and attics. The chances of turning up a Brady photo of the Civil War or one of the few other collectible photographs of past photographers are remote. Modern photographers are producing books of their works and one-man or -woman shows in museums and galleries that are attracting the art critics.

Should you have a fine old photograph that you feel is of historical value (perhaps it is of a famous person, place, or event), you can contact a rare-book dealer as well as an art dealer for appraisal, for many book dealers buy old prints and photographs and are experts in this field.

CHAPTER 5

Books, Pamphlets, Maps, Autographs, and Manuscripts

Looking for rare or valuable out-of-print books is one of the most fascinating hobbies in the world. Books are everywhere! Chances are there are thousands of valuable books, pamphlets, maps, and autographs buried on book shelves, in attics and trunks across the nation, with their owners unaware of the treasures they have been hiding all these years. When Van Allen Bradley started his first antiques column in the Chicago *Daily News,* back in 1957, he told of a New England woman who found a dusty copy of Edgar Allan Poe's *Tamerlane* that turned out to be the rare 1827 first edition, paperbound, of which only five hundred copies were printed; it was valued at $20,000.

Men and women who like to spend their spare time "antiquing," browsing through out-of-the-way country shops and auctions, should keep an eye out for books, even if they are more interested in other antiques. One Virginia man I know complained constantly about driving his wife through the countryside every weekend to browse through the antique shops—that is, until he found two valuable books for 25 cents each and discovered that one of them contained two Civil War autographs. She doesn't have to beg him to take her any more!

I learned from Mr. Bradley that a first edition does not always say "First edition." Many books are identified as such by mistakes on certain pages, a change in type on one of the pages, or a change of the dedication in the front of the book. If a book has any value to a collector, an autographed copy is worth even more.

In the past publishers sometimes issued a limited number of copies of a book with special bindings, to be sent out in advance of the publication date. These were first editions, as those to follow would be, but, because of their differences, more valuable to the collector. I've learned that the physical state of a book is the single most important factor affecting a book's price, aside from rarity and scarcity. The importance of describing your books accurately can't be stressed too emphatically.

I highly recommend both of Mr. Bradley's books, *Gold in Your Attic* (Fleet Press Corporation) and *The Book Collector's Handbook of Values* (G. P. Putnam's Sons), and also *American Book-Prices Current*. All are available at most public libraries and are a big help in determining if your old books are of exceptional value.

There are old books and rare books, not necessarily the same. The rarest books are not always the oldest books. In many fields second, third, and fourth editions may join the rare-book category. It is the subject, the rarity, and the demand that set some books apart on the "rare"-book list.

First editions of most books are more valuable than later editions. Exceptions may occur when extensive revising is done by the author in a later edition, making the book more desirable.

First editions of classics (Poe, Emerson, Longfellow, Whitman, etc.) and of art and discovery books are very valuable.

Old books with large illustrations of birds, flowers, or people dressed in clothing of the period, as well as steel engravings, are more valuable than most books without illustrations.

Generally speaking, a leatherbound book is more valuable than a clothbound or paperbound book, except for rare editions (such as of personal travel, histories, and discoveries) that were never published in leather editions.

One would think that very old encyclopedias would have some value, but they do not. Except for the first edition, sets of the *Britannica* published before around 1946 have no sale value, and the more recent sets are valuable only as reference works, not as collectibles. This applies to other encyclopedias as well.

The Antiquarian Booksellers Association of America was established in 1949 to maintain high standards in the rare-book field. To ask about rare-book dealers or collectors, you can write to them at 630 Fifth Avenue, New York, New York 10020, enclosing a self-addressed, stamped envelope for reply. This nonprofit organization recommends the following query when writing a dealer about a book: "Give the author; title and size of book (size of pages in inches). Publisher and place of publishing. Binding (full leather, half leather, cloth or paper cover). Number of pages and illustrations (plain or colored); condition of overall book (inside and out. State if pages are stained or there are tears.)."

The ABAA adds this to its instructions:

The bookseller can then decide whether the book is worth anything to him and if so will ask to see it. It should be sent by insured parcel post (book rate) and he will return it the same way if you do not come to an agreement. If the books to be sold are numerous and important enough to justify the expense, the bookseller will travel to see them. Before he can decide to do this, he must have a general description of the contents of the library (for example: Americana, theology or old novels, etc.), a detailed description of the more important titles, and the approximate number of volumes. Valuable books must be seen before an appraisal can be given; pages have to be counted, illustrations and plates carefully checked. It is obvious that a valuation cannot be given over the telephone.

A book's condition is described or judged much as is a coin's. A book in perfect condition is catalogued as "mint condition"; if it is in fine condition but not perfect, it is called "very fine"; if it is in good condition but not very fine, it is described as "very good." A book that is badly stained or soiled is described as only "fair."

More people ask about selling old Bibles than about any other book. This is what the Antiquarian Booksellers Association says in a bulletin it put out on Bibles:

> It should be borne in mind that the Bible is the most frequently reprinted book of the Western world, and by its nature the one book most carefully treasured by its owners. In many households it was the only book. Therefore, as a text it is not scarce. Many editions, even of the later 15th century, during the first 50 years of printing are comparatively common and worth very little. Rare and important editions are easily recognized by experts—the *Gutenberg Bible,* circa 1450–1455, generally considered to be the first printed book; the *Mentelin Bible* of 1460, in German; the first Bible in each language; the first polyglot; the first authorized King James version; the first Indian Bible, etc. Then there are oddities such as the Breeches Bible, the Vinegar Bible, the Wicked Bible, which command special prices for some misprint or curious phrase in the text.
>
> Although of sentimental value, it is fairly safe to say of all the rest that they are valueless in the commercial market, and by this is meant anything in excess of $10.00. An exception to this might be if the Bible belonged to a distinguished or important family and has extensive family records written in it.

Collecting books is a hobby open to everyone, no matter how little you have to spend. Rare books have a way of turning up at auctions and rummage, yard, and garage sales more often than you think. I know two collectors who would rather spend their Saturday mornings in the Salvation Army bookstore than on the golf course, and both are golf enthusiasts. The important thing is that they know what to look for. You can learn too.

Books that are valuable to collectors, according to Bradley's *Gold in Your Attic,* include the whole range of printed materials, from a paperbound guide for emigrants of the gold-rush period to the poems of Edna St. Vincent Millay on Japan vellum.

Books dealing with Americana and the American scene and with history, exploration, and development head the list: any book published up to about 1875 relating to state, county, and local history; books of adventure, travel, and exploration; Indian books, almanacs, and overland narratives, especially first-person accounts of early travel and adventure; books on Utah and the Mormons; books on the old Northwest and Midwest; accounts of early explorers, such as Davy Crockett and Daniel Boone; histories of railroads and canals and other businesses in the opening of the West.

These are very general categories, and there are many others; I merely want to give you an idea of the breadth of the field of potentially valuable books that rare-book dealers and collectors are looking for.

If you ever have attended an antiquarian book fair, you know that old maps, magazines, railroad timetables, advertisements, manuscripts, and letters hold an honored place in written memorabilia. Some are rare and expensive, such as a handwritten manuscript offered in the Washington, D.C., area in 1976 of a short story by Sir Arthur Conan Doyle, "The Death Voyage," priced at $4,500; some are inexpensive by today's standards, such as a July 1936 issue of *Popular Science* magazine (originally priced at 15 cents) selling for $3.50. These book fairs hold something for everybody interested in books, and usually at prices everybody can afford.

Out-of-print books by almost any writer are collectible; the first and last issues of a magazine and letters written and signed by famous people today are collectible. Millions of books, pamphlets, letters, and magazines that are not considered rare are collectibles that have a potential market value. I know several people who make a good living buying and selling these collectibles. It is possible in a big city to scour the thrift shops and auctions and find collectibles in this field. Yard and garage sales are excellent sources too. Once you learn what the dealers and collectors are looking for and what distinguishes an exceptional book from the run-of-the-mill types, you may well open new doors to a profitable and fascinating hobby that can be worked in with the other collectibles you've been interested in for a long time.

The advantages of book collecting are many. It doesn't take a fortune to start a collection. You may find valuable books or related materials for a few cents at rummage sales and thrift shops. Unlike glass and other easily damaged pieces, books don't require special handling. You never need to hire a truck for transporting your books. The best thing of all about buying books is that there are so many dealers and collectors waiting to buy your find. There are collectors all over the country looking for books on all kinds of subjects. I once had a collector who would buy anything on horses (including horse diseases!), so I had a ready market for any such book I came across.

At a recent book sale I was shocked to see the "Better Little Books," which originally sold for 10 cents in the early 1940s, going for from $4 to $8 each. These tiny, thick books, printed on pulp paper with hard covers, covered many subjects attractive to children: Mickey Mouse, Dick Tracy, Captain Midnight, Popeye, Little Orphan Annie, and others. Being a Lone Ranger fan, I bought *The Lone Ranger and the Silver Bullets,* for $4.

A first edition of Lewis Carroll's *Alice's Adventures in Wonderland,* with forty-two illustrations by John Tenniel, was priced at $500.50 at the sale.

If a book you have is not dated on the title page or in a copyright notice or elsewhere, you should consult a bookseller or the catalogue of a large library to determine from the printer, and perhaps from certain irregularities peculiar to the first edition, whether you have a first edition.

I suggest that beginners visit the book fairs, study the conditions and prices of books offered by the experts, and then study the market. In this field, more than any other, knowledge is more valuable and essential to you than money, for only if you know what to look for, what to buy, and how much you can safely pay for a book in order to make a profit can you expect to enjoy a profitable and exciting hobby.

Should you have or find a historical autograph that you're not sure about, send it by registered mail to the Library of Congress, Manuscript Division, for authenticating. This service is free.

In 1973 a New York auction house sold a George Washington letter, signed by our first President but with the text in the handwriting of a secretary, for $27,500. At that time, it was the highest price ever paid for a Washington letter and one of the highest ever paid for an autograph of an American.

Sometime earlier that same year, another auction house sold a Washington autograph for the small sum of $800.

According to the experts, the difference in the two prices lay in the contents of the two letters. The higher-priced letter was twenty-three pages long and was a version of a State of the Union message written in 1783, with personal accounts of the times dictated to his secretary. The lower-priced letter was a business document, a voucher for the Potomack Company, dealing with the canal venture in which Washington was interested.

Obviously, the contents of the material accompanying the autograph is of prime importance in determining the value. If you have an autograph attached to a "little bit of history" it is more valuable than the same autograph on a check or document.

Civil War autographs are the most avidly sought. This war produced more leaders than any other in our history. Abraham Lincoln's signature is the most sought and seldom brings under $500. A voucher signed by Robert E. Lee sells for around $100.

Because of the extensive destruction in the South during the War between the States, most of the valuable papers of the South were destroyed. Because of this, Confederate autographs are harder to find and more valuable than Yankee ones. A Stonewall Jackson autograph is valued at about ten times as much as a Ulysses S. Grant.

Experts say it is almost impossible to find autographs of General Jeb Stuart. There seem to be a lot of Jefferson Davis's autographs on the market, but here the collector must beware. Many of Davis's postwar letters were signed by his wife, Varina, who was quite an expert at copying her husband's handwriting.

The best market for your autographs will be one of the "autographs only" dealers listed in the back of this book. They are specialists in their field and the fairest to do business with.

As for maps, early maps of exploration are most valuable, selling in the thousands of dollars. The most sought by American collectors are the crude maps used in opening up the West.

Nineteen seventy-six saw the discoveries of several

valuable manuscripts, which reinforces my opinion that many valuable original manuscripts may still be hidden in attics and trunks throughout the world.

A batch of nineteenth-century papers, valued at between $425,000 and $850,000, which had lain undisturbed for more than 150 years, was uncovered under the Pall Mall branch of Barclays Bank in London during remodeling in December 1976. They were hailed as a literary gold mine. Among them was an original Byron manuscript, several unknown poems by Shelley, and an eyewitness description of Napoleon's arrival in exile on St. Helena in 1815. Experts say it will take years for scholars to fully evaluate and complete their examination of the contents. The papers apparently were left in the bank vault of scholar Scrope Bergmore Davis, a friend of the poets, who fled England in a hurry in 1820 to avoid prosecution for gambling debts.

Meanwhile, in Boston, half of what may be the long-lost final draft of the Declaration of Independence, in Thomas Jefferson's own handwriting, was turned up in a Dorchester attic.

"I don't have any doubt that it's the document lost two hundred years ago," said the Reverend James K. Allen, who discovered the two-page document among papers given him by a friend who knew of his interest in history.

Should you come across an old document such as this, I suggest you take it (or send it insured mail) to the Library of Congress, Division of Manuscripts, Washington, D.C., for authentication. Chances are you will receive an appraisal as well. If you decide to sell, you can safely contact any one of the rare-book dealers listed in this book. I would advise selecting one near you and perhaps making a personal visit (by appointment) to his or her establishment if the material you have seems of exceptional value.

CHAPTER 6

Bottles, Flasks, and Jars

Since bottles, flasks, and jars are most often made of glass, I considered putting them in the chapter on glass, but I was astonished to find that there are so many bottle collectors that this really belongs in a category of its own. The glass dealers listed in Part IV, however, are interested in bottles. There are also a few "bottle only" dealers listed.

Bottle collectors are so serious about their hobby that many are using mine detectors to find the discard pits of our ancestors. The enormous increase in their numbers is attested to by the way antique dealers are moving their bottles to ever more prominent places in shops and shows.

The older the bottle, the cruder it may be, and the more valuable to the collector. A friend recently found a Prohibition whiskey flask for 50 cents at a church rummage sale in Alexandria. When she asked the curator at the Smithsonian to tell her what he could about the bottle, he asked her to donate it to the museum, which she did.

The first bottle-making machine was not perfected until 1903, when an employee of Libbey Glass Company in Toledo, Ohio, reversed the earlier method of bottle making and made the lip of the bottle first.

Blown bottles made before that time are becoming more valuable year after year. Recently I've seen dirty old medicine bottles, still caked with mud from being buried for many years, selling like hotcakes for $10 each at a flea market.

Our Midwestern glass factories turned out some of the prettiest whiskey flasks of the early nineteenth century. Many glass experts claim that only Stiegel glass surpassed the colors and delicacy of the mold of the early flasks. It isn't unusual to find a pretty flask priced from $100 up.

Back in 1972, a two-hundred-year-old bottle of sour milk was brought up out of a fifty-five-foot well on the thirty-six-hundred-acre Kingsmill Plantation, six miles east of Williamsburg, Virginia. For two centuries the milk bottle had lain in the well, its contents preserved because the sealing cork had remained firmly in place, submerged underwater.

Another treasure hunt, in 1973, produced tall bottles of French champagne, beans canned in jars, pickles, and more than four thousand bottles of bitters, all over a hundred years old, buried in the hold of the steamboat *Bertrand,* which was sunk in the Missouri River in 1865 while on her maiden voyage to Virginia City.

Almost every old bottle is collectible and has a commercial value if you want to sell it. Visit almost any large excavation and you will find bottle collectors digging for "buried treasure" with enthusiasm. Collectors everywhere are looking for bottles, from the primitive medicine, poison, hair tonic, and liquor bottles to the late Avons. Bottles come in all sizes, shapes, and colors, and may be found almost anywhere.

The colored ones (cobalt blues, aquas, violets, bluegreens, and pretty ambers) are perhaps the most sought, and *bottles retaining their original label of contents* bring far higher prices than those without labels—unless, of course, the name of the contents and/or the manufacturer is embossed on the glass.

If the bottles you find have no identifying marks, it is fairly easy to determine their approximate age by the way they were made. Most bottles blown after 1840 were blown into two- or three-part molds. This means the bottles were pressed together from two or three parts and show ridges at the edges of contact. Those made before 1860 had mold seams that did not reach the neck of the bottles. From around 1880 on, the seams extended to the neckline of the bottles, and from 1900 on the seams usually penetrated the lip of the bottles.

Early bottles had cork stoppers, not screw-on lids. Don't be misled if a bottle or fruit jar has a patented date embossed in it. I've had many people try to sell me items they claimed were over a hundred years old simply because of the patent date of 1858. The fact that it was *patented* in that year doesn't necessarily mean that that particular bottle or jar was *made* that year. (I mentioned earlier how an auctioneer was able to get $12 for a jar he claimed was made in 1858.)

If you are an Avon collector, you should send for the *Western World Avon Collectors Newsletter,* which is published bimonthly and reaches up to thirty thousand members. By joining (the fee is $6.50 per year), you are granted free advertising privileges in the newsletter for selling or swapping your bottles with other collectors. It also publishes all the latest news on Avon collectibles, their values and market potentials. The address is: Western World, 511 Harrison Street, San Francisco, California 94105.

There are over two thousand Avon items being collected today. Most are bottles and jars which housed the early California Perfume products, which later became Avon products.

While some of the early California Perfume items sell in the hundreds of dollars, the average "old Avons" bring around $20. Avon collectors identify the Avon years 1900 to 1930 as "those old Avons," 1930 to 1950 as the "middle years of Avon," and 1950 to the present day as the "now years of Avon."

Avon 3, published by Western World, is the best guide for dealers and collectors. There are fully illustrated pages with values which will help you identify your items and put a value on them.

If you collect or have White House Vinegar bottles to sell, you should send for the White House Vinegar book, which lists the approximate ages and values of all White House bottles. This book is not available in stores, but can be ordered directly from the publisher. The address is: White House Vinegar Book, Levin J. Smith Enterprises, P.O. Box 102, Independence, Virginia 24348, and the price is $3 at this printing.

The vinegar book shows the earlier jugs, from about 1923, shaped like a big apple and with a picture of the White House embossed on the front, as being worth $65 for the set of five (all five sizes). The half-pint size is the most difficult to find and brings the highest prices. A gallon jug with wire handle and original paper label, sold around 1900, is worth about $15. Any White House bottle with the White House embossed in the glass is collectible and worth from about $10 up.

Since milk dairies all over the country have replaced their glass bottles with plastic ones, more and more folks are collecting the old milk bottles. Any bottle collector or dealer who specializes in bottles will buy these milk bottles, but they are not worth as much as the vinegar bottles and jugs.

When I first began contacting collectors and dealers for listing in this book, I found a collector, Robert L. Daly (1480 Dyemeadow Lane, Flint, Michigan 48504), who was offering upward of $1,000 for old bitters bottles. When I wrote to him, I told him about a purple bitters bottle I'd had for several years, describing the embossed name, "Berrings," on the bottle. I am not an expert on bottles and wasn't sure how old the bottle might be, but Mr. Daly promptly wrote back: "I think your Berrings Apple Bitters bottle is a reproduction. Look on the bottom of the bottle. If you see the words: 'Nuline, N.J.,' or, 'Wheaton, N.Y.,' you can be sure you have a reproduction. If you cannot find the words on the bottom, please take a picture of the bottle and send it to me."

I looked and sure enough the words "Wheaton, N.Y." were on the bottom. I realized from Mr. Daly's card, enclosed with the letter, that what he would really like to find are bitters bottles shaped like a log cabin. Apparently they are very scarce, and if you have one you're lucky indeed, for it is worth about $1,500.

The *Old Bottle Magazine* (Box 243, Bend, Oregon 97701) is a must for every bottle collector. It lists all the bottle shows and has one of the largest classified-ad sections on bottles, and you will find a market in its pages for every kind of bottle imaginable. Bottle dealers are listed by state, making it easy for you to find the dealers near you specializing in bottles.

Historical bottles are popular with collectors and bring high prices. A half-pint aqua Washington Sheaf of Rye flask is listed at $59.00, a pint aqua double-eagle flask at $42.50, and a half-pint deep aqua "For Pikes Peak," showing prospector, walking right, and on the reverse a hunter shooting deer, $110.00.

It is always advisable to sell your bottles to bottle specialists, for the average antique dealer may not place its true value on an ordinary-looking bottle that is in fact quite rare. The bottle experts will recognize a rare bottle and have a market for it. Remember that the rarest bottles are not always the prettiest bottles; in fact, they're sometimes actually ugly by most antique-glass standards.

CHAPTER 7

Clocks, Cameras, Lamps, Telephones, and Primitives

American factory-made clocks that were cheap and made strictly for keeping time do not interest serious clock collectors. Most collectors will snub any clock that was factory-made.

As late as seven years ago I was selling pretty walnut and oak "steeple" clocks (from the late Victorian era), in good repair, for from $25 to $45. I bought my clocks from a man who imported truckloads of them from some source in Pennsylvania. He always had hundreds to select from. These clocks now sell for around $150 and up.

I hated selling clocks. Old mantel clocks with their pendulums do not keep time unless they sit perfectly level, and despite my telling customers this, someone was always bringing one back because "it would not run."

A nonrunning clock will not bring even half as much as it would in running condition, although many dealers and collectors know how to repair their clocks themselves. Should you sell a clock by mail, make sure the pendulum is removed and the suspension braced. Stuff paper inside the clock case so that no part shakes loose in shipment.

There is a lot of literature available on clocks. The best

and latest information can be obtained by subscribing to the *Bulletin of the National Association of Watch and Clock Collectors of America,* which is largely concerned with American clocks. The address: P.O. Box 33, Columbia, Pennsylvania 17512.

According to E. J. Tyler, an English clock collector, in an article in the Antique Collector's Club monthly magazine, *Antique Collecting* (Clapton, Woodbridge, Suffolk, [England]):

> The thousands of American factory-made clocks that flooded into this country (England) during the second half of the 19th century have always been held in low esteem. They never set out to be anything but cheap; most of them have been neglected during their lives and yet many are still in existence today, capable of being restored and taking their place among household timekeepers once again.
>
> There is a feeling among clock collectors that a factory-made article is not worth collecting, but it has been established that many of the 18th century London makers had their clocks produced for them in specialist workshops, and it is possible that this practice goes back even earlier. The interest in an American clock is not in the fine engraving on its dial nor in the fine wood of its case, but in the way that the factory that produced it worked to put on the market an article that could compete with others being sold at the time. Not only did this point have to be taken into consideration, but also the cost of production had to be kept down.

Early European clocks, on the whole, were more beautiful, encased in carved wood and trimmed lavishly with brass and sometimes ivory. These fine clocks are worth much more than most American-made clocks and should be sold only through the most exclusive auction galleries or clock dealers.

After telling you about selling a seventy-five-year-old "antique" clock for $25, I feel ashamed to quote the prices listed in a current price guide for children's watches and clocks from the 1930s.

	Cost	Value
Betty Boop watch, 1935 (Ingraham)	$0.98	$300
Big Bad Wolfwatch, 1934 (Ingersoll)	1.98	350
Buck Rogers pocket watch, 1935 (Ingraham)	1.89	225
Official Boy Scout watch, 1935 (Ingraham)	1.89	200
Mickey Mouse watch with fob, 1935 (Ingersoll)	1.29	275
Mickey Mouse electric clock, 1933 (Ingersoll)	—	500

These are only samples of the fantastic prices on children's novelty timepieces.

I was surprised in researching this book to find so few camera dealers and collectors. More surprising was the low value placed on early photographic equipment in general, including cameras.

A year or so ago I could have bought four very old Kodak cameras for $1 each in a Salvation Army store. Not knowing very much about cameras, I let them slip by, and have since regretted it. I'm sure they would have brought much more from one of the collectors listed in the back of this book, or perhaps from one of the general antique dealers.

I guess my past disappointment as a dealer trying to sell mechanical things that worked capriciously or were missing an irreplaceable part made me wary. I suspect that camera collectors, like clock collectors, are familiar with the inner workings of their collections and can make repairs when needed.

Antique Cameras by R. C. Smith, published by David & Charles, North Pomfret, Vermont ($12.95), will help you evaluate old cameras. It covers the history from the use of the camera obscura and the perfecting of the daguerreotype in 1839 through the latter nineteenth century.

Almost every one of the general antique dealers listed in Part IV will buy old clocks, cameras, telephones, and primitives, but there are a few dealers who deal almost exclusively in these items, and it seemed only fair that they be listed separately.

Clocks and cameras are distinctive in that many of the dealers who deal exclusively in them will buy nonworking items or even parts, since, as already mentioned, many dealers repair as well as buy and sell. An antique clock that doesn't work may have a great deal of value to a dealer who can repair it. I've seen people throw away an old clock simply because the weight had been lost and the clock would not run without it. In the years that I was in business, I had several "clock men" who would even buy clock cabinets, empty of works, in which they would put rebuilt clocks. Since antique parts of almost anything mechanical are hard to come by, it is wise to query a dealer before throwing away *any* parts you may have. (This applies to early lamps and fixtures as well; many dealers will buy them despite the fact that they need rewiring or repairing. Tiffany shades are always in demand, even damaged ones, so take a second look before you throw anything away. It may have value to someone looking for that specific item.)

A telephone lineman, who supplied me with glass insulators for resale, was also an avid telephone collector. I remember his excitement one day when he returned from a week on the road. He had come across an old schoolhouse that was being torn down to make way for a new highway and it was "loaded with old wall telephones."

Collectors often find old phones in buildings being demolished in urban-renewal programs (wreckers let them go for practically nothing). Even junkyards have them occasionally, and unless the owners are up on market prices they will sell them for very little.

The old wall phones bring anywhere from $25 to $100 or more, depending on where you live. I think they are cheaper in the North than in the South, for many places in the South had no phones until the thirties, when President Roosevelt instigated the rural electrification program in the South and electric lights and phones became a part of Southern country life.

Most telephone companies in the United States will hook up an antique phone for you as an extension.

Not so in England. Mick Joannou, of Talworth, in Surrey, England, has collected over 113 telephones, some dating back to an original Alexander Bell. His collection is so impressive (all in working order) that an official of an American telephone company paid him a visit in 1974 and offered a blank check for the entire collection. Mr. Joannou would not sell. With the walls of his home covered with antique phones—French, Belgian, German, English, and American—the only phone that is hooked up to the outside world is a blue plastic instrument sitting on a hall table.

Early electric lamps from the twenties and thirties are becoming collectibles now and bringing high prices.

The old bridge lamps are favorites, and I buy every one I can find for a few dollars. Until a year or so ago, the charity-run thrift shops sold them for $1 to $3 or $4, depending on wiring and whether they had shades (it is almost impossible to find the screw-on shades for them). Now the same shops are asking up to $35 for them. Almost overnight they have become spotlighted as collectibles for the future.

Many of these standing lamps are solid brass and polish up beautifully. We have found that lamps "marry" well; we buy all the inexpensive broken ones we can find and put two or three together to make a whole lamp.

A few years back, when we had a shop in North Carolina, we came across a bushel basket of old gaslight fixtures, which we bought for a few cents. Out of them we had three sets of sconces (sold for candles) and a gorgeous Williamsburg chandelier. After the huge gaslight crystal chandelier I bought for $15 out of a Pittsburgh church that was being torn down, the basket was one of the best buys of my career.

There are dealers who will buy lamp parts, so throw away nothing in the old-lamp department.

The very word "primitive" to me indicates anything nonprofessional, crudely made, yet serving a useful purpose. Webster defines it as "being the first or earliest of the kind in existence." My definition is different, but has helped me to identify items worth buying over the years.

The general antique dealers listed will most likely buy any primitives you have to sell, but there are special dealers listed in this book who sell only primitives: Tim and Cindy Weir, friends of mine who are dealers in Prairietown, Indiana, sell only Shaker primitives—boxes, tools, kitchen utensils, and furniture. Another friend, with a country store in the mountains of North Carolina, specializes in country primitives of all kinds.

Primitive items are selling for higher prices than ever before, and being sought by more collectors. If you do not find a collector for your items, query the general antique dealers in your area, for more and more of them are including primitive Americana in their stock and displays at antique shows.

Old wooden dough boards and bowls are bringing up to $50 in some areas. Many of them are simple hollowed-out trees or logs, and not too many years ago could be bought for from $3 to $5. Hand-hewn spoons, paddles, and forks bring several dollars in today's market; ten years ago I could buy most pieces for a dime each.

Old blacksmith tools, fireplace equipment, wooden handmade butter churns are just a few of the primitives bringing high prices today.

All primitives are entirely handmade, usually from materials at hand. Those bringing the highest prices are the ones that were carved or distinctly decorated in some way. Dated pieces are more valuable. There is a very thin line between folk pieces and primitive pieces. Many experts classify both types as primitives.

CHAPTER 8

Old Clothes...The Collectibles Ones

As clothes from the past have grown popular as collectibles, shops all over the United States have become eager to buy them. If you held on to the styles you or your parents wore back in the twenties, thirties, and forties, you may have a gold mine hanging in your closet.

Ten years ago, when I had two shops in North Carolina, one of which sold clothing, I sold dresses and accessories from the twenties and thirties to owners of old cars who wanted clothing from the same period as their automobiles for parades and "show" affairs. I sold other fancy or unique clothes to theater groups from the universities in the area, but never did I dream that outdated clothing for both men and women would become collectible in the antique field. Oh, the valuable things I threw away or donated to the state hospital for the mentally ill in Raleigh! If only I'd held on to those raccoon coats, flapper dresses with their tassels, fringes, and beads, the ostrich-feathered gowns and Spanish shawls that were so popular during the twenties! I'd be rich today, for so many people loaded me down with those early vintage clothes that I eventually had to discontinue selling clothing altogether. Now they are very much in demand.

A woman I once knew never threw away anything.

"Every twenty years or so," she used to tell me, "the styles come back." I could never understand why anyone would clutter up her closets with outdated garments, but now I see the wisdom of it. Many old garments are bringing more in the used market than they did brand-new.

A Southern governor's wife and Elizabeth Taylor both had dresses made from a batch of "secondhand" lace a London designer bought from an old warehouse. An ambassador's wife from one of the Middle Eastern countries boasted at a Washington party that she was wearing a dress that had belonged to a great-aunt, and allowed photographers to photograph her in it.

Vintage clothes are found in many museums. One of the most interesting exhibits in recent years was the 1973 Smithsonian "Suiting Everyone—200 years of American Clothing and Its Manufacture." Although the clothing examples began with the colonial times—when what a person wore instantly identified his or her station in life—to the present, there were over fifty pieces from the "roaring twenties," the most colorful fashion period in our history, and the most collectible in the antique market.

When querying an antique-clothes market, take color photographs of what you have for sale. Here again, condition is important. Every garment must be clean; in most states it is against the law to sell used clothing that has not been laundered or dry-cleaned, and most dealers will not buy soiled garments from anyone.

Do not expect to get a price offer from any dealer until he or she has actually seen the merchandise. It is impossible to make an offer from a photograph. The photograph is used only to let the dealer see what the styles and period of the clothing are so he can determine whether he wants to see them. Remember, too, that the dealer must hold the garments until the right person comes along to buy them, and he must make a profit. Consequently, he cannot pay you more than half or perhaps even a third of what he expects to get for them. Clothes are different from other salable items in an antique store. They're easily soiled, torn, or otherwise damaged. They're often stolen, and, if kept a long time, they may have to be cleaned again before they can be sold.

If a dealer makes you an offer and you feel you should get more, ask if he will consider selling the garments on consignment. You will wait longer for your money, but it may well be worth it. The dealer can afford to make less, since he has no investment in the garments but will simply take his percentage of the sale price.

Jacki Bailey, buyer for the Encore secondhand clothing shop on New York's Madison Avenue, buys quite a few of Jacqueline Onassis's discarded clothes. "I think she's shrewder than I when it comes to secondhand clothes, and I've been in the business for twenty years," Mrs. Bailey says. "Jackie has a good knowledge of what secondhand clothes are worth, and she's not about to be cheated."

Charles Barry, husband of the owner of Encore, says that Jackie has made thousands of dollars selling her old clothes through the shop.

"We've been dealing with Mrs. Onassis for about fifteen years," he said. "We have a fifty–fifty arrangement with her. For example, if she's selling a thousand-dollar gown for three hundred, she gets one hundred fifty dollars and the store gets one hundred fifty dollars. We never tell women which clothes belong to Mrs. Onassis, but our business has boomed since it got around that she sells through our shop."

Jackie never goes to the shop; she phones, and Mrs. Bailey goes to her Fifth Avenue apartment to appraise the clothing. "Jackie is usually waiting for me when I go to her home," Mrs. Bailey said. "We go to her bedroom, where the clothes she wants to sell are laid out for me to examine.

I'll tell her what I think they'll bring on the market, and if she agrees I'll write out a receipt for the clothes. If she thinks the clothes are worth more than the amount I've offered, we'll bargain until we agree on a price."

When asked what sort of clothing Jackie sells, Mrs. Bailey said, "Just about anything a woman wears. She sells gowns, blouses, skirts, pantsuits, slacks, dresses—all of them the very best by big-name designers. The last batch of Jackie's clothes sold for thirty-five hundred dollars."

There is such a demand these days for vintage clothing, both men's and women's, that you have more markets than just the antique shops. Men and women are buying and wearing the clothes they find from the thirties and forties and even the fifties.

In addition to the antique shops that advertise for vintage clothing, you might consider selling to used-clothing shops in your area. You will find them listed in the Yellow Pages under "Clothing—Bought and Sold." You may get more money from the antique market, but your clothing will sell faster in one of these secondhand shops.

The most salable items are real silk dresses and shirts, fancy chiffons and satins, anything with hand embroidery, feathers, or beads, and velvet capes and raccoon and other old fur coats. Clothes that look dated are most popular and will bring the highest prices.

CHAPTER 9

Coins and Stamps

Back in 1972, when the wrecking ball smashed an old brick mansion in Charlottesville, Virginia, once described as "the most disorderly house in Virginia," old coins and bills began popping up all over the place.

Just as the wrecking crew spotted the first wad of "the madam's greenbacks," over two hundred fifty men, women, and children began combing the remains with rakes, hoes, shovels, and pitchforks. Money surfaced everywhere! No one knows exactly how much money was turned up, but between thirty and forty individuals discovered hundreds of dollars each. One sixteen-year-old, Darlene Harris, found $8,000 in a rusty metal box buried four feet underground. Money found that first day varied in denominations from thousand-dollar bills to coins that had been hidden in glass jars and tin cans, or molded into the plaster walls of the twenty-three-room house.

The mansion, about two miles from the campus of the University of Virginia, was built in 1918 and turned into a bawdyhouse shortly after. The Charlottesville *Daily Progress* wrote that some of Charlottesville's most distinguished residents visited the house over the years, "perhaps to view what some said were the finest furnishings of any house in the city." The place was also known as a subcampus of the then-all-male university, and was jokingly referred to as the "student union," according to the paper.

A friend of mine, who was an antique dealer in the area, told me of one youngster who found a rusty, decaying can of silver and gold coins caked with rust and residue under a pile of rocks. Ignorant of their numismatic value as antique coins, he dropped them into a bath of acid for quick cleaning, and of course they were ruined. A representative of Deak & Company, of Washington, D.C., which is among the nation's top coin dealers, advises that coins should never be cleaned by amateurs. Only experts know how to clean them without destroying their value. If you should find a buried coin you might safely soak it in warm water to get the mud off, but any other cleaning should be done by an expert.

Graham Rayner, in his numismatic column in *Hobbies* magazine, says there are three basic rules for handling coins: First, hold them by the edges (perspiration can harm them); second, store them carefully—coins kept unwrapped in a box or purse will develop scratches; third, never drop them to see if they ring (the way we used to test to see if a coin was lead or silver). Coins are delicate, and every scratch detracts from value.

If you have a question about a coin in your possession, do a pencil tracing (place paper on top of flat coin and run pencil over it repeatedly and lightly until the face of the coin is duplicated on the paper) and send the tracing with 50 cents (stamps, check, or money order) for handling to Graham Rayner, c/o *Hobbies,* 1006 South Michigan Avenue, Chicago, Illinois 60605, for expert evaluation.

In late 1976, the Gaithersburg Coin Exchange, in my area, advertised the following rates they would pay for silver coins:

90% U.S. silver coins (pre-1965) . . . . . .$3.32 per $1.00
40% U.S. silver halves (after 1965). . . . . .$1.44 per $1.00
Wartime nickels (1942–1945) . . . . . .$9.15 per roll ($2.00)

Canadian silver (pre-1966) . . . .$2.55 per $1.00
Silver dollars (fine to better) . . . .$3.80 each

It is well to remember that prices fluctuate, reflecting world economic conditions, and anyone with coins to sell should consult the latest coin books for current values.

As an amateur coin collector, I've found pennies the most fascinating coins to collect. For several years I have watched my change, for pennies that may be of value.

In the July 4, 1976, issue of *Numismatic News* there is an ad in the classified section offering $36 for a *good-*condition 1914–D cent; $38 for *very good* condition; $46 for *fine* condition; $62 for *very fine;* and $112 for *extra fine.* These differences in prices indicate how important the condition of a coin is in determining the price. If you're an amateur, as I am, leave the judging of condition to an expert, for many factors come into play.

If you decide to mail your coins to a dealer, check the dealer's references first. Most reputable dealers are members of leading numismatic organizations, such as the Professional Numismatic Guild and ANA, and will offer bank references. You can trust the integrity of these dealers.

Although the $2 bill has the most colorful history of any U.S. currency, it is the least liked and most collected of all our paper money. Since they are a curiosity, many of them are being tucked away in safe places, in the hopes that someday they may increase in value. The Treasury Department has not decided how many $2 bills they will have to keep printing to prevent hoarding, but there is talk of issuing as many as 800 million in a year in order to cancel their value as collectibles.

The history of stamps is interesting indeed, and stamp collectors are some of the most enthusiastic collectors in the world. If you have stamps to sell, it would be well to remember these instructions from the Greg Manning Company of South Orange, New Jersey, one of the top dealers in stamps:

> Arrange your holdings in a format others can follow. Orderly albums and files of labelled glassines are always easier for buyers to check than cartons of stamps heaped to overflowing. Know not only what you have, but also how much you have. Buyers are helped by knowing if there are quantities of any particular items, the amount of duplication, and your estimate of net value. Describe the more valuable items in your collection. Any knowledgeable buyer is most interested in the scarcer material. Determine the true condition of your stamps. Quality will be a major factor in deciding the price you get for your collection. Establish a realistic price for your holdings, considering each of the factors above.

After you have received the go-ahead to send your stamps or coins to a dealer, send them, well packaged, by registered mail, insured, and give the recipient adequate time for reply. Remember that the mails are not always as fast as they should be and it may take days for a package to travel even a short distance.

CHAPTER IO

Comic Books, Magazines, and Catalogues

Many of the rare-book dealers listed in Part IV will also buy old magazines, comics, and catalogues, but there are so many collectors and dealers specializing in them that it seemed more advisable to list them separately. If you do not find the market you want under dealers and collectors listed for this chapter, go back to the rare-book dealers and query the markets there.

Comic books are no longer simply child-oriented amusement reading. Adults are taking old comic books (from the twenties, thirties, and forties, and possibly even the fifties) seriously as collector's items and enthusiastically collecting and exhibiting them all over the country. Those most popular with collectors are *Superman, Batman, Captain America, Captain Marvel, Spider-Man, Flash Gordon, Buck Rogers,* and similar cliffhanger comics that were originally created to stir the imagination of children.

The average comic book is worth from $1.50 to $5.00, except for first editions, such as the *Batman* first edition, priced at $1,250.00 in a New York shop.

If you have collections to sell, it will pay you to check the selling prices in shops, shows, and collectors' publications (listed in the back of the book) to see what they are

71

currently selling for. Prices are changing constantly, mostly going up.

Monster magazines, published by the Warren Publishing Company, are selling for from $2.50 to $3.50 generally, although certain issues are bringing more. The *Monster* yearbooks bring in the neighborhood of $8.00 to $10.00.

The first issue of *Playboy* is valued at $150 to $200 in mint condition (cover and centerfold intact). This issue came out in 1953, and later issues are valuable, too. January 1954 is valued at $40, other 1954s at around $25 each. Later issues decrease in value on down to 1966, worth only about 50 cents.

I have saved the October 1976 issue, containing the controversial interview with Jimmy Carter. I believe it is a collector's item and will one day be worth a great deal.

Although old-magazine collecting has not taken on the popularity of comic-book collecting, it is gaining in popularity. Perhaps the most sought and highest-priced is the first issue of *National Geographic* magazine (1888). Next would be the January 1954 *Playboy,* with Marilyn Monroe on the cover and as the nude centerfold. I have many collectors going for old *Saturday Evening Posts* with Norman Rockwell's famous covers.

All old catalogues are valuable, but you must be careful, for many are being reproduced. Several years ago, for a nominal sum, you could order reproductions of Sears, Roebuck and Montgomery Ward catalogues of the early 1900s. They too are collectible, but not worth as much as the originals.

You will find that the collectors in Part IV are looking for all types of catalogues. If you're a frequent visitor to old-book stores, auctions, and rummage sales, it might pay for you to start a file on all the collectibles that people are looking for and be on the lookout for them. I've kept files on all my collectors for many years.

Early in the seventies, an Academy of Comic Art was established to maintain a microfilm library of comics published in a thousand magazines and periodicals. The organization publishes a bimonthly magazine and sponsors annual conventions. You can write to P.O. Box 7499, North End Station, Detroit, Michigan 48202, for further information. A museum of cartoon art opened in August 1976 in Greenwich, Connecticut—the first of its kind, dedicated to the preservation and exhibition of the ever-growing popularity of cartoon art.

CHAPTER II

Firearms, Knives, Military Items

It is fairly safe to say that collecting weapons and related items is a "man's hobby." In all my years as an antique dealer, I never came across a female gun collector—although I am sure that somewhere there may be some.

Rifles, muskets, pistols, once purchased for a reasonable price, are now selling in the hundreds and thousands of dollars and are quite out of the reach of most collectors. A Kentucky rifle, once priced in the low hundreds, now sells for several thousand, depending on condition. Many "military-oriented" collectors have turned to knives, swords, and World Wars I and II items, including buttons, patches, and uniforms.

A young friend of mine, while visiting Gettysburg, excitedly paid $5 for what he thought was an authentic Union cavalry button, only to find out later that it was a restrike.

The experts warn that collecting military buttons is a highly specialized field. A collector must learn the backmarks of the buttons he buys—and collects. Backmarks were first used on the backs of martial buttons early in the nineteenth century; they do not appear on most of the War of 1812 buttons. They are, simply, marks pressed into the backs of buttons.

There is reason to doubt the authenticity of buttons without backmarks, even when accompanied by letters claiming their authenticity. Civil War restrike buttons have been pouring into this country from England, and buyers should beware. An expert in the field claims a buyer should "buy the backmark instead of the face of a button." The face of a button sets the price—the back tells you if it's worth it. To check the buttons you have, get A. H. Albert's book *Record of American Uniform and Historical Buttons* from the library and study it.

It is advisable for anyone planning to send guns or knives through the mail to ask for a copy of 18 U.S.C. 1715 and 124.4 Postal Service Manual, relating to what can and cannot be mailed. When I talked to Thomas A. Ziebarth, attorney for the postal service, regarding this, he warned that one should not take the advice of a postmaster, but should read the law before preparing any firearms for shipment.

Here are a few points from the manual that I feel are important to know:

(1) Pistols, revolvers, and other firearms capable of being concealed on the person are unmailable.

(2) The term "antique firearm" means any firearm (including those with a matchlock, flintlock, percussion cap, or similar type of ignition system) *manufactured in or before 1898,* or any replica thereof if such replica is not designed or redesigned for using rimfire or conventional centerfire fixed ammunition, or uses rimfire or conventional centerfire fixed ammunition, which is no longer manufactured in the United States and is not readily available in the ordinary channels of commercial trade.

(3) Antique firearms sent as curios or museum pieces can be accepted for mailing without regard to the provisions of 124.413 through 124.416 of the manual.

(4) No markings of any kind that would indicate the

nature of the contents should be made on the outside wrapper or container of any parcel containing firearms or switchblade knives.

Mr. Ziebarth advises that anyone planning to send firearms through the mail should check on the state, city, and county laws in his vicinity—it might be legal to mail firearms in one area and not in another. These postal regulations are available in every U.S. post office for the asking.

Over the past twenty years, values of antique guns have risen to the point where collectors on small budgets have found it impossible to find collectible guns in their price range. For that reason, more and more collectors are turning to World Wars I and II Army rifles, bayonets, and related military items.

During the Civil War many officers and enlisted men purchased Number 2 Smith and Weston revolvers for their personal use. The size of the gun made it easy to carry. The Smith and Weston Number 2 is not a rare gun today and frequently can be found in near-perfect condition for about $150. If you have one to sell, remember that a dealer will pay only about half of the retail value.

If you have a gun you're not sure about, take it to a pawnbroker and ask to borrow the limit on it. The average pawnshop will lend about a quarter to a third of its value. You do not have to actually borrow, but this is one way to get an approximate value for your gun.

There are over six hundred manufacturers of knives of various kinds in the world today. The most valued of all the pocket knives listed in a current price guide are the Remington Mumbly Peg, valued at $500, Remington Quick Point, St. Louis, Missouri, $400, and the Remington Radio Electrician's knife, which sold originally for $4, at $75.

There are many other pocket knives valued in the

hundreds of dollars. Consult a value guide before selling any knife.

Gordon A. Abbott, an avid knife collector of Dallas, Texas, says, "An old knife is any knife not manufactured any more. If it is rare enough and in mint condition, it could be worth as much as five hundred dollars." Remington and Winchester knives, made by the same people who make guns, are "old knives." Although the companies still make guns, they gave up making knives in the 1930s.

CHAPTER 12

Glass and China

There are, without a doubt, more collectors of glass than of any other category in the antique field. I combine the glass markets with the china, to avoid repetition of dealers. Shops that buy and sell glass also buy and sell china.

The products of America's first industry—glass making—have become the most popular of antique collectibles. A signed 20″ Tiffany dragonfly lamp, originally costing around $100, sold in 1976 for $12,500; a signed Oriental poppy-table went for $6,500 at the same sale.

Over the years styles in furnishings have changed many times, and for a time the popular Tiffany pieces went out of favor and found their way to attics and storerooms, to be replaced by more modern styles. Now collectors are clamoring for them. So much in demand are the Tiffany pieces that experts, like Robert Koch, professor of art at Southern Connecticut State College, in New Haven, are cautioning buyers to beware. "The name 'Tiffany' is being used for lots of things that only remotely resemble the real thing," warns Professor Koch, who has involved himself with Tiffany for twenty years. "The name 'Tiffany' should be used only to refer to those period pieces made in Tiffany studios."

Tiffany is one of the few glass antiques that retain their value when damaged. Fred Dikeman of Flushing, New York, wrote me that he apprenticed under his father, John Dikeman, forty years ago, when his father was the head of the lamp-shade department of Tiffany studios in New York. His father had worked for Tiffany studios from 1892 to the day the doors were padlocked, when he took all the remaining glass sheets of Tiffany's supply and continued restoring damaged windows and lamp shades until his death, in 1967.

Fred Dikeman has continued restorations to date with only the original, authentic glass. He owns a great portion of the original price lists and brochures of everything that was turned out of Tiffany studios. With this information, his wife does appraisals of Tiffany objects for insurance companies and others.

All of Mr. Dikeman's work is done with the original tools, workbench, blocks, patterns foil, and techniques. His address is: 42-66 Phlox Place, Flushing, New York 11355, for those of you who would like to have a damaged piece of Tiffany repaired or a perfect piece appraised. The Dike-mans also buy damaged pieces.

There are so many different varieties of glass that it would be impossible to mention them all, but collectors are enamored of every kind of glass, and there are markets for all of them.

Glass wire-insulators of our not-too-distant past have become one of the most interesting kinds of collectibles. These were used on telegraph, telephone, and electric poles all over the country until recent times.

Ten years ago my telephone-lineman customer used to bring me boxes of glass insulators of various colors. Back then I sold them for $1 each. I imagine they are bringing three or four times as much today.

Sandwich glass, including the lacy "historical" pieces, portraying events, places, and people in our history are popular with collectors everywhere, but the early flint lacy ware (1825–88) is the most sought. Unlike other collectible glass of this century (Cambridge, Tiffany, Heisey, Steuben, etc.), which carried an impressed trademark in the glass, Sandwich, with one exception (the *Lafayet* boat salt dish), was never marked.

Teapots, cups, and cup plates are among the most sought collectibles. The early teacups were handleless and the saucers large. Frequently drinkers referred to "a dish of tea," since the tea was poured into the saucer (dish) and the cups put to rest on cup plates (small glass plates that were placed beside the cups and saucers).

Sandwich Glass Company made nearly a thousand different cup plates from 1825 to 1850, and they sold for as little as 3 or 4 cents. They are very popular collectibles, and welcomed by most dealers.

Reproduction Sandwich glass is categorized as "Depression" glass. Depression glass is the mass-produced, cheap (even for the time) glass of the Depression years, most of which were copies of earlier pressed glass. Depression glass includes Sandwich, Carnival, and others, much of which was given away by soap companies as bonuses. According to N.H. Mager, an expert in the field and a producer of antique shows and flea markets, this glass is much in demand and brings high prices in the collecting field.

Heisey Glass (marked with an H inside the diamond) was produced until 1957, when the molds and trademark were sold to the Imperial Glass Company. Heisey collectors are growing steadily in numbers. The Heisey Museum in Newark, Ohio, also houses the headquarters of the Heisey Collectors of America (P.O. Box 27, Newark, Ohio 43055), whose membership fee is $3. Membership entitles one to receive a monthly publication of news and ads involving Heisey collectors.

It is said that the erection of a Libbey Glass factory at the World Columbian Exposition in Chicago in 1893 may have been responsible for the beginning of the "brilliant period" of American cut glass. Leading to the mass production of this heavy cut glass in the early 1900s was the important innovation of mechanized cutting lathes with electric power, which made possible a quality product at a reasonable price.

The word "Corning" to many people brings to mind squarish casserole dishes decorated with blue cornflowers. But to the rare-glass collector the name "Corning" means the town in the lower reaches of New York State's Finger Lakes and wine country, a few miles from the Pennsylvania border, where Steuben glass is blown.

Over the years the cornflower casserole dishes produced by Corning Glass Works have paid the rent for the glass furnaces in Corning, where the expensive, exquisitely delicate Steuben glass is hand-blown.

The Steuben 1903–1932 pieces signed by Frederick Carder are among the most highly valued glass in today's market—$10,000 for a piece of Intarsia, $5,000 for a small bowl of Tyrian. *The Glass of Fredrick Carder,* written by Paul Gardner (once an associate of Carder's), the curator of glass and ceramics at the Museum of History and Technology of the Smithsonian Institution in Washington, has been credited with much of the rise in value of the Carder pieces.

A signed piece of glass is far more valuable than the same piece would be unsigned. Often the signature may be hidden in the fold of the glass, along a rippled edge or in some other inconspicuous place. I learned this when I had a shop outside of Pittsburgh, and was rewarded many times with a signature in cut glass or art glass that I might never have seen without searching for it.

The ancient craft of glass blowing was a dying art until recently, when many young artisans in the United States began creating contemporary art glass. A list of ninety-six glass artists can be found in a recent book, *Contemporary*

Art Glass, by Ray and Lee Grover, published by Crown, and thirty-three of the artists are American. Fine pieces of contemporary blown art glass are finding their way into expensive collections, at prices comparable to those for antique glass.

There are as many variations of china as there are of glass. As I mentioned earlier, the exquisitely hand-painted, eggshell-thin old china pieces from Germany, France, Prussia, Austria, and other European countries are the most beautiful and cherished of all antiques. English bone china, though fine and desirable, in no way (to my way of thinking) compares with these others.

The destruction of German china factories, museums, and old homes during World War I and World War II destroyed so much of the fine German porcelain and china that German pieces have joined the "rare" category of collectibles. Dresden, one of the finest German products, is rare indeed, and not too often found at antique shops and shows.

If you're not a knowledgeable collector or dealer, as I wasn't for years, something to watch out for in china is pieces with decals that may look hand-painted to the inexperienced eye. Sometimes it is difficult to tell the difference, but there is a big difference in the price you will receive for the pieces.

A jeweler in Pittsburgh once advertised for hand-painted "Bee Hive" pieces and offered top dollar for them. I had several beautiful "Bee Hive" plates and took them to his store, expecting to get a great deal more than I was asking in my small shop, only to find out that the beautiful "paintings" on them were decals and not hand-painted at all. Sometimes, if pieces are used frequently and washed often, parts of the decals will rub off. This jeweler showed me how to run my finger over the edges of the pictures to feel the difference where the decals end. Also, touching a whole decal lightly with your fingers gives you a feel of uniformity not present in oil painting, where certain sections would naturally have heavier paint than others.

Recently I came across a September 1911 issue of *Ladies' Home Journal,* in which there was an interesting article about the meeting of John Wesley (founder of the Methodist Church) and Josiah Wedgwood (founder of Wedgwood pottery). It seems that in 1760 John Wesley passed through Burslem, England, and stopped to chat with Wedgwood, who was weeding his flower garden beside the "Ivy Cottage." A year later, Josiah Wedgwood made a teapot for Mr. Wesley, decorating it with a floral wreath surrounding the "Blessing" on the one side and "Return Thanks" on the other. According to the article, this John Wesley teapot could be seen at Wesley's house, City Road, London, England.

Be that as it may, I believe the pot was copied many times, for I saw two pots in my years as an antique dealer. They were marked "The John Wesley Teapot" and, in smaller letters, "Wedgwood, Etruria, England." There were other marks that I do not remember, but it seems apparent that Mr. Wedgwood made more than one John Wesley teapot.

Marie Longworth Nichols, a wealthy woman in Cincinnati, who painted china as a hobby, became so excited at the exhibition of Japanese art at the Centennial Exposition of 1876 that she was inspired to found the Rookwood Pottery Company in 1880. Her first pottery included beautiful tableware, with floral decorations blended over rich browns, oranges, and yellows. Until about 1910, all Rookwood art pottery was individually decorated by the hundred or more artists who signed their work.

Plate collecting today involves limited-edition plates made each year right up until the present time. There are many American companies that sell plates only by subscription. Many of the plates, which are just a few years old, are selling for fantastic prices, which makes this a most profitable hobby. According to a major plate company, if you bought a 1965 Lalique crystal plate for $25, you could have sold it in 1976 for $1,750—a 6,900 percent profit.

The most popular design ever to be used in china is the Blue Willow pattern. It was first used about two hundred years ago, imported from the ports of Nanking and Canton to the Western world. According to legend, the Blue Willow pattern told the story of two Chinese lovers, Koong-shee, daughter of a mandarin, and Chang, her father's secretary. Although she was in love with Chang, Koong-shee had been promised to an old, wealthy merchant. On the day of her wedding, amid confusion and celebrating, Chang slipped into the pagoda (on the right of the pattern) and captured his love. They had gone as far as the bridge beside the willow when the father saw them and set off after them, his whip raised in his right hand. The lovers managed to elude the father and were later married. According to the legend, the lovers were looked on favorably by the gods and changed into two immortal doves, the emblem of constancy. United forever in death, they can be seen in the center of the design, looking down on the scenes of their romance.

The original Blue Willow designs were hand-painted in cobalt blue in the great pottery centers of China and exported to European and later American cities. The pattern was changed in 1780 by Thomas Turner, of the Caughley Pottery Factory, in Shropshire, England. He combined many of the Oriental designs with the original Blue Willow, and most of the china we find today is of his pattern.

So much of the world's history has been represented in our glass and china that it is no wonder that collecting it has become one of the most fascinating hobbies in the world.

China and glass prices are increasing almost daily, and some of the prices asked in shops and shows boggle my mind. I can't help remembering what I got for similar pieces back in the forties and fifties. For example: an 8" satin-glass vase (coralene on satin, heavily decorated) recently sold for $495, a Tiffany 12" H. harp desk lamp (shade not original) for $625, and a small Steuben atomizer for $200. I could go on, for I always note the prices when I visit shops or shows, and it never fails to amaze me how the prices have skyrocketed.

The best advice I can give any person preparing to sell, for example, some of the treasures your grandmother left you is: Know what you have before marketing. If you are unable to find out from the value guides listed in the back of this book or from talking with dealers in your area, then pay a reputable appraiser for an honest written appraisal. It may put many dollars in your pocket.

When Christopher Hugh Hildesley, vice-president of Sotheby Parke Bernet, Inc., and head of its appraisal department, spoke in Washington, D.C., in 1976 on the subject "Techniques of Buying at Auction," he gave some priceless advice to his audience:

"Most important in buying is to know a great deal about the object you're bidding [on]. There's no substitute for an eye. To develop the collector's eye, you have to read a great deal on your subject, go to museums and look at good things, and then read auction catalogues and compare the catalogues with the sale price. Then you'll be ready to take a flyer."

Mr. Hildesley says it's possible to learn a good bit from talking with the heads of the different categories at Sotheby's. "They never mind if you bring in the odd object to be identified. They charge nothing for a verbal opinion rendered on the premises [980 Madison Avenue, New York City]. Actually, they like looking at oddities."

To get a written appraisal from Sotheby's—say, for tax or estate purposes—they charge $1\frac{1}{2}$ percent of the appraisal value up to $50,000 and 1 percent for appraisals of greater value.

"We'll negotiate when the appraisal goes over a million dollars," he said. He told a most interesting story of a very rare find. "I had gone up to appaise some statues at a Catholic teaching order in Yonkers. The statues were not of great interest. But I happened to notice a small bowl which the sisters were using for sugar. I brought our china expert—kicking and screaming that it couldn't be anything of interest—out to the convent. And he actually turned a brilliant red when he saw the bowl. It was a piece commissioned in the sixteenth century, in imitation of Chinese porcelain, by the Medicis. It carried the maker's mark. It sold eventually for eighteen thousand dollars. Only fifty-four pieces of the china are known to exist."

His final advice to collectors was "always buy the very best you can afford. The top range always keeps its value better. Currently, we see a drop in price for the middle-priced object.

"Collectors should keep good records. Objects are more valuable if their provenance [history] is well documented. You should note what you paid for it and keep up with the prices in your field of interest. And you should have photographs of your collection in a safety deposit box—for insurance, among other reasons."

If you have glass, china, or pottery to sell and do not find a collector here who is specifically looking for what you have, you should be safe in contacting any of the dealers listed in Part IV.

CHAPTER 13

Memorabilia

Memorabilia covers one of the most popular phases of collecting. It is said that Americans are on a nostalgia kick, and because of it old-fashioned, "yesterday" items are becoming more valuable day by day.

Even the Smithsonian Institution has become an avid collector of Americana. During the 1976 Democratic and Republican conventions, a special representative was sent to both conventions with instructions to bring back at least five hundred political items from each. This was done with collections of state banners, hats, buttons, programs, and many other items.

Most collectors collect anything and everything surrounding or related to their chosen subjects.

As I said earlier, although bicentennial items are collectible and will become valuable in time, do not expect to get fantastic prices for any of them. You must remember that they are available all over the country, and will be for some time to come. These are what I would call the collectibles of tomorrow, for age will add to their value.

Many general antique dealers will buy memorabilia, but collectors of special memorabilia are your best bet for marketing.

Political memorabilia is more popular than most other categories.

Immediately after Senator Thomas Eagleton's unprecedented withdrawal as a Vice-Presidential candidate in

1972, an ingenious young man, Ron Beatus, realized that the campaign material that had been produced for the McGovern-Eagleton ticket would make fantastic items for collectors, investors, historians, and dealers.

"I immediately got in touch with all the manufacturers and political organizations," said the young man, "and bought up every authentic McGovern-Eagleton button I could find. A small ad for these buttons in one of the local newspapers and I was in business! The letters and orders poured in, and I found a totally neglected area in the antiques and collecting field. I had to move out of my home, where I was conducting business, and move into an office in midtown Manhattan."

Make sure your political material (especially buttons) are not reproductions. The Hobby Protection Act passed by Congress on November 30, 1973, requires that all political buttons, stamps, and coins that are reproduced from originals must be clearly marked "Reproduction," along with date of reproduction.

Mr. Beatus warns that any buttons that represent Presidential candidates who ran before 1896 are definitely fakes—the first political button was not made until 1896.

The Davis-Bryan buttons from the early 1900s are so scarce and rare that they sell for upward of $1,000. It is believed by many that political-button collecting will become the most popular phase of collecting after coins and stamps. (Current estimates show over 100,000 collectors in the United States.)

If you want to be put on Mr. Beatus's political-memorabilia mailing list, there is no charge. Simply send your name and address to: Joy Products, 24 West Forty-fifth Street, New York, New York 10036.

Beatles memorabilia is near the top in popularity. (I mentioned earlier the New York shop selling the 1966 album cover for $150.) Almost any early Beatles material is collectible. Posters, programs, and early advertising items are bringing terrific prices. The same holds for Shirley Temple, *Gone With the Wind*, World's Fair, and many other nostalgia items from our not-too-distant past.

Back in 1975, the Kennedy family intervened to prevent the Chemical Bank of New York from auctioning off President John F. Kennedy's 1939 Harvard report card and other historic memorabilia until ownership of the articles could be determined. The bank happened to have possession of the papers, including handwritten letters from John to his parents, because Gene Shoor, an author of juvenile books, who had written a book, *Young John Kennedy*, had presented the papers as collateral for a loan which had not been paid. Shoor claimed, through his telephone-answering service, that the papers had been given to him by President Kennedy.

Chemical Bank planned to sell eleven items, which had been tentatively appraised at a minimum of $8,000. One letter from JFK to his mother, Rose Kennedy, was valued at $1,500; another, to his father, which contained a drawing, was valued at $3,000. The report card, which contained "mostly C's," was valued at $75.

Almost anything that has belonged to a famous person or was used by one has great value to collectors. Elvis Presley's tremendous following will pay just about anything for something that belonged to him personally. Because of his popularity, a few years ago he was able to auction off an old basketball glove, a portable oven, and a painted bathtub for $11,000. Those same items belonging to just plain folks probably wouldn't have sold in a junkyard or thrift shop at any price.

CHAPTER 14

Musical Items

Records and music boxes are by far the most-collected items in the musical category. There was a time when radio disc jockeys were the foremost collectors of records, having access to the radio stations' huge record libraries and able to take home the discards when the stations "cleaned house" or culled the obsolete records from their files. Not so any more. The records have become valuable, and stations often sell them.

A young opera singer, who was a friend of my daughter's, collected every recording by Frank Sinatra she could find, paying as much as $12 for an early one.

In compiling the listing of dealers and collectors in the back of this book, I discovered more seeking or selling records (primarily 78 rpm and radio transcriptions) than any other musical item. In the thousands of letters received from *Woman's Day* readers after the magazine excerpted *Antiques for Amateurs on a Shoestring Budget,* more folks wanted to know where to sell 78 rpm records than any other single item.

I have found that Salvation Army stores, which used to sell these records for 5 and 10 cents, are now asking $1 for run-of-the-mill recordings. Some are scratched and in generally poor condition. If there were not a great demand for them, I'm sure the prices would not have risen so substantially in so short a time.

Musical boxes of all varieties are next on musical

collectors' lists—any music box, from the rare cylinder types to the ornate one- or two-tune boxes that flooded the country during the early 1900s. There áre musical snuffboxes, singing birdboxes, and even musical pieces of jewelry. (Musical clocks are not categorized as music boxes.) Even old stuffed teddy bears and other musical toys have joined the collectible ranks.

It is believed that the first makers of musical box movements were watchmakers and that the first musical tones were housed in watches. They probably originated in Switzerland about 1770, and it was there that the industry developed and thrived. There had been musical clocks as much as three hundred years before, but the tunes were played with bells, not pegs set in cylinder discs. In the early 1800s music boxes were being made in France (by a Swiss), and soon thereafter in Germany.

The early boxes were novelties, rare treasures, often made of solid gold and silver, set with precious stones. From the early 1800s the music box became the accepted means of producing fine music, generally the most popular operatic selection of that day. Many music boxes can be dated by the tunes they play.

The production of bigger music boxes during the Victorian era made it possible to produce selections from the operas that thrilled the people of that time. Many of them played more than one selection, whereas the earlier, smaller ones played only a single tune. A few years later (1877) the phonograph was invented, and R. Mosoriak, in his *Curious History of Musical Boxes,* declared, "It was the development and wide public acceptance of this human voice recorder and reproducer which doomed the musical box—it was the death blow!"

With the improvements of the phonograph in the early 1900s, the manufacture of music boxes was halted, and in a very short time they became collector's items. There are collectors of musical snuffboxes, although the small space inside the boxes would hardly have held snuff, collectors of the larger types, which were elaborate and ornate, and others, but it is obvious that collectors are not so concerned with the tunes or music as they are with the cases that house them.

Although many thousands of old music boxes do not bear the maker's mark or even a trademark, this does not mean that these boxes are inferior. Most likely they were distributed or sold through agents to retailers who preferred to put their own identity on the boxes.

Over the years, as an antique dealer, I sold hundreds of music boxes. Victorian photograph albums with tiny music boxes encased in the back were by far the most popular of all I sold. Depending on condition and how elaborately decorated the albums were, prices ranged from $25 to $100 or more. Small musical jewel boxes varied as much in price.

Today all antique prices have escalated, and music boxes are more in demand than they were when I had a shop. Any antique shop is a potential market for selling your boxes. It might be wise to get an offer from more than one dealer before selling, for there is no set value placed on them, to my knowledge. One dealer may have collectors or some special customer in mind and be willing to pay much more than another dealer would.

There was a time when pawnshops were the most likely places to buy or sell a musical instrument, but today most antique shops both buy and sell them, as do music shops which handle only used or old musical items.

In my search for values I found almost no prices or guides to instrument values. I think you will find that the prices offered depend on how badly a collector or dealer wants what you have. Ten years ago I sold beautiful old pump organs for as little as $50, and today I see them advertised for $1,500 and up.

There is one thing that is almost a certainty: Collectors of and dealers in musical items know all there is to know about their wares or collectibles and will ask questions about performance and condition that you may not be able to answer. The average person who might have an instrument to sell may know very little about strings, bellows, or felts, so this is one category that the amateur would do best to avoid in the buying-to-sell aspect of antiquing.

CHAPTER 15

Paper:
–Postcards, Valentines,
Paper Dolls, Etc.

Paper collectibles cover a wide range of items, many of which fit into other chapters of this book. Maps, pamphlets, and related paper pieces are sought by book and comic-book dealers, posters and paper advertiques by a special set of dealers and collectors. Many book dealers also buy postcards and valentines, just as many toy dealers buy paper dolls, but there are enough dealers and collectors who specialize in postcards, valentines, paper dolls, and other paper collectibles to warrant a chapter of their own.

Topical-postcard collectors are dedicated in their pursuit of that rare, hard-to-find addition to their collection. Some folks collect only cards with firehouses or fire engines on them; others want locomotives or early automobiles. The kinds of collected post cards are limitless, and somewhere a collector is probably looking for exactly what you have.

Sally S. Carver, an expert on topical-postcard collecting, writes in *Hobbies* magazine that she's seen collectors travel great distances to auctions just to buy one card. Collectors will not be frustrated when they have to pore over thousands of cards to find one of their specialty.

A hundred years ago it was mostly the rich who collected picture postcards, for only they could afford to travel to exotic and interesting places.

Cards from the last half of the nineteenth century are not only valuable historically but extremely beautiful as well, for the photographers took great pains in developing their work. They might well show the interior of the roofless Hotel de Ville, burned down during the siege of 1871, the interior of castles, and attractions you would see on a personal "Grand Tour." Many places photographed on those old cards no longer exist, which makes the cards more valuable. If some famous landmark burned to the ground or was destroyed, as in the San Francisco earthquake, picture postcards of them are very valuable.

Our nostalgic longing for quaint old cards has been responsible for reviving interest in the famous Kewpies by Rose O'Neill. When *Ladies' Home Journal* published the first Rose O'Neill Kewpie drawing in December, 1909, it carried a footnote explaining the name: "The reason why these funny, roly-poly creatures are called Kewpies is because they look like cupids. You can tell by their tiny wings Kewpie means a small cupid, just as a puppy means a small dog."

Rose O'Neill described her Kewpies as "cheerful elves, bursting with kindness," and declared she put all of her "love of humanity into those little images." They had then, as now, those starfish hands, rounded tummies, broad elfin smiles, sprouting wings, and the distinctive topknots that would always characterize the whole Kewpie tribe.

From the pages of magazines, Kewpies began to spring forth on postcards, valentines, and "kutouts" all over the country. An original Kewpie card in good condition will bring as much as $10 on today's market.

Kewpiana collectors number in the thousands, and there are hundreds of Kewpie clubs both in this country and in Europe. Each April many gather for a Kewpie festival in Branson, Missouri, which is headquarters for the International Rose O'Neill Clubs. If you're interested in contacting one of the Kewpie clubs in your area, write to: Kewpie Clubs, Shepherd of the Hills Farm, Branson, Missouri, or call (417) 334-4191.

The Kewpies' appearance in magazines, both in the form of paper dolls and as illustrations for a full page of rhymes by Rose O'Neill, evoked such a response that Jell-O quickly signed up the elfin figures to advertise their product. The association of paper dolls and food advertising brought on a profusion of paper dolls, used as giveaways for all kinds of household products.

The Campbell Kids, designed by Grace Dayton, were more earthbound. Gawky and Clumsy stared at you with wide-eyed astonishment, toddlers who could not tie their own shoelaces or cope with their own coat buttons.

Grace Dayton's magazine and book items, postcards, paper dolls, and comic strips tumbled from her desk in profusion. Her paper dolls of Dolly Dungle and friends appeared in *Pictorial Review* for over twenty years and today are worth many dollars if in good condition. Many Kewpiana collectors also collect these. Any of the paper dealers or collectors in the back of this book will be interested in them.

I mentioned earlier the prices the Shirley Temple paper dolls were bringing. Any set of paper dolls depicting clothing styles of an earlier era are good. Often they can be dated by the fashions they wear. They usually bring from $5 to $10.

The spirit of the past has crept into modern-day Christmas cards. The Hummel-like, wistful figures, the snow-covered landscapes depicting "Grandma's house," and copies of the works of the Old Masters are collectible.

Daniel Yankelovich, a pollster, was hired by Hallmark

in 1972 to ask people what they wanted in Christmas cards. He reported back that the demand was for cards that gave the illusion that the buyer had made them himself or herself.

An invalid I know who has artistic ability creates cards from his bed and sells them for $3 to $6 each. They are beautiful and collectible, as most handmade paper items are.

I had the occasion to write Jimmy Carter early in his campaign for the Presidency, and he replied promptly with a postcard with his picture on it. As a result of my letter, I was put on his mailing list and later received an invitation to the inauguration festivities and a beautiful inaugural book with sketches of Carter and Mondale, a pictorial map of Washington, and other related material.

The postcard, invitation, and commemorative booklet are collector's items for my three-year-old granddaughter, Sarah (with these I will put the issue of *Playboy* with the controversial interview), and by the time Sarah reaches her teens she will have the start of a collection she may want to continue.

Old calendars are collected by many. Although the age of the calendar is a determining factor in evaluation, more important are the illustrations. For example, World War II calendars with their "Buy Bonds" and other patriotic scenes are collectible to many who are interested in military or historical material.

I've had collectors of fancy, old-fashioned valentines who pleaded to be called the minute I found a box of old correspondence or a "memory book," where such valentines might be found. Finding one piece for their collection was worth a trip. One customer had a removable glass top in her large cocktail table, and beneath the glass she displayed one of the prettiest assortments of valentines I've ever seen.

There are several things to remember when you are marketing paper items:

(1) Paper dolls are more valuable when uncut.

(2) Postcards that were postmarked (dated) and sent through the mail are more valuable than unused ones.

(3) Calendars are more valuable with no dates torn off, and those old ones on which household records were kept (marketing notes and especially prices paid for things) are more valuable than plain ones.

Banks, railroads, airlines, insurance companies, drug and hardware stores, not to mention your oil company and the corner gas station, once passed out free calendars year after year. I can remember arguing with my children about which of the dozens we received should be hung in the kitchen. Sandy wanted the one with kittens and Sally the one with dogs.

Count yourself lucky if you get a decent-looking one free any more. Paper shortages and high postage and packaging rates make the old-fashioned "big as life" calendar, which you could see from across the room and which had space for writing around the dates, a thing of the past. Selling the days of the month is big and competitive business these days, and the days of the free calendar are gone forever, which probably makes these items more valuable than ever as collectibles.

CHAPTER 16

Silver, Gold, Pewter, Jewelry, and Fountain Pens

The best friends a young dealer or collector of silver, gold, or jewelry can have are a druggist and a pawnbroker.

When I spoke to a group of general antique dealers at a seminar last summer, they were shocked at that statement, but I think my experiences over the years will bear me out.

Almost from the beginning of my career, I've kept a scrap gold and silver box. Long before prices reached such inflationary heights and our country went off the silver standard, my scrap boxes paid the rent on my shops many months out of the year. Without my two "friends" this might not have been possible.

Silver and gold are weighed by the troy ounce (12 ounces to the pound), and my druggist has a troy scale on which he has weighed many "so-so" pieces of jewelry to see if it would be more profitable to sell them for scrap or as individual pieces. You'd be surprised how often a piece will be worth more as scrap than sold "as is."

Many old pieces may not be marked, or the marks may have worn off. The druggist is equipped to test these unmarked pieces with an acid to determine if they are solid or plated.

The pawnbroker is a priceless friend in getting free appraisals—particularly of stones. A pawnbroker in Pittsburgh became my teacher concerning silver and gold; I found him more than willing to help me after I allowed him first chance to buy unusual pieces—at my price, not his. I found him completely trustworthy, but remember, you do not have to sell to any pawnbroker if you doubt his sincerity.

Most pawnshops will buy your scrap metal at the current market rate.

Before you offer for sale any silver, gold, or jewelry, know what you have. Remember that silver marks from 800 up usually mean silver content that is equivalent to sterling—and often better. Much Mexican silver is marked this way.

Both solid silver and gold are soft metals, so other metals are added to harden them. A watch fob, over years of rubbing against a man's woolen pants, may have all marks literally rubbed off. We've all seen old rings worn thin in the back.

Few of us ever have 18-karat-gold dishes to eat from, nor would many of us want to eat our meals from such precious plates, but one family owned such a service. Back in June 1974, a seventy-five-piece 19-karat-gold dinner service for twelve was sold by Sotheby Parke Bernet Galleries in Los Angeles for a total of $185,000. This fabulous gold service belonged to Edward and Julia Bodman, who were advised back in 1930 to purchase gold as an investment. Taking the advice of their financial adviser, they sent a representative to China to purchase 1,100 ounces of gold. The representative returned with 1,100 ounces of gold jewelry he had purchased for them for about $18 an ounce, for a total of under $20,000. When the Bodmans received the jewelry, they had it melted down and made into the dinner service, which sold in 1974 for $148 an ounce. It had been a good investment!

Seldom, if ever, will you come across solid-gold pieces of tableware, but often you'll see sterling-silver pieces that have been washed in gold. The House of Kirk, America's oldest continuing silversmiths, made flatware for President James Madison, which was gold fired on silver, and the Madison service was used by subsequent tenants of the White House. Somewhere along the way it ended up in storage, but Jackie Kennedy found it during her stay at the White House and brought it out again. Many of the pieces were missing, but she liked it well enough to have copies made of these pieces, and the set is now used by the President and Mrs. Carter for formal White House dinners.

The House of Kirk (founded by Samuel Kirk, a direct descendant of two great seventeenth-century silversmiths: John Kirk, registered in Goldsmiths Hall, England, 1696–97, and Sir Francis Child, Lord Mayor of London in 1669, and a practicing silversmith) has used dozens of marks. The early pieces are fairly easy to date, for marks similar to the English hallmark system were used in Baltimore from 1814 to 1830. This system was not used anywhere else in America.

The marks have the Assay Office stamp, which is the Maryland arms in shield, the head of Liberty, the Cominical letter mark, indicating the year, and the firm's mark. Early pieces, from 1815 to 1818, were marked K & S (the S for John Smith, a partner at that time). After 1818, the mark KIRK & KIRK was used. Early in 1821 it was changed to S. KIRK. In 1846, after Kirk took his son into the business, it became "Samuel Kirk & Son."

Another Early American silversmith, Paul Revere, was a second-generation silver- and goldsmith, and one of America's outstanding artisans.

Early silversmiths also used a lot of pewter. Called "everyman's alloy," pewter was less expensive and was useful in many ways. Composed mainly of malleable tin, it was turned into plates, spoons, cups, and tankards, and during the War of 1812 it was even melted down to make ammunition for American guns.

Pewter had its greatest popularity from 1750 to 1850. It was made into everything from candlesticks to babies' bottles. It had its advantages, being tarnishproof and much easier to care for than silver, but it had its disadvantages, too. Pewter is not a perfect alloy. Early pewter contained lead with the tin, and today we know not to use any vessels containing lead for food. (Modern pewter is 90%–93% tin, 1%–2% antimony—a hardening agent—and copper, a formula set down by the American Pewter Guild.)

Pewter is a soft metal and easily bent or dented; it has a low melting point, which means it cannot be used in cooking and should not be placed too near the stove or other heat.

The Stieff Company of Baltimore, Maryland, began reproducing copies of Early American pewter after the Korean War, for sale at Williamsburg. Americans were quick to buy copies of the pieces their ancestors had used. Many think the swing back to pewter in recent years may be attributed to the high cost of silver, since pewter is a perfect substitute for the more precious metal. Leading jewelers and department stores now feature a full line of pewter products. The Stieff Company is now reproducing old pieces for the Smithsonian as part of the Smithsonian's Product Development Program, and all of the pieces are copied from pieces in the museum's collection. These are collectible and have resale value, since they are limited in number.

Christopher Hugh Hildesley, appraiser for Sotheby Parke Bernet, says about a visit to an English castle, "The chase for the valuable object is the thing. Just as we were leaving the castle after appraising some paintings, one of the owners said, 'Oh, you wouldn't be interested in a bit of silver, would you? We have some we use every day.' The bit of silver turned out to be the largest collection of Huguenot silver [eighteenth-century] ever sold. It brought seven hundred fifty thousand dollars."

Prices for older gems, in both silver and gold mountings, are frightful. Since the prices of gold and silver have skyrocketed, those old, out-of-style pieces of jewelry with their old-fashioned mountings are being sought by dealers and collectors alike. Jewelers who never sold secondhand jewelry before are advertising for "antique jewelry," which could very well cover almost any piece made up to the present time, although the old-fashioned designs are by far the most popular. According to the president of one of the largest Washington, D.C., jewelry stores, local shops are virtually flooded with old jewelry around income-tax time. "Many people," he said, "are looking for ready cash to pay their taxes, so they scrounge around and come up with all the old jewelry they can find lying around the house."

Another jeweler said that some fabulous pieces show up at a time like that, including old watches, which are very much in demand. In one jeweler's window was a 14-karat-gold "Keywind watch" dated on the back of the case, "Dec. 1855." The price was $585. A later Elgin watch, dated 1920, was offered for $385. This same jeweler told of a client he'd had once who wanted to invest $15,000 in diamonds. He put together a package for her of 1-karat and 1½-karat diamonds. Since she bought them, several years ago, values have jumped from $1,000 to $3,000 a karat, and he estimates that his customer's investment of $15,000 would bring her $30,000 or more on today's market.

Another jeweler recently paid $30,000 for an emerald the seller had purchased for between $8,000 and $9,000 only fifteen years ago.

Glenn Nord of the Gemological Institute of the American Gem Society in Los Angeles declares that fine gems have skyrocketed in price over the last few years. Many buyers from Japan, Europe, and Arabian countries "know no price limit." In a speech before the American Gem Society's annual gathering in New Orleans in 1973, he said, "Seven years ago, there was a fifty-five-karat sapphire which sold for $65,000. The same stone sold seven years later for $195,000.—three times the original sale price."

Diamonds have always been good investments, according to the experts. Today there is a great demand for black opals, and even the semiprecious stones, such as garnets, have come into their own. Anything set in gold has potential value for dealers and collectors. Jade pieces have mounted in value in recent years. Jade is more than a precious stone to the Chinese; it means magic spells and charms that they believe influence their lives. In recent years, when more people from all walks of life are clamoring for jade, the prices have soared as much as 500 percent.

The commercial value of a piece of jade depends on its color. The highest quality is "glassy jade," so transparent that when placed on a sheet of white cloth it looks like a drop of green oil. The stone comes in many colors and varieties, however: grayish-olive (celadon jade), "butter yellow," the whitish "mutton fat," and dark green (the color of spinach). It has been suspected that many greenish tombstones in China and Japan have been stolen, crushed, and sold as pieces of jade, but there is a way to tell the real from the imitation. Real, genuine jade, when scratched on the surface with a steel-pointed object, won't be marred.

Another valuable jewel is the pearl. Unlike minerals, the organic pearl does not have to be cut or polished. The first step in determining if your pearls are real is to hold them between your teeth. If they feel gritty, like sand, chances are they are real. The final test is to have them

X-rayed by a jeweler.

A woman called me long distance after reading my previous book to tell me that I had changed her whole life. It seems that after reading how to identify pearls, she attended a church rummage sale and bought a pair of pearl-and-sapphire earrings for 50 cents. They were appraised at $150. This just proves that there are still valuable pieces around—if you are able to identify them among the worthless pieces at sales or in thrift shops. Many people do not know what they have, or place too little value on pieces that may be worth a small fortune.

There are markets for all kinds of jewelry, even broken or damaged pieces, for the stones are valuable and can be set in other pieces, and, of course, the precious metals have value.

Perhaps nostalgia or sentiment has played a role in the revival of the faithful old fountain pen. Almost a century ago, Louis E. Waterman invented the fountain pen, and it occupied a prominent place in almost every pocket, purse, and desk as the quality writing instrument until the advent of the ballpoint. Now the old pens are being collected, bought and sold, and even worn as jewelry. Robert Edison, in an article appearing in *The New York Times* in 1976, wrote, "In Los Angeles, a funky new fashion fad is wearing jazzy antique pens as jewelry. Teen-agers who have never seen a blotter or an inkwell are having pens made into clips, pins and necklaces (a harking back, intended or otherwise, to the 1920's and 30's, when petite ladies' models, worn from the neck on ribbons or chains, were the rage). This penchant for pen jewelry has caused one New York collector to come up with a charm bracelet for his young daughter which has dangling pen points of various sizes as charms."

The "Big Red" or Parker Duofold, which sold in 1921

for $7, is bringing $150 on today's market. Les Sackin, owner of Sarsaparilla, a Manhattan shop that specializes in nostalgia items from the twenties and thirties, claims he began selling these old fountain pens as long as seven years ago and they are increasing in popularity and scarcity every day.

Many jewelers and antique shops will buy old "working" pens, but here are a few New York City shops that handle them:

Sarsaparilla, 1179 Second Avenue, New York, New York 10022. Pens average about $15 and are sold in working condition.

As-Is, 561 Hudson Street, New York, New York 10014. A mixed bag of old pens, displayed in a real pen case. Prices range from $3 to $125, for a sterling-silver Tiffany pen-and-pencil combination. Pens are guaranteed to work.

Cherchez, 141 East Seventy-sixth Street, New York, New York 10021. Some interesting old pens, with prices that average about $12 to $15. Pens are sold in working condition.

Country Cousins Antiques, 369 Canal Street, New York, New York 10013. Pens in working condition, in a range of prices from $8 to $35.

Council Thrift Shop, 842 Ninth Avenue, New York, New York 10019. When fountain pens are available here, they are sold at giveaway prices, particularly if you buy a handful.

CHAPTER 17

Toys

Many toys from the twenties, thirties and forties are worth several hundred times what they cost when new. For example, at a London auction recently a toy delivery truck, 2¹/₂ " long, which cost a dime in 1934, sold for $230. With the introduction of plastic into the toy business, almost all pre-plastic toys jumped in value. Iron, tin, and wooden toys are much in demand in the collecting field. Mechanical toys from the early years of this century are bringing fantastic prices. These early toys were made to last. The toys you buy on the market today are not. It isn't unusual to find mechanical toys from the twenties and thirties that still operate as well as they did when bought.

Dolls and doll-house equipment are by far the most popular of the toy collectibles.

Miniature doll furniture is both expensive and much sought. A hand-carved miniature sofa may cost you as much as $100 or more, even new. How much more the old handmade pieces are worth!

Children's tea sets were made by all of the fine china companies. Recently I found an incomplete set marked with the crossed-swords Meissen mark. In the past, many plain white sets were sold to be hand-painted, for china-painting was a popular hobby for women during the eighteenth and nineteenth centuries. Complete sets with covered tureens may sell for $100 or more.

Of all these, dolls are the most collectible. I was amazed in compiling this book to find so many dealers specializing exclusively in dolls. There are so many exclusively "doll dealers" that they are listed separately in the back of this book; however, any toy dealer will most likely sell dolls. Dolls come in all sizes and price ranges, the most desirable and expensive being the bisque from Germany and France and the English porcelains, but many of the later forty- and fifty-year-old composition dolls have joined the ranks of the collectibles, as have the character dolls.

A primitive "slave" doll, made of clay and papier-mâché around 1860, was sold recently for $175 at auction.

As I've said, the famous Kewpie dolls (4½" tall) that sold for 25 cents in 1913 are selling for $80 today. There are Kewpie Clubs all over the world, whose members are eager to buy anything with a Kewpie on it, toy or not.

Character dolls are skyrocketing in prices. A 25" Deanna Durbin doll is priced at $37; a 14½" Margaret O'Brien doll at $18; and a 15½" Judy Garland doll at $30. A few months ago I saw this same Judy Garland doll (listed in a guide for $30) bring $52 at auction, which reinforces my opinion that price guides are not always a dependable yardstick for measuring value.

The earliest American toys date from the mid-nineteenth century, when mass production began in this country. Handmade American toys are so scarce that few of them have been collected. Tin toys (trucks, cars, etc.) were often made by tinsmiths as a way to use up the scraps they had left over from some other job, and often these early tin toys sold for as little as a penny. Things with wheels fascinate most collectors.

Comic-strip and movie idol toys from the twenties through the early fifties are also being collected. Popeye, Charlie Chaplin, and Highway Harry are just a few. These are doll figures representing the popular comics.

A current price guide lists a Mickey Mouse movie projector at $100 and a box of film at $5; a Mickey Mouse "Movie Jector" at $75 and a record for it at $25; and a Mickey Mouse "wood pull toy" at $50. There are many other Mickey Mouse items, and I doubt if any of them originally cost more than $5.

The same guide book lists a 27½" Shirley Temple doll "with flirty eyes, original dress, shoes and wig," marked "Ideal," for $150.

Riding toys (Irish Mail, the Marmom, Velocipede, etc.) that sold originally for less than $10 are priced up to $125 in good condition.

Mechanical banks, valued by collectors, were toys of a sort in their day. Santa frequently brought them to children to encourage thriftiness. The dancing, moving figures delighted the children, and it wasn't difficult to get them to drop their pennies into the banks to get the figures to perform. Banks have become so scarce that collectors will often travel great distances to obtain one. Many sell for as much as $500.

The values of old electric trains change constantly. If you have a Lionel train for sale, you might write to Ladd Publications, Inc., P.O. Box 137, Jacksonville, Illinois 62650, for a list of their Lionel publications, including a current price guide.

PART III

From Your Hands to the Buyer's

CHAPTER 18

Crafts

Americans, stimulated by nostalgia and turned off by shoddy mass-produced merchandise, are turning more and more to the do-it-yourself arts and crafts. Basements and sewing rooms all over America are turning out all sorts of handmade items, from quilts to pottery to hand-carved birds and plaques.

Collectors today are haunting antique shops and auction houses searching for objects made by hand.

Crafts shows and folk festivals all over the land are doing more business, attracting more crowds, and making more money than ever before. Crafts centers, where craftsmen and women may take their wares to sell, are springing up all over the nation. Our nation's capital may soon have its own crafts center. A bill introduced in Congress by Senator Charles Mathias, of Maryland, would establish a National Center for American Handcrafts in the District of Columbia, along with an increased crafts program under the direction of the National Endowment for the Arts.

In nearby Grantsville, Maryland, the Penn Alps, a nonprofit organization, serves the Appalachian-area crafts folks with a shop selling the handiwork of over 775 craftspeople. The shop, located in a remodeled 1818 log stagecoach stop between Cumberland, Maryland, and Wheeling, West Virginia, is open every day of the year except

Sundays and Christmas.

In addition to the shop, Penn Alps arranges for folk festivals at which everything handmade, from woven table mats colored with natural dyes, pottery, hand-carved birds, wooden lamps, apple and cornshuck dolls, to quilts, rugs and tin cookie cutters, is sold.

Another crafts center, famous for mountain-folk handicrafts, is the WE-DO (Western Economic Development Corporation), started several years ago in Hazelwood, North Carolina. From the mother craft center, thirteen craft cooperatives were established, allowing people to sell their homemade objects to wholesale and retail markets with no middleman to eat into their profits.

"The women started quilting because they needed covers, and now because it's in their systems. The men carved because when it rained they couldn't work the tobacco fields. They whittle to kill time," said Eddie Lail, director of WE-DO.

The Smithsonian Institution sponsors a folk festival, to which artisans from all over the country bring their crafts to sell.

There are craft co-ops all over the United States, and most likely there is one in your area. Three shops in my area stock crafts (all kinds) from some of the best craftsmen in the country:

(1) Appalachian Spring, 1655 Wisconsin Avenue, N.W., Washington, D.C. 20007; (202) 337-5780.

(2) The American Hand, 2904 M Street, N.W., Washington, D.C. 20007; (202) 338-4588.

(3) The Craftsmen of Chelsea Court, 2909 M Street, N.W., Washington, D.C. 20007; (202) 338-4588.

If you have exceptionally fine handwork you'd like to sell, you might write to them.

Sewing crafts are by far the most popular of all handwork. A beautifully sewn pattern quilt, even new, will find a ready market in almost any antique shop. It is the beauty of the design and the quality of the work that make a new quilt as valuable as the heirlooms of the past.

Museums, including the Smithsonian, have eagerly sought bicentennial quilts, and many beautiful, historical quilts have emerged. A well-made historical quilt portraying our past, yet made in the twentieth century, may bring thousands of dollars at auction.

I used to refer to pattern or historical quilts as "instant antiques," for I discovered they were more desired than old, poorly made, or badly worn quilts. The age was not the most important factor.

Experts, who judge quilts, give this advice when buying:

> In looking for value, check all cotton fabrics and hand sewing. In the best quilts, the pieces will be small, many and stitched together by hand as well as hand-quilted. Look for evenly spaced stitches. Anything machine-quilted is poor quality and of little value. Quilting that follows the pattern of the fabric is better than a superimposed checkerboard pattern over the design.
> The stuffing should be either cotton or dacron. Cotton is more traditional, but dacron washes easily and dries quickly.
> In crazy quilts, the pieces should be small, and the best have different embroidery stitches joining each piece, as if it were a sampler.

Samplers of embroidery or needlepoint are the most collectible of crafts. Old samplers, dated and tracing the history of a family or commemorating a special occasion or date, are much sought. "New" samplers, tracing a family history or honoring some famous person, place, or time (such as the bicentennial), are easy to market, for they are heirlooms of the future. Needlepoint chair-seat covers often sell for $50 to $75 each. Old samplers, dated and in good condition, bring as much. The average samplers bring about $20.

Our "history in stitches," whether done many years ago or yesterday, are crafts I consider "instant antiques," to be collected and sure to grow in value as the years pass.

A woman I know in Maryland makes quilts on order, allowing her customers to select their own patterns. She averages a quilt a month and gets $900 for each one; the customer furnishes all materials.

When she made her first quilt (just because she liked to sew) and took it to her office, where she worked as a typist, she became swamped with orders. She quit her job to make quilts, and loves every moment of it, and it pays better than her former job.

"The secret of marketing your hand-sewn items," she told me, "is in turning out good work. Shoddy and careless work will not bring top prices anywhere. If I make a mistake or break a thread, I go back and do it all over again.

"It helps me," she said, laughing, "to pretend I am making a quilt for the First Lady, to become a part of the White House furnishings. While I sew, I imagine all the famous people who may sleep beneath my cover, and I can't help doing my best work."

Where my friend plays a game with herself, I've always found it easier to work well on anything by asking myself: Would I be proud to put my name on it?

Not all quilts will sell for $900. Some may sell for more and some for much less, but there is a big demand for them, and they are usually the first things to sell at a crafts show.

If macramé is the craft you do best and you are not able to get your pieces to a crafts show, try contacting the florist in your area. Many florists feature macramé hanging baskets and wall decorations. In my area they are priced from $18 to $25.

If churches or museums in your area have gift shops, ask about putting your things in on consignment. I cannot imagine any craftsperson having any difficulty selling well-done handmade items, since the demand for them is widespread and news travels fast if you are an expert in what you do. My friend who makes the quilts has never had to advertise. Her business has grown by word of mouth.

Candle making is another craft of the past that has made a terrific comeback. The days of the nickel or dime candle are gone forever. Making candles today is an art and has come a long way since our pioneer ancestors made them to illuminate their homes.

Candles are being created in many kitchens across the nation. They are more decorative than useful. They are used today to create an atmosphere, as centers of floral arrangements, and to add an appealing touch to any decor. They make unusual gifts and are selling at gift shops, stationery stores, florist shops, and just about every craft show. You should have no trouble marketing unusual ones in your own home town. I paid $8 for the last "fat" one I bought, and there were many in the shop selling for much more.

If you're interested in a candle-making "cookbook," write to Steve Ellingson, P.O. Box 2383, Van Nuys, California 91409, for details and price. He also sells candle patterns.

Since the late sixties, leather shops have sprung up all over the nation. Men and women make and sell belts, purses, and many other oddities that our younger generation seem to clamor for: bracelets, headbands, necklaces, etc.

Many shops sell only their own work, much done on order to specification, but any craft or hobby shop that sells all kinds of crafts will most likely take your work on consignment. After talking with several "leather men" at the Folk Festival in Washington, D.C., I learned that leather goods sell better when the craftsmen have a "working" booth at fairs and shows, where they are continually making things right in front of people. One man told me that watching a leather piece materialize right before their eyes fascinated some folks so much that they would buy it even though it wasn't the sort of thing they'd ever use.

Perhaps that is why the Torpedo Factory, in Alexandria, Virginia, is attracting so many people. It opened in the fall of 1974, renting booths to artists and craftsmen of all sorts. Right after opening there were 144 tenants occupying the booths, which rented for about $60 per month. There were 60 painters, 24 sculptors, 15 fiber artists, 15 potters, 15 print makers, and another 15 miscellaneous craftsmen, including a jewel maker and a blacksmith. The occupants are allowed to sell only what they make themselves and aren't allowed to hire anyone to serve as salespersons, even when business is booming. This way the buyer deals directly with the "maker" and can ask questions to his heart's content, which may account for the success of the program.

Woodcarvers and whittlers do well at craft shows with their wooden toys and children's items, such as carved animals and birds, whistles, and popular toys like the "gee-haw whimmy diddle" made by many of the mountain men. The explanation for this toy's popularity was "It goes this-away and haws that-away."

There are a few "giants" in the furniture-making crafts. One of them is George Nakashima, of New Hope, Pennsylvania, who has been making handmade furniture for thirty years. He has a large following in the Washington area. The Nelson Rockefellers filled their Japanese country house with Nakashima furniture.

At a recent craft showing at the Renwick Galleries, in Washington, a most unusual wooden bathtub designed by Mark Baldwin of Surrey, Maine, was shown. Made of hardwood, it was dovetailed and finished in natural wood,

118

with spigots attached. It reminded me of a hollowed-tree bathtub I saw at a southern auction that sold for $1,000.

Pottery is bringing higher prices than ever before. Single bowls at one potter's place of business in Virginia are bringing $60 and up.

Warren and Catherine Pfefferle, who have been making and selling ceramics in New Jersey since the mid-sixties, tell me you have no trouble selling through crafts shops and shows if your things are pretty and different.

Catherine said when they first moved to Gibbsboro, New Jersey, she selected one crafts-shop dealer in each of the eight nearby towns from the Yellow Pages of the phone book and visited them. Each of the shops gave her orders from the samples she carried with her. Now she sells regularly through those shops, and at the booth she and Warren rent at the Philadelphia Flower Show every spring.

She tells me that *Ceramic Arts and Crafts* magazine is a must for anyone selling ceramics. It is available through crafts shops, or by subscription: 30595 West 8 Mile Road, Livania,Michigan 48152. It lists all forthcoming shows.

In pricing her wares, Catherine adds the costs of all supplies, plus a fair price on time spent making, and transporting to sales, plus a nominal profit. For example, if a mold cost $10, finished ware 40 percent more on the $10, paints and other supplies an additional $4, the actual cost of a piece would be $18. Four hours' time at $4 per hour would increase the price of the finished article to $34, plus miscellaneous expenses, such as transportation and commission, if the piece is to be sold on consignment. These are strictly ball-park figures, since molds, time, and other expenses will vary with each individual piece.

In pricing your crafts remember that comparison pricing does not come into play as it would with antiques. You should keep records of time and materials spent on each item and add a fair profit in determining what price to ask. If your work is in some way different (more decorative or distinctive) you may be able to get a much higher price than someone else does for the same item.

The beauty and creativity that go into any handmade object have a great deal to do with how quickly it sells and how much you can ask for it. If your items are "look-alikes" with your neighbor's, you can't expect to get a cent more than she does. It's the *difference* that pays off in craft work.

Hobby and craft shops all sell kits for sewing, painting and weaving, but you should bear in mind that these kits are mass produced and no matter how well you follow the instructions, your finished product will not be worth as much as an original work. In crafts, *one of a kind* puts money in your pocket.

Handmade jewelry is so popular that the largest department stores as well as hobby shops and antique shops are buying from craftspersons. There is a ready market for this type of jewelry, whether it be crafted silver, beads, cut stones, or woodcarvings.

PART IV

Markets for Your Collectibles and Crafts

ANTIQUE PUBLICATIONS AND
ADVERTISING RATES

The Antiques Journal
P.O. Box 1050
Dubuque, Iowa 52001
10 cents per word, $1.50 minimum

The Antique Monthly
P.O. Drawer 2
Tuscaloosa, Ala. 35401
20 cents per word, 25-word minimum

Old Bottle Magazine
Box 243
Bend, Ore. 97701
Regular type, 7 cents a word; double-size type, 15 cents a word; $2 minimum monthly charge

Coin World
911 Vandemark Road
P.O. Box 150
Sidney, Ohio 45365
$11.25 per column inch

Hobbies Magazine
1006 S. Michigan Ave.
Chicago, Ill. 60605
10 cents per word

Numismatic News
Iola, Wis. 54945
Up to 20 words, $1.95; $1.95 minimum

Spinning Wheel
Fame Ave.
Hanover, Pa. 17331
Single insertion, 15 cents per word

Sinn's Stamp News
P.O. Box 29
Sidney, Ohio 45365
Up to 25 words, $2.90; minimum $2.90

VALUE GUIDES

Price Guide to Country Antiques and American Primitives. Dorothy Hammond. Funk & Wagnalls, $6.95.

The Complete Antiques Price List. Ralph M. Kovel and Terry H. Kovel. Crown, $5.95.

Thirteenth Antiques and Their Current Prices. Edwin G. Warman. Warman, $9.95.

Comic Strip Toys, A Price Guide. Harmon. Wallace-Homestead, $8.95.

Mechanical and Still Bank Price Guide. Edwin G. Warman. Warman, $4.85.

Price Guide to Dolls. Robert W. Miller. Wallace-Homestead, $9.95.

Pocket Watch Price Guide, Book 1. Roy Ehrhardt. Heart of America Press, $6.95.

Carnival Glass, Vols. 1–10, with 1975–76 Price Guide. Hartung, $35.00.

Flow Blue China and Mulberry Ware—Similarity and Value Guide. Petra Williams. Fountain House East, $9.75.

The Book Collector's Handbook of Values, 1976–1977. Van A. Bradley. Putnam, $20.00.

Third Value Guide to Old Books. Edwin G. Warman. Warman, $7.95.

Rare and Expensive Post Cards. John M. Kaduck. Wallace-Homestead, $6.95.

Old Magazine Price Guide. R. Clear, $5.00.

Paper Americana. Cotten, $5.00.

Cast Iron and Tin Toys. Crammer, $6.95.

Encyclopedia of Pocket Knives. Roy Ehrhardt. Heart of America Press, 2 vols., each $6.95.

Collectors Book on Toothpick Holders. Mignell. $7.95.

Steins and Prices. Dimsdle, $6.95.

Official Guide to Silver and Silverplate. H. L. Cohen. House of Collectibles, $5.00.

American Kitchen Collectibles. Mathews, $5.95.

If you can't find these books in your library or bookstore, you may order them through R. J. Beck Co., 2108 Hunter St., Huntertown, Ind. 46748

The following lists are organized by category. Each category is organized alphabetically by state, then alphabetically by city, and finally by person or business. Phone numbers are provided where possible.

(C) indicates a collector.
(D) indicates a dealer.

ADVERTIQUES

Dealers and Collectors

ARIZONA

(D) King Richard III, Pipe & Tobacco
10639 N. 71st Way
Scottsdale 85254
(602) 948-0498
(Wants old tobacco tins, tobacco posters, and related items in tobacco advertising.)

CALIFORNIA

(D) Humphrey House Antiques
2019 W. Magnolia
Burbank 91505
(Wants advertising buttons.)

(C) Quentin Ogen
837 5th Ave.
Los Angeles 90005
(Wants cigar-band collections.)

(D) Independent Eureka Mine
227 S. San Mateo Dr.
San Mateo 94403
(415) 347-2267
(Wants trade cards.)

(D) The Antique Company
12429 Ventura Blvd.
Studio City 91604
(213) 980-4844
(Buys advertising items.)

CONNECTICUT

(C) Peter A. Tavera
27 Howard Ave.
Bristol 06010
(Wants early, colorful beer and tip trays. Northeast brewers preferred. Also tobacco tins.)

(C) Charles B. Gardner
Box 27

New London 06320
(Will buy flasks, documents, advertisements, pictures from Early American Glass works.)

(D) Peter's Antique Center
857 S. Main St.
Plantsville 06479
(203) 621-2280
(Wants early, colorful beer and tip trays.)

(D) Larry Shapiro
Box 101 .
Rocky Hill 06067
(203) 563-1348
(Wants advertising trays, signs, tobacco and food tins, syrup dispensers, spool cabinets, and advertising and country-store items.)

ILLINOIS

(C) J. R. Mautner
2948 Arlington Ave.
Highland Park 60035
(312) 432-4595 (after 7 P.M. and on weekends)
(Wants Sears, Roebuck & Company items: catalogues, buttons, ribbons, letters, guarantees, grocery and tobacco tins and containers, tape measures, mirrors, toys,

watches, pamphlets. No stereo cards.)

IOWA

(C) Nancy E. Kayser
RR 3
Webster City 50505
(Wants any sale catalogues, sale posters, brochures, or anything advertising or related to Aberdeen-Angus cattle, 1880–1930.)

MASSACHUSETTS

(C) R. MacDowall
106 Hathway Circle
Arlington 02174
(Will buy old advertising cards, loose or in albums.)

NEW JERSEY

(C) Bob Slawsky
P.O. Box 423
Rockaway 07866
(201) 361-1603 (after 7 P.M.)
(Wants trade tokens, all types: merchant trade, love tokens; collections or odd lots.)

NEW YORK

(C) Metzler
Box 2206

Astoria 11102

(Wants hair combs,
beer-tap knobs, foam
scrappers, swizzle sticks,
whiskey pitchers,
cigarette tins, and
related items.)

(C) D. H. Hubert
140 E. 56th St.
New York 10022
(212) 751-7885

(Wants beer trays, foam
scrappers, tin trays, beer
cans, openers, mini beer
bottles, signs, buttons
with brewing advertising,
and older beer
advertising items.)

NORTH CAROLINA

(C) Bill Ricketts
Box 9605
Asheville 28805
(704) 298-6348

(Wants any Coca-Cola,
Pepsi, or other soft-drink
advertising items. Top
prices paid.)

OREGON

(D) The Old Timers
4759 N.E. Fremont
Portland 97213
(503) 281-5154

(Buys unusual
advertising items.)

PENNSYLVANIA

(D) House of Gabler
71 N. Main St.
Chambersburg 17201

(Wants old
mechanical-bank
advertising cards.)

(C) Yartz
628 N. Main St.,
Extension
Meadville 16335

(Old watch fobs,
mirrors, stickpins,
pinback buttons, and
signs.)

VERMONT

(C) David Begin
148 Maple St.
Essex Junction 05452

(Wants tobacco cards;
any quantity of old cards
on any subject—movie
stars, sports, animals,
etc.)

WASHINGTON

(C) Forest Dunham
201 N. 107
Seattle 98133
(206) 362-5270

(Wants old merchant's
trade tokens—"Good for
5¢," etc.—with
town/state on them.)

(C) Vada Belle Bledsoe

Star Rte., Box 151
Underwood 98651
(509) 493-1543

(Wants "Flying Red
Horse" Mobil Oil
advertising items,
especially neon signs.)

WISCONSIN

(C) Richard Bucht
Land O'Lakes 54540

(Wants beer advertising,
glasses, mugs, trays,
syrup dispensers, etc.)

(C) Schachter
7312 W. Marine Dr.
Milwaukee 53223

(Wants medical and
pharmaceutical
advertising items. Send
detail in first letter.)

(C) Albert Goetz
1763 Poplar
South Milwaukee 53172

(Wants old strap-type
machinery advertising.)

ART

Dealers

ARIZONA

David Adler
6815 N. 2nd St.
Phoenix 85012
(602) 264-9146

CALIFORNIA

The Icart Vender
3146 Purdue Ave.
Los Angeles 90066
(213) 390-2472
(Specialty: Louis Icart,
Mucha, and Maxfield
Parrish original prints.)

CONNECTICUT

Namon Gallery
715 Danbury Road
Ridgefield 06877
(203) 438-6229
(Contemporary folk artists.)

Marguerite Reordan
Stonington 06378
(203) 535-2511

DELAWARE

Stuart Kingston Galleries
264 Thomas Dr.
Monroe Park 19801
(302) 652-7978

DISTRICT OF COLUMBIA

The American Folk Art
Shop
3214 O St., N.W.
Washington 20007
(202) 338-8250

Adam A. Weschler & Son
905 E St., N.W.
Washington 20004
(202) 628-1281

IDAHO

Daniel J. Trublood, Broker
of Fine Arts
719 8th Ave., S.
Nampa 83651

ILLINOIS

Chicago Art Galleries, Inc.
5960 N. Broadway
Chicago 60660
(312) 561-7256
(Buys all types art objects.)

Webberly Galleries
202 S. State St.
Chicago 60604
(312) 922-5278

U. Armbruster
1509 Dobson
Evanston 60202
(Paintings and prints.)

LOUISIANA

Norton's Auction Exchange, Inc.
643 Magazine St.
New Orleans 80130
(504) 561-1196

Marsha Oliver, Ltd.
3951 Magazine St.
New Orleans 70115
(504) 897-6670

MAINE

F. M. O'Brien
38 High St.
Portland 04101
(207) 774-0931
(Wants paintings.)

MARYLAND

Ruth's Antique Shop, Inc.
41 E. Baltimore St.
Funkstown 21734
(301) 739-0311

MASSACHUSETTS

Brodney Gallery of Fine Art
811 Boylston
Boston 02116
(617) 536-0500
(Buys paintings, bronzes.)

MISSOURI

Quality Art & Antique
  Imports
7803 Clayton Road

St. Louis 63117
(314) 725-4009

Selkirk
4166 Olive
St. Louis 63108
(314) 533-1700

NEVADA

Astrid's Antiques
67 E. Reno
Las Vegas 89119
(702) 736-9715
(Specialty paintings.)

NEW JERSEY

Collector's Gallery
310 Springfield Ave.
Summit 07901
(201) 273-6877

NEW YORK

Ace Galleries
810 Broadway
New York 10003
(212) 260-2720

Asian Art Gallery
5 E. 57th St.
New York 10022
(212) 688-7243
(Far East art.)

Astor Galleries
754 Broadway
New York 10003
(212) 473-1658

Bijan Royal, Inc.
60 E. 11th St.
New York 10003
(212) 533-6390
(French works of art.)

Chinese Gallery of Art
15 E. 71st St.
New York 10021
(212) 535-1730
(Chinese art and antiques.)

David Gallery
220 5th Ave.
New York 10001
(212) 532-6483
(Wants Persian art.)

Lubin Galleries
72 E. 13th St.
New York 10003
(212) 254-1080

Manhattan Art & Antique
  Center
1050 2nd Ave.
New York 10022
(212) 355-4400

Ira Spanierman, Inc.
50 E. 78th St.
New York 10021
(212) 879-7085

Barbara N. Cohen
13 E. Park Road
Pittsford 14534
(716) 586-4744

NORTH CAROLINA

Gallery Clinton Lindley,
Ltd.
220 Church St.
Hillsborough 27278
(919) 732-4300

VIRGINIA

Liros Gallery, Inc.
628 N. Washington St.
Alexandria 22314
(703) 549-7881
(Fine paintings, prints,
icons.)

Dean Wilson Antiques
Box 102
Fort Defiance 24437
(703) 885-4292

Collectors

CALIFORNIA

Collector
Box 1122
Burbank 91507
(Wants any engraving, print,
or painting showing dogs.)

T. Fair
Box 1227
Santa Monica 90406
(Wants Vanity Fair
lithographs, Spy prints.)

133

FLORIDA

J. Schlossberg
9620 N.W. 39th Court
Coral Springs 33065
(Wants reverse-painted glass
pictures from 1930s.)

KENTUCKY

Southern Galleries
P.O. Box 321
Hopkinsville 42240
(Wants original Prang Civil
War prints. Also Kutz and
Allison *Battle of Cold
Harbor,* original Currier and
Ives, *Jefferson Davis,* original
Gilbert Gaul prints.)

MICHIGAN

G. Wickersham
1848 Humphrey
Birmingham 48008
(Wants abstract paintings.)

NEW YORK

R. G. Myers
22 Chapel St.
Canton 13612
(Wants Remington prints
and lithographs.)

A. R. Davison
126 Girdle Road
East Aurora 14052
(Wants Currier and Ives.)

Chazz Schoenfeld
525 Moffitt Ave.
Hewlett 11557
(Wants Remington prints.)

Jacques Schurre
280 9th Ave.
New York 10001
(Wants Currier and Ives and
other early American prints.)

OHIO

Collector
Box 2001
Cincinnati 45201
(513) 561-7668
(Wants original paintings of
Indians by Sharp, Hauser,
Burbank, Seltzer, and
others.)

R. E. Frye
RR 1, Brookville Road
College Corner 45003
(Wants B. DeLoose oil
paintings.)

PENNSYLVANIA

Eli Fleisher
41 S. Dawes
Kingston 18704
(Wants Wallace Nuttings.)

BOOKS: RARE AND OUT-OF-PRINT

Dealers

ARIZONA

Southwest Books
Box 55
Alpine 85920
(602) 339-4574

Readex Book Exchange
Box 1125
Carefree 85331
(602) 488-3304

Purple Possum Bookshop
212 W. McNeil Dr.
Phoenix 85041
(602) 276-0233

Guidon Books
7117 Main St.
Scottsdale 85251
(602) 945-8811

William R. Hecht
5001 E. Tomahawk Trail
Box 67
Scottsdale 85252

The Bookshelf
21 E. 7th St.
Tempe 85281
(602) 968-2262

Rosetree Book Shop
Box 7
Tombstone 85638
(602) 457-3326

Arizona Bookshop
  Schaeffers
803 E. Helen St.
Tucson 81510
(602) 622-1963

The Bookstop
2504 N. Campbell Ave.
Tucson 85719
(602) 326-6661

Boyer Gallery
2540 E. 6th St.
Tucson 85716
(602) 327-0653

Joe's Books
3652 E. Fort Lowell
Tucson 85716
(602) 325-4114

Kerber's Book Store
622 W. Prince Rd.
Tucson 85705
(602) 887-6082

Overland Book Shop
903 E. Hendrick Dr.
Tucson 85719
(602) 623-5092

ARKANSAS

Donald Choffel, Bookseller
Cane Hill 72712

Marshall D. Vance,
  Bookseller
Box 27
Forrest City 72335
(501) 633-1980

Lucyle's Shop
1319 W. 6th St.
Pine Bluff 71601
(501) 534-3840

CALIFORNIA

Alta California Bookstore
1407 Solano Ave.
Albany 94706
(415) 527-7711

John L. Riemer
1042 Concha St.
Altadena 91001
(No phone)

Volkoff & Von Hohenlohe
545 E. Mariposa
Altadena 91001
(213) 797-3342

Amor Librorum
Box 430
Aptos 95003
(408) 688-1473

Dusty Tomes
322 Chester Ave.
Bakersfield 93301
(805) 322-4814

Ostby's Americana
8758 Park Ave., Box 89
Bellflower 90706

(213) 925-7767

Castro Books
1919 University Ave.
Berkeley 94704
(415) 845-3743

Ganymede Graphics
15 Maybeck Twin Dr.
Berkeley 94708
(415) 849-0279

Joseph Rubinstein
84 Uplands
Berkeley 94705
(415) 653-3131

Serendipity Books
1790 Shattuck Ave.
Berkeley 94709
(415) 841-7455

Urban Books
295 Grizzly Peak Blvd.
Berkeley 94708
(415) 524-3315

Maxwell Hunley
9533 Santa Monica Blvd.
Beverly Hills 90210
(213) 275-7466

Harry A. Levinson, Rare
  Books
9527 Brighton Way, Box 534
Beverly Hills 90213
(213) 276-9311

Harold B. Diamond,
  Bookseller
Box 1193

Burbank 91505
(213) 846-0342

Gamut Book Shop—Alpha
   to Zulu
723 California Dr.
Burlingame 94010
(415) 343-7428

Donald La Chance
5105 Bridge St., Box L
Cambria 93428
(805) 927-4145

Chula Vista Bookstore
322 Third Ave.
Chula Vista 92010
(714) 427-9518

Goodman Brier
452 W. 8th St.
Claremont 91711
(714) 626-5623

Joyce Bookshop
2187 Salvio St.
Concord 94520
(415) 689-7412

Apollo Bookshop
545 W. 18th St.
Costa Mesa 92627
(714) 646-7045

The Museum
1201 Wanda St.
Crockett 94525
(415) 787-1351

Indus Books
Box 812

Davis 95616
(916) 756-4495

P. K. Slocum, Bookseller
7733 Corey St.
Downey 90242
(213) 862-9435

Alpha Books
18046 Ventura Blvd., Box
   1783
Encino 91316
(213) 344-6365

New Albion Bookshop
1820 Sir Francis Drake Blvd.
Fairfax 94930
(415) 456-1464

Pacific Book Supply
   Company
Box 337
Farmersville 93223
(209) 594-4155

Book House
3043 E. Tulare St.
Fresno 93721
(209) 266-0956

Monroe Books
1465 E. Escalon Ave.
Fresno 93702
(209) 439-2479

Talisman Press, Booksellers
Box 455
Georgetown 95634
(916) 333-4486

Roy V. Boswell, Antiquarian

Books & Maps
Box 278
Gilroy 95020
(408) 842-9072

Arthur H. Clark Company
1264 S. Central Ave.
Box 230
Glendale 91209
(213) 245-9119

Family Bookshop
1367 E. Colorado St.
Glendale 91205
(213) 242-0069

London Book Company
244 W. Broadway
Glendale 91204
(213) 244-0828

Jax Used Book Shop
2670 E. Florence Ave.
Huntington Park 90255
(213) 589-4500

John H. Shuster Books
294 Chiquita St.
Laguna Beach 92651
(714) 494-4519

Lawrence McGilvery
Box 852
La Jolla 92031
(714) 454-4443

Aide Bookpost
1465 Neptune
Leucadia 92024
(714) 753-3392

Rair Literature
Box 2488
Leucadia 92024
(No phone)

Art & Book Barn
1943 Pacific Coast Hwy.
Lomita 90717
(213) 325-5222

Green Door Books &
    Antiques
3850 E. Ocean Blvd.
Long Beach 90803
(213) 867-6204

Rodden's Bookshop
344 E. Broadway
Long Beach 90802
(213) 432-5896

Blitz Books
Box 64
Los Altos 94022
(408) 253-0418

Abbey Book Shop
8813 Allcott St.
Los Angeles 90035
(213) 278-0146

ABC Book & Magazine
    Research Company
7055 Hollywood Blvd.
Los Angeles 90028
(213) 462-1766

Aldine Books
4663 Hollywood Blvd.
Los Angeles 90027
(213) 666-2690

Belle's Bookshop
2009 W. 7th St.
Los Angeles 90057
(213) 483-7750

Bennett & Marshall Rare
  Books
8214 Melrose Ave.
Los Angeles 90046
(213) 653-7040

Boulevard Bookshop
10634 W. Pico Blvd.
Los Angeles 90064
(213) 837-1001

Caravan Book Store
605 S. Grand Ave.
Los Angeles 90017
(213) 626-9944

Cherokee Book Shop
6607 Hollywood Blvd.
Los Angeles 90028
(213) 463-6090

Peggy Christian, Bookseller
769 N. La Cienega Blvd.
Los Angeles 90069
(213) 652-5695

Collings Bookshop
8424 Melrose
Los Angeles 90069
(213) 655-4119

Cosmopolitan Book Shop
7007 Melrose Ave.
Box 85218
Santa Western Sta.
Los Angeles 90072

(213) 938-7119

John Parke Custis,
  Booksellers
412 S. Benton Way
Los Angeles 90057
(213) 381-2141

Dawson's Book Shop
535 N. Larchmont Blvd.
Los Angeles 90004
(213) 469-2186

Lee Freeson
Box 922
Los Angeles 90028
(213) 463-5848

Heritage Book Shop, Inc.
6707 Hollywood Blvd.
Los Angeles 90028
(213) 466-6527

Hollywood Book Gallery
6631 Hollywood Blvd.
Los Angeles 90028
(213) 466-2525

Hollywood Book Service
1654 N. Cherokee Ave.
Los Angeles 90028
(213) 464-4164

Robert L. Link, Bookseller
2428 Canyon Dr.
Los Angeles 90068
(213) 466-1565

James Meachum
5331 Raber St.
Los Angeles 90042

(213) 254-3225

Needham Book Finders
11613 San Vincente Blvd.
Los Angeles 90049
(213) 826-6533

John B. Nomland,
  Booksellers
404 S. Benton Way
Los Angeles 90057
(213) 389-9745

Regent House
108 N. Roselake Ave.
Los Angeles 90026
(213) 389-0678

Rose Rose Books
Box 27659
Los Angeles 90027
(213) 660-2087

Kurt L. Schwarz
738 Bristol Ave.
Los Angeles 90049
(213) 828-7927

Third World Ethnic Books
Box 38237
Los Angeles 90038
(213) 737-3292

Tower Book Shop
7952 W. 3rd St.
Los Angeles 90048
(213) 653-3524

Universal Books
6258 Hollywood Blvd.
Los Angeles 90028
(213) 467-6887

Yesterday's Books
451 N. Western Ave.
Los Angeles 90004
(213) 462-3851

Zeitlin & Ver Brugge
815 N. La Cienega Blvd.
Los Angeles 90069
(213) 655-7581

Green River Bookshop
6509 Wandermere Road
Malibu 90265
(213) 457-2066

G. F. Hollingsworth
Box 1725
Manhattan Beach 90266
(213) 374-1641

Mithra Books
24811 San Fernando Road
Newhall 91321
(805) 259-4861

R. E. Lewis, Inc.
Box 72
Nicasio 94946
(415) 456-6393

Gregory Paul Books
9430 Encino
Northridge 91324
(415) 652-3095

Acme Books
3386 Piedmont Ave.
Oakland 94611
(415) 652-3095

H. F. Bowker, Bookseller
1716 Gouldin Road

Oakland 94611
(415) 339-1074

Clare's Collectors Cooks
818 E. 21st St.
Oakland 94606
(415) 834-5431

De Freitas Bookstore
373 12th St.
Oakland 94607
(415) 452-4533

Gull Bookshop
538 15th St.
Oakland 94612
(415) 834-8108

Joyce Book Shop
1116 Franklin St.
Oakland 94607

Northwest Books
3814 Lyon Ave.
Oakland 94601
(415) 532-5227

Roskie & Wallace Bookstore
1809 San Pablo Ave.
Oakland 94612
(415) 893-9166

Bacon's Books
1459 S. Euclid Ave.
Ontario 91761
(714) 983-8235

International Bookfinders,
  Inc.
Box 1
Pacific Palisades 90272

(No phone.)

Chimaera Books
405 Kipling
Palo Alto 94301
(415) 329-9217

William P. Wreden Books
200 Hamilton Ave., Box 56
Palo Alto 94302
(415) 325-6851

Daniel H. Deutsch Books
141 Kenworthy Dr.
Pasadena 91105
(213) 681-9638

Old Town Book Shop
17796 Sintonte Dr.
Poway 92064
(714) 487-0867

Acoma Books
Box 4
Ramona 92065
(No phone.)

Baily Search Service
Box 326
Redondo Beach 90277
(No phone.)

Personal Book Shop
7219 Reseda Blvd.
Reseda 91335
(213) 343-5951

G. A. Bibby Books
714 Pleasant St.
Roseville 95678
(916) 783-3270

Academic Library Service
6489 S. Land Park Dr.
Sacramento 95831
(916) 428-2863

Argus Books
2741 Riverside Blvd.
Sacramento 95818
(916) 443-2223

J. B. Muns Books
Box 711
San Anselmo 94960
(415) 453-4495

William Bledsoe, Bookseller
Box 763
San Carlos 94070
(415) 593-6878

Carlos Book Stall
1115 San Carlos Ave.
San Carlos 94070
(415) 593-7466

Out of State Book Service
Box 1253
San Clemente 92672
(714) 492-2976

Antiquarian Book Service
Box 17201
San Diego 92117
(714) 274-3680

Bargain Book Store
1053 8th Ave.
San Diego 92101
(714) 234-5380

Herweg & Romine,

Booksellers
958 5th Ave.
San Diego 92101
(714) 233-0880

Otento Books
3817 5th Ave.
San Diego 92103
(714) 296-1424

Theodore Reed, Antiquarian
  Books
3789 Ocean Front Walk
San Diego 92109
(714) 488-8001

John Roby Books
3703 Nassau Dr.
San Diego 92115
(714) 583-4264

Albatross Book Store
166 Eddy St.
San Francisco 94102
(415) 885-6501

Argonaut Book Shop
792 Sutter St.
San Francisco 94109
(415) 474-9067

Brick Row Book Shop
251 Post St.
San Francisco 94108
(415) 398-0414

Compass Bookstore
689 Clay St.
San Francisco 94111
(415) 397-0663

Discovery Book Shop
245 Columbus Ave.
San Francisco 94111
(415) 986-3872

Eldorado Book Shop
Box 14-036
San Francisco 94114
(No phone.)

John Howell Books
434 Post St.
San Francisco 94102
(415) 781-7795

Jabberwock Books
143 Clement Ave.
San Francisco 94118
(415) 752-8611

David P. Johnson,
  Booksellers
1473 Pine St.
San Francisco 94109
(415) 776-8520

Lion Book Shop
1415 Polk St.
San Francisco 94109
(415) 474-5522

McDonald's Book Shop
48 Turk St.
San Francisco 94102
(415) 673-2235

David Magee Antiquarian
  Books
3108 B Fillmore St.
San Francisco 94123
(415) 567-1888

H. J. Molloy
Box 5267
San Francisco 94101
(No phone.)

Jeremy Norman & Company
442 Post St.
San Francisco 94102
(415) 781-6402

Old Book Shop
1104 Sutter St.
San Francisco 94109
(415) 776-3417

Perry's Antiques & Books
1884 W. San Carlos
San Francisco 95128
(415) 286-0426

Recycle Books
235 S. 1st St.
San Francisco 95113
(415) 286-6275

Lester Roberts Bookshop
47 Golden Gate Ave.
San Francisco 94102
(415) 431-0348

Bernard M. Rosenthal, Inc.
251 Post St.
San Francisco 94108
(415) 982-2219

Round Up Book Company
166 Eddy St.
San Francisco 94102
(415) 885-6501

State Book Shop

389 S. 1st St.
San Francisco 95113
(415) 297-4797

E. L. Sterne
Box 22041
San Francisco 94122
(415) 752-4160

Horizon Book Shop
832 B St.
San Rafael 94901
(415) 453-6830

Mandrake Book Shop
817 4th St.
San Rafael 94901
(415) 453-3484

Book Center
207 N. Main St.
Santa Ana 92701
(714) 542-8839

Saddleback Book Shop
Box 10393
Santa Ana 92711
(714) 637-6086

Book Den
15 E. Anapamu, Box 733
Santa Barbara 93102
(805) 962-4956

Drew's Bookshop
Box 163
Santa Barbara 93101
(805) 966-7083

W. T. Genns Books
116 E. De La Guerra St.

Studio I, Box 1328
Santa Barbara 93102
(805) 965-5817

Hare in the Field Books
630 N. Milpas
Santa Barbara 93103
(805) 963-2882

Harvey Taylor Books
430 Hot Springs Road
Santa Barbara 93108
(805) 969-1678

Book Service of Santa Cruz
510 Errett Circle, Box 511
Santa Cruz 95060
(408) 426-3486

Book Land
1615 Montana Ave.
Santa Monica 90403
(213) 394-0726

Emerald Shop
434 26th St.
Santa Monica 90402
(213) 393-4402

Santa Monica Book Bazaar
131 Broadway
Santa Monica 90401
(213) 451-2710

Cipriano's Books
402½ Mendocino Ave.
Santa Rosa 95401
(707) 542-1986

Wendell P. Hammon
20200 Hill Ave.

Saratoga 95070
(408) 867-3216

West Coast Library Service
210 S. Navarro Dr.
Scotts Valley 95060
(408) 438-2382

Nickelodeon
13826 Ventura Blvd.
Sherman Oaks 91403
(213) 981-5325

Lighthouse Book Company
Box 666
South Pasadena 91030
(213) 441-1337

John Makarewich Books
Box 395
Tarzana 91356
(No phone.)

Joyce Book Shop
303 Kelly Road
Vallejo 94590

Bargain Books
14426 Friar St.
Van Nuys 91401
(213) 782-2782

J. E. Reynolds, Bookseller
16031 Sherman Way
Van Nuys 91406
(213) 785-6934

Family Book Shop
6725 Comstock
Whittier 90601

Rudolph William Sabbot,
    Natural History
5239 Tendilla Ave., Box 772
Woodland Hills 91364
(213) 346-7164

COLORADO

Stage House 11, Books &
    Antiques
1936 14th St.
Boulder 80302
(303) 447-1433

Henry A. Clausen Bookshop
224 N. Tejon St.
Colorado Springs 80902
(303) 634-1193

Abco Bookshop
304 E. Colfax Ave.
Denver 80203
(303) 255-2151

Collector's Center, Rare
    Books
654 Emerson St.
Denver 80218
(303) 244-8287

Fred A. Rosenstock Books
1228 E. Colfax Ave.
Denver 80218
(303) 222-9883

Old Corner Bookshop
619 S. College Ave.
Fort Collins 80521
(No phone.)

CONNECTICUT

Alfred W. Paine Books
50 Wolfpits Road
Bethel 06801
(203) 748-4125

Christmas Tree Bookshop
Bethlehem 06751

Pages of Yesteryear
429 Hawley Ave.
Bridgeport 06606
(203) 335-1252

Book Barn
Rte. 183, Box 108
Colebrook 06021
(203) 379-3185

Lawrence F. Golder Rare
  Books
Box 144
Collinsville 06022
(203) 693-8110

Edward Myers Country
  Lane Books
Box 47
Collinsville 06022
(203) 693-2245

Durham Book Store
Haddam Quarter Road
Drawer B
Durham 06422
(203) 349-3130

John M. Skutel Americana
251 Carroll Road
Fairfield 06430
(203) 259-1997

Evelyn Bottome
571 Glenbrook Road
Glenbrook 06906
(203) 324-0180

N. Flayderman & Company,
  Inc.
Squash Hollow
New Milford 06776
(203) 354-5567

Elliots Books
Box 6
Northford 06472
(203) 484-2184

Hillcrest House
Drawer 279
Old Greenwich 06870
(203) 637-3981

Old Mystic Bookshop
58 Main St., Box 189
Old Mystic 06372
(203) 536-6932

Douglas M. Jacobs Old Rare
  Books
268 Nod Road
Ridgefield 06877
(203) 438-8088

Cydon Books
Roxbury 06783
(203) 354-5016

Housatonic Bookshop
Main St., Box 466
Salisbury 06068
(203) 435-2100

Chiswick Book Shop, Inc.
Walnut Tree Hill Road
Sandy Hook 06482
(203) 426-3220

Charles B. Wood, III, Inc.,
    Antiquarian Booksellers
The Green
South Woodstock 06267
(203) 928-4041

Eddie Welch's Gallery
246 Old Post Road, Box 544
Southport 06490
(203) 255-0740

Books For Collectors
322 Main St.
Stamford 06905
(203) 323-0088

Joh Bridge
26 Lanark Road
Stamford 06541
(203) 324-0541

Stamford Book Store
127 Bedford St.
Stamford 06902

Crossoner Books
Stonington Road
Stonington 06378
(203) 535-1119

Ardent Bookfinders
61 Winton Place
Stratford 06497
(203) 377-4760

DELAWARE

Attic Books
RD 3
Newark 19711
(302) 738-7477

Blue Hen Book Shop
Box 523, RD 2
Smyrna 19977
(302) 653-7021

DISTRICT OF COLUMBIA

Albion Book Shop
1319 F St., N.W.
Suite 408
Washington 20004
(202) 783-6698

Bargain Book Shop
808 9th St., N.W.
Washington 20001
(202) 347-5007

Capitol Hill Book Shop
525 Constitution Ave., N.E.
Washington 20002
(202) 547-1121

Q. M. Dabney & Company,
    Inc.
P.O. Box 31061
Washington 20031
(202) 423-9077

Duff & M. E. Gilford
1722 19th St., N.W.
Washington 20009
(202) 387-1418

Estate Book Sales

1724 H St., N.W.
Washington 20006
(202) 298-7355

Nada Kramer
927 15th St., N.W.
Washington 20005
(202) 737-1305

Park Reifsneider's Book
  Gallery
1310 19th St., N.W.
Washington 20004
(202) 833-8082

Saddle Horn Sales
P.O. Box 8933
Washington 20003

FLORIDA

Jean Cohen Books
P.O. Box 654
Bonita Springs 33923
(813) 992-7421

Apollo Bookfinders
4295 Harbor City Blvd.
Eau Gallie 32935
(305) 254-9517

Davis Bookstore
Box 194
Eustis 32726
(904) 357-6149

I. E. Deibert, Bookseller
1100 S.E. 6th St.
Fort Lauderdale 33301
(305) 522-8766

Hoosierland Books
Box 932
Fort Myers 33901
(813) 334-0448

Old Book Shop
108 E. Adams St.
Jacksonville 32202
(904) 355-6159

Alla T. Ford, Rare Books
114 S. Palmway
Lake Worth 33460
(305) 585-1442

Irving Levy Books
1034 South Blvd.
Lakeland 33803
(813) 683-1015

Richard G. Uhl
6319 Pine Dr.
Lantana 33460
(305) 582-4029

The Old Book Shop
3110 Commodore Plaza
Miami 33133
(305) 661-4913

The Bookfinders, Inc.
Box 2021 Oceanview
Miami Beach 33140
(305) 538-4795

Thompson's Book Store
416 W. Main St.
New Port Richey 33552

A & Z Book Service
Box 813

North Miami 33161

Carroll Miner Robinson,
  Book Appraiser
Park Ave.
Palm Beach 33480
(305) 833-2028

Long's Books
711 W. Lakeview Ave.
Pensacola 32501
(904) 438-1956

John C. Daub
9656 42nd St., N.
Pinellas Park 33565
(813) 527-2595

Quincy Book & Antique
  Shop
14 E. Washington St.
Box 766
Quincy 32351
(904) 627-9080

Charlotte Street Shop,
  Books & Prints
32 Charlotte St.
St. Augustine 32084
(904) 829-2361

Appletree Books
4035 38th Ave., N.
St. Petersburg 33734
(813) 527-4819

Dorothy Bell Books
2712 9th St., N., Box 7045
St. Petersburg 33734
(No phone.)

Yesterday's Books

538 Pineapple Ave.
Sarasota 33577
(813) 959-4084

Arthur L. Mittell
11180 4th St.
Treasure Island 33706
(813) 360-4169

GEORGIA

Harvey D. Abrams,
  Bookseller
1633 N. Rock Springs Road,
  N.E.
Atlanta 30324
(404) 874-9033

Peachtree Book Store
598 Peachtree St., N.E.
Atlanta 30308
(404) 874-0955

T. E. Bradley
1200 Clairmont Road
Decatur 30030
(404) 373-7150

O. G. Lansford
Powersville 31074
(912) 956-3484

Elizabeth Albers Books
Columbia Drive, Box 241
Rincon 31326
(912) 816-5870

Whistles in the Woods
Rte. 1, Box 265A
Rossville 30741
(404) 375-4326

HAWAII

Pacific Book House
2109D Kuhio Ave.
Honolulu 96815

ILLINOIS

Craig's Bookshop
110 S. Cook St.
Barrington 60010
(312) 381-3772

Putman's Bookshop
304 W. Jefferson St.
Bloomington 61701
(309) 828-1016

A-1 Book Store
1112 N. State St.
Chicago 60610
(312) 787-7830

Richard S. Barnes,
  Bookseller
1628 N. Wells St.
Chicago 60614
(312) 642-8005

Herbert Biblo, Bookseller
5225 S. Blackstone Ave.
Chicago 60615
(312) 643-2363

The Book Box
4812 N. Broadway
Chicago 60640
(312) 334-5311

Book Stack
5221 N. Damen Ave.
Chicago 60625

(312) 334-2821

Buckingham Book Shop
65 E. Van Buren St.
Chicago 60605
(312) 939-7306

Canterbury Bookshop
538 S. Wabash Ave.
Chicago 60605
(312) 939-2923

Celmer's Book Store
4433 N. Broadway
Chicago 60640
(312) 334-9237

Owen Davies, Bookseller
1214 N. LaSalle St.
Chicago 60610
(312) 642-6697

Edgewater Book Store
5941½ N. Broadway
Chicago 60660
(312) 271-4657

Michael R. Fleischhacker
1642 N. Fairfield Ave.
Chicago 60647
(312) 276-4512

Hamill & Barker
230 N. Michigan Ave.
Chicago 60601
(312) 236-9782

Alexander J. Issacs
5116 S. Blackstone Ave.
Chicago 60615
(312) 288-3646

Jayar Books
4715½ Sheridan Road
Chicago 60640
(312) 878-0659

Edgar Krebs
5849 N. Talman Ave.
Chicago 60659
(312) 275-4611

Abraham Lincoln Book
  Shop
18 E. Chestnut St.
Chicago 60611
(312) 944-3085

Henry Litke
236 E. 115th St.
Chicago 60628
(Mail order.)

Reid Michener, Bookseller
5309 S. Kimbark
Chicago 60615
(312) 493-6872

Kenneth Nebenzahl, Inc.
333 N. Michigan Ave.
Chicago 60601
(312) 641-2711

J. E. Pearson, Bookseller
Box 446
Chicago 60690
(312) 523-8713
(Mail order.)

Petelles International
  Booksearch
56 W. Maple St.
Chicago 60610

(312) 787-5533

Elsie M. Phalen
4922 N. Claremont
Chicago 60625
(312) 271-4120
(Out-of-print mail order.)

A. C. Prosser, Jr., Books
3118 N. Keating
Chicago 60641
(312) 685-7680
(Mail order.)

Charles Reitsma, Bookseller
Box 27066
Riverdale Branch
Chicago 60627
(Mail order.)

Paul Romaine Books
192 N. Clark St.
Suite 516
Chicago 60601
(312) 348-7551

John Rybski, Bookseller
2319 W. 47th Place
Chicago 60609
(312) 847-5082

Otto Soukup Art & Book
  Shop
6720 Ashland Ave.
Chicago 60636
(312) 778-5499

Sullivan Sporting Books
3748 N. Damen Ave.
Chicago 60618
(312) 472-2638

(Mail order.)

Robert Thompson Books
1401 E. 56th St.
Chicago 60637
(Mail order.)

M. Von Berg
2243 W. Leland Ave.
Chicago 60625
(312) 271-4551
(Mail order.)

Morris Yanoff Books
6159 N. Wolcott Ave.
Chicago 60660
(312) 274-3163

Zollinger's Book Shop
1150½ W. Belmont Ave.
Chicago 60657
(312) 549-5990

Chicago Book Mark
Box 613-W
Chicago Heights 60411
(Mail order.)

The Athenaeum
1937 Central St.
Evanston 60201
(312) 475-0990

Richard Booker Books
1307 Chicago Ave.
Evanston 60201
(312) 328-4424

The Cogitator Bookstore
919 Foster, Box 1274

Evanston 60204
(312) 869-7783

Kennedy's Bookshop
1911 Central St.
Evanston 60201
(312) 864-4449

Van Norman Book
  Company
422-424 Bank of Galesburg
  Bldg.
Galesburg 61401
(309) 343-4516

Valley Book Shop
122 Hamilton St.
Geneva 60134
(312) 232-2636

Colophon Book Store
700 S. 6th Ave.
La Grange 60525
(312) 354-7062

J. R. Burdett & R. E.
Stocker
Box 77
Lombard 60148
(312) 469-3647
(Mail order.)

The Book Store
123 Westmoreland Dr.
Mundelein 60060
(312) 362-2011

Richard P. Germann
Box 42
North Chicago 60064
(312) 623-8547

(Mail order.)

Harry Busck
710 N. Humphrey Ave.
Oak Park 60302
(312) 848-2850

D. & D. Antiques & Books
205 South St., Box 206
Ridge Farm 61870
(217) 247-2764

Wilbur D. Smith, Bookseller
2244 S. 10th St.
Springfield 62703
(217) 544-5255
(Mail order.)

Modern Times Booksellers
600 S. Webster St.
Taylorville 62568
(217) 824-5921

G. W. Shoenbeck
1942 Greenwood Ave.
Wilmette 60091
(312) 251-6399
(Mail order.)

Leekley Rare & Scholarly
  Books
711 Sheridan Road
Box 337
Winthrop Harbor 60096
(312) 872-2311

INDIANA

Capitol Book Store
11802 E. Washington St.

Cumberland 46229
(317) 894-4491

Foster's Book Service
2218 E. Jackson Blvd.
Elkhart 46514
(219) 522-6991

Donald Beck
1828 Ida Ave.
Fort Wayne 46808
(219) 437-1801

Hoosier Bookshop
3820 E. 61st St.
Indianapolis 46220

Indiana Book Store
320 N. Illinois St.
Indianapolis 46204
(317) 637-7556

William S. Johnson,
  Bookseller
829 East Dr.
Box 33
Indianapolis 46206
(317) 639-1256

Ms. Helen Windle, Rare &
  Used
715 Allen St.
South Bend 46616
(219) 234-9627

IOWA

Broken Kettle Book Service
RR 1
Akron 51001
(712) 568-2114

The Source Book Store
305 W. 2nd St.
Davenport 52801
(319) 324-8941

McBlain Books
Box 971
Des Moines 50304
(515) 274-3033

William A. Graf Books
717 Clark St.
Iowa City 52240
(319) 337-7748

Bibliophiles, Inc.
3829 Jones St.
Sioux City 51104
(712) 277-4429

KANSAS

Wagon Wheels Book
2901 Colt Dr.
Lawrence 66044
(913) 841-3954

T. N. Luther Books
Box 6083
Shawnee Mission 66206
(913) 381-9619

Marsh Bookstore
113 E. 6th St.
Topeka 66603
(913) 232-4388

Welda Books & Antiques
Welda 66091

Al's Old Book Store

731 W. Douglas
Wichita 67213
(316) 264-8763

Pied Piper Book Shop
1749 N. Fairmont
Wichita 67208
(316) 686-0401

KENTUCKY

Dennis Book Store
257 N. Limestone St.
Lexington 40507
(606) 252-1969

W. C. Gates Books
1279 Bardstown Road
Louisville 40204
(502) 451-3295

Ace Book Exchange
104 S. 2nd St., Box 1092
Paducah 42001
(502) 443-6744

LOUISIANA

F. J. Federico
265 Glenwood Dr., Box 9186
Metairie 70005
(504) 835-0758

Southern Book Mart
742 Royal St.
New Orleans 70116
(504) 525-6835

Ark-La-Tex Book Company
319 Ward Bldg., Box 564
Shreveport 71162

(318) 423-6820

Carol's Book & Magazine
  Service
355 College St.
Shreveport 71104
(318) 423-2350

City Book & Coin Store
521 Crockett St.
Shreveport 71101
(318) 425-5142

Coronet Book Shop
1622 Front St., Box 807
Slidell 70458
(504) 643-6740

MAINE

Christian F. Verbeke,
  Antiquarian
Park Street, Box 407
Bethel 04217

Leon Tebbetts Book Shop
164 Water St.
Hallowell 04347

F. M. O'Brien, Antiquarian
34-36 High St.
Portland 04101
(207) 774-0931

Daniel MacGelvray,
  Bookseller
144 Fort Road
South Portland 04101
(207) 799-5143

Lobster Lane Book Shop

Spruce Head 04859
(207) 594-7520

Aimee B. MacEwen
Stockton Springs 04981
(207) 567-3351

MARYLAND

John Gach Bookshop, Inc.
3322 Greenmount Ave.
Baltimore 21218
(301) 467-4344

Hispanic Americana
Box 3580, Hamilton Sta.
Baltimore 21214
(301) 254-4890

Cecil Archer Rush
1410 Northgate Road
Baltimore 21218
(301) 323-7767

Sherlock Book Detective
2624 St. Paul
Baltimore 21218
(301) 235-2326

Old Hickory Bookshop
Brinklow 20727
(301) 924-2225

William F. Stewart
4804 Brinkley Road
Camp Springs 20031
(301) 449-4257

Wharf House Books By Mail
Box 57
Centreville 21617

(301) 758-0678

Jeff Dykes Western Books
Box 38
College Park 20740
(301) 864-0666

Doris Frohnsdorff
Box 831
Gaithersburg 20760
(301) 869-1256

Alvin Lohr
Conococheague
Hagerstown 21740
(301) 582-0234

Old Book Store
7600 Adelphi Road
Hyattsville 20783
(301) 422-7682

Riverdale Book Shop
6104 Rhode Island Ave.
Riverdale 20840
(No phone.)

Merritt Book Shop
630 E. Church St.
Salisbury 21801
(301) 742-4625

D. R. Spaight Bookseller
Rte. 249 to Piney Point
Tall Timbers 20690
(301) 994-0311

MASSACHUSETTS

Mark A. Kalustian
259 Pleasant St.

Arlington 02174
(617) 648-3437
(Mail order.)

Mariner's House
19 Tanager St.
Arlington 02174
(617) 643-1317
(Mail order.)

Don French Antiques
1755 Main St.
Athol 01331
(617) 249-8830

Sunrise Hills Books
Sunrise Ave., Box 64
Barre 01005
(617) 355-4015

Dish Hollow, Old Books
Rte. 8
Becket 01223
(413) 623-8810

Dunham's Book Store
34 South Road
Bedford 01730
(617) 275-9140

Brattle Book Store
5 West St.
Boston 02111
(617) 542-0210

Goodspeed's Book Shop,
Inc.
18 Beacon St.
Boston 02108
(617) 523-5970

Edward Morrill & Son, Inc.
25 Kingston St.
Boston 02111
(617) 482-3090

Starr Book Company, Inc.
37 Kingston St.
Boston 02111
(617) 542-2525

H. S. Victorson, Bookseller
44 School St.
Boston 02108
(617) 227-9326

Williams Book Store
52 Providence St.
Boston 02108
(617) 227-7520

Hoffman & Freeman,
   Antiquarian Booksellers
4 Trowbridge Place
Cambridge 02138
(617) 868-8070

Pangloss Bookshop
1284 Massachusetts Ave.
Cambridge 02138
(617) 354-4003

Starr Book Shop
29 Plympton St.
Cambridge 02138
(617) 547-6864

Old Colony Book Shop
Main St.
Carver 02330
(617) 866-3647

Atlantic Book Service
287 Main St.
Charlestown 02129
(617) 242-0188

Cynthia Elyce Rubin
28 Sakville St.
Charlestown 02129
(617) 241-9549
(Mail order.)

Elsie Sexton
212 North Road
Chelmsford 01824
(617) 256-2347
(Mail order.)

Barrow Bookstore
86 Thoreau St., the Depot
Concord 01742
(617) 369-6084

Norman Alexander Hall
Normandie Road
Dover 02030
(617) 785-1744

Elmwood Bookshop
35 N. Bedford St.
East Bridgewater 02333
(617) 378-7587

The Paper Barn
Rte. 6A
East Sandwich 02537

D. R. Nelson, Bookseller, &
   Company
107 Main St.
Fairhaven 02719

(617) 994-0663

Jane Field Books
14 North St.
Georgetown 01833
(617) 352-6847

George Robert Menkoff,
Inc.
Rowe Road, RFD 3, Box 147
Great Barrington 01230
(413) 528-4578

Robert L. Merriam, Rare &
  Used
574 Bernardston Road
Greenfield 01301
(413) 773-7912

Poor Mans Shop
Old Plymouth St., Box 5
Halifax 02338
(617) 293-6648

Paul S. Clarkson Books
3 Lowell Ave.
Holden 01520
(617) 829-4076
(Mail order.)

University Book Reserve
75 Main St., Box 905
Hull 02045
(617) 925-0570

Bucklins Books
Ipswich 01938
(617) 356-2413
(Mail order.)

Islington Book Company

217 Washington St.
Islington 02090
(617) 326-2912
(Mail order.)

Roderick Hilton
13 Main St.
Marion 02738
(617) 748-0136

C. & M. Hutchinson
108 Webster St.
Marshfield 02050
(617) 834-9509

Aceto Bookman
Bedford St., RFD 3,
Box 120A
Middleboro 02346
(617) 947-0913

Fonda Books & Antiques
Box 1826
Nantucket 02554
(No phone.)
(Mail order.)

Hudson Book Shop
Box A 2091
New Bedford 02741
(617) 997-3801
(Mail order.)

Anne Maxted
124 Dickerman Road
Newton Highland 02161
(No phone.)

New Englandiana
46 Ashland St., Box 787

North Adams 01247
(413) 664-9417

Old Book Store
32 Masonic St.
Northampton 01060
(413) 586-0576

Incredible Barn
Main Street, E.
Orleans 02653
(617) 255-1259

New England Books
Petersham 01366
(617) 249-6724

Gulliver Books & Press
120 Commercial St.
Box 561
Provincetown 02657
(617) 487-0228

Jewett's Bookshop
Rowley 01969
(617) 356-4553

Olde Book Shop
53 Washington St.
Salem 01970
(617) 744-4193

Andy's Antiquarian
   Exchange
1566 Fall River Ave., Rte. 6
Seekonk 02771
(617) 336-7236
(Mail order.)

Howard S. Mott
S. Maine St.

Sheffield 01257
(413) 229-2019

M. Douglas Sackman
Saw Mill Plain Road
South Deerfield 01373
(413) 665-4241

Ralph F. Cummings
161 Pleasant St.
South Grafton 01560
(617) 839-4622
(Mail order.)

Murray's Bookfinding
Service
115 State St.
Springfield 01103
(413) 335-5598

Herbert Reichner
Stockbridge 01262
(413) 298-3477
(Mail order.)

Aerophilia
1613 Central St.
Stoughton 02072
(617) 344-8200

Henry J. Vickey
9 Brook St.
Stoughton 02072
(617) 344-3649
(Mail order.)

Quaboag Bookshop
47 High St., Box 83
Thorndike 01079
(413) 283-8456

Harold M. Burstein, Literary
  Mailer
16 Park Place
Waltham 02154
(617) 893-7974

Paul E. Belisle
74 Spruce St.
Watertown 02172
(617) 923-9079
(Mail order.)

Bromer Booksellers
127 Varnard Ave.
Watertown 02172
(617) 926-3150
(Mail order.)

Books Unlimited
45 Russell Road
Wellesley 02181
(617) 237-5829

William Young & Company
Box 242
Wellesley Hills 02181
(617) 235-3424

Malcom M. Ferguson
1489 Main St.
West Concord 01781
(617) 369-2898
(Mail order.)

M. & S. Rare Books, Inc.
45 Colpitts Road
Weston 02193
(617) 891-5650

Philip Lozinski

1504 Drift Road
Westport 02790
(617) 636-2044

Jan Thornton Books on
  Antiques
195 Pond St.
Winchester 01890
(617) 729-1359

MICHIGAN

The Raven Book Shop
413 Capital Ave., S.W.
Battle Creek 49015
(616) 965-6469

Roy Newton Books
208 Rust Ave.
Big Rapids 49307
(616) 796-6175
(Mail order.)

Angelescu Book Service
3645 Barham St.
Detroit 48224
(313) 861-5432

Big Book Store
3769 Woodward Ave.
Detroit 48201
(313) 831-8511

Bruce's Books on Art
444 W. Margaret
Detroit 48203
(313) 869-9189

The Cellar Book Shop
18090 Wyoming, Box 6
College Park Sta.

Detroit 48221
(313) 861-1776
(Mail order.)

B. C. Claes Book Shop
1670 Leverette St.
Detroit 48216
(313) 963-4267

Blaine Ethridge Books
13977 Penrod St.
Detroit 48223
(313) 838-3363
(Mail order.)

Mid-West Book Service
4301 Kensington Road
Detroit 48224
(313) 885-2450

A. F. Rand Books & Coins
132 W. Lafayette Blvd.
Detroit 48226
(313) 961-4814

Rouse's Books
Box 242
Manistee 49660
(616) 723-2144
(Mail order.)

Max S. Primmer
394 W. Southern Ave.
Muskegon 49441
(616) 722-4742
(Mail order.)

Ye Olde Curiosity Shoppe
3720 Red Arrow Hwy.
St. Joseph 49085

(616) 429-5321

MINNESOTA

J. & J. O'Donoghue Books
1920^1/$_2$ 1st St., S.
Anoka 55303
(612) 427-4890

McCosh's Book Store
Dundas 55019
(No phone.)

B & H Books
809 4th St., S.E.
Minneapolis 55414
(612) 378-0129

Oudal Book Shop
71 S. 12th St.
Minneapolis 55403
(612) 332-7037

Ross & Haines, Inc.
11 E. Lake St.
Minneapolis 55408
(612) 823-2146

ABC Antiques & Books
Territorial Road
Monticello 55362
(612) 295-2950

Ken Crawford Books
2719 E. 16th Ave., N.
St. Paul 55109
(612) 777-6877

Gordon Gladman
441 Desmoyer Ave.
St. Paul 55104

(612) 644-3564

Harold's Book Shop
186 W. 7th St.
St. Paul 55102
(612) 222-4524

Arthur B. Primeau
246 E. Stanley Ave.
St. Paul 55118
(612) 222-7693
(Out-of-print.)

James Cummings,
Bookseller
320 N. 4th St.
Stillwater 55082
(612) 439-8944

Mennetonka Antiquarian
Bookshop
639 E. Lake St.
Wayzata 55391
(612) 473-8341

MISSOURI

D. C. Book Service
211 Gipson, Box 122
Columbia 65201
(816) 442-0001

Hall's Book Shop
202 Taylor Ave.
Crystal City 63019
(314) 937-4048

William J. Cassidy
109 E. 65th St.
Kansas City 64113
(816) 381-4271

Glenn Books, Inc.
1227 Baltimore Ave.
Kansas City 64105
(816) 842-9777

Smoky Hull, Booksellers
Box 2
Kansas City 64141
(816) 531-2524

Jesse James Bank Museum
Bookshop
104 E. Franklin St.
Liberty 64068
(816) 781-4458

Amitins Book Shop
811 Washington Ave.
St. Louis 63101
(314) 421-9208

R. Dunaway, Bookseller
6138 Delmar
St. Louis 63112
(314) 725-1581

Lillian Orr Leverett
7523A S. Broadway
St. Louis 63111
(314) 638-1246
(Mail order.)

The Book Mark
511 Hudson, Box 114
Wellsville 63384
(314) 684-2776

MONTANA

Flathead Lake Galleries
Box 426

Bigfork 59911
(406) 837-6633

David A. Lawyer, Bookseller
Plains 59911
(406) 826-3229

NEBRASKA

G. N. Dupley
9118 Pauline St.
Omaha 68124
(402) 393-2906

Louise Stegner Books
1029 S. 32nd St.
Omaha 68105
(402) 345-5626
(Mail order.)

NEVADA

Charleston Books & Rare
   Coins
1907 E. Charleston Blvd.
Las Vegas 89104
(702) 384-8528

Grahame Hardy Books
Box 449
Virginia City 89440
(No phone.)
(Mail order.)

NEW HAMPSHIRE

Richard Mills
91 Front St.
Exeter 03833
(603) 934-4837

Carry Back Books
Franconia 03580
(603) 823-8892

Herbert West
Box 82
Hanover 03755
(603) 643-3249

Book Farm
Concord Road, Box 515
Henniker 03242
(603) 428-3429

J. C. Perry Company
7 Court St.
Keene 03431
(603) 352-4132

Harold R. Scammell Books
Rte. 152
Nottingham 03290
(603) 942-8196

Frank E. Reynolds Books
152 Middle St.
Portsmouth 03801
(603) 436-7109

Edward C. Fales
150 Turnpike Road, Box 56
Salisbury 03268
(603) 648-2484

Cricket Hill Books
Box 66
Stratham 03885
(603) 772-5166

Old Settler Bookshop
RFD 1

Walpole 03608
(603) 756-3685

NEW JERSEY

White's Galleries, Inc.
607 Lake Ave.
Asbury Park 07712
(201) 774-9300

Paper & Ink Bookshop
44 Beech Ave.
Berkeley Heights 07922
(201) 464-2391

William F. Kelleher
544 Westview Ave.
Cliffside Park 07010
(201) 943-2125

Frank Z. Edwards
11 N. Essex St.
Dover 07801
(201) 366-5540
(Mail order.)

Thomas Kelly Books
227 Midland Ave.
East Orange 07017
(201) 672-9238
(Mail order.)

Heinoldt Books
Central & Buffalo Ave.
Egg Harbor City 08215
(609) 965-2284
(Mail order.)

Leon Zakian
35 E. Demarest Ave.

Englewood 07631
(201) 567-1822

Book Roundup
Box 162
Flemington 08822
(Mail order.)

Broadwater Books
Box 783
Freehold 07728
(201) 462-2936

Archie's Resale Shop
Meyersville Road
Gillette 07933
(201) 647-1194

Robert A. Paulson
39 Downing Place
Harrington Park 07640
(201) 768-6926

Bob Dawson Americana
  Books
21 Marlpit Place, Box 38
Hazlet 07730
(201) 671-3611
(Mail order.)

Elizabeth Woodburn
Booknoll Farm
Hopewell 08525
(609) 466-0522
(Mail order.)

Alfred H. Arwe
3 Commodore Dr., Rte. 1
Lake Hopatcong 07849
(201) 663-0056

(Mail order.)

Past History
136 Parkview Terr.
Lincroft 07738
(201) 842-4545
(Mail order.)

Keen Books
Box 698
Long Branch 07740
(201) 229-5060
(Mail order.)

Chatham Bookseller
8 Green Village Road
Madison 07940
Mailing address:
38 Maple St.
Chatham 07928
(201) 822-1361

Trans Atlantic Books
Box 44
Matawan 07747
(No phone.)
(Mail order.)

Robert K. Black
57 Union St.
Montclair 07042
(201) 744-3219
(Mail order.)

Patterson Smith
38 Prospect Terr.
Montclair 07042
(201) 744-3219

Fera's Book Shop

199 Washington St.
Newark 07102
(201) 622-3596

Frank Michelli Books
45 Halsey St.
Newark 07102
(201) 623-4289

Lawrence Lane
1187 Dakota Road
North Brunswick 08902
(201) 667-6830

Martin F. Duffy & Sons
229 Coeyman Ave.
Nutley 07110
(201) 667-6830

Book Bazaar
10th & Boardwalk
Ocean City 08226
(609) 399-4137

The P.M. Book Shop
321 Park Ave.
Plainfield 07060
(201) 754-3900

Witherspoon Art & Book
  Store
12 Nassau St.
Princeton 08540
(609) 924-3582

Ernest S. Hickok
382 Springfield Ave.
Summit 07901
(201) 277-1427

Joseph Liptak

750 Cedar Lane
Teaneck 07666
(201) 836-5398

Books-On-File
Box 195
Union City 07087
(201) 869-8786
(Mail order.)

Harold Nestler
13 Pennington Ave.
Waldwick 07463
(201) 444-7413
(Mail order.)

Mennone Selected Books &
  Magazines
95 Lyons Ave.
Wayne 07470
(201) 696-1680

NEW MEXICO

El Paisano Books
2323 Central Ave., N.W.
Albuquerque 87104
(505) 242-9121

Quivira Bookshop &
  Photograph Gallery
111 Cornell Dr., S.E.
Albuquerque 87106
(505) 266-1788

Jack D. Rittenhouse Books
600 Solano Dr., S.E.
  Box 4422
Albuquerque 87106
(No phone.)

(Mail order.)

Harkins Book Supply
824 7th St.
Las Vegas 87701
(505) 425-8817

L. E. Gay-Southwest Books
209 E. Wabash, Box 548
Lordsburg 88045
(505) 542-9845

Abacus Books
652 Canyon Road
Sante Fe 87501
(505) 983-2424

Ancient City Bookshop
Sena Plaza, Box 1986
Santa Fe 87501
(505) 982-8855

Jack Potter, Bookseller
203 E. Palace Ave.
Santa Fe 87501
(505) 983-5434

NEW YORK

Cottage Bookshop
206 Lark St.
Albany 12210
(518) 434-0946

John F. Schultz
Box 73
Ancramdale 12503
(518) 329-0193
(Mail order.)

J. Howard Woolmer Books

Gladstone Hollow
Andes 13731
(914) 676-3218

Kemstark Bookshop
548 Front St.
Binghamton 13905
(607) 724-9465

Editions
Rte. 28A
Boiceville 12512
(914) 657-8354
(Mail order.)

Charles Baron
55 Knolls Crescent
Bronx 10463
(212) 548-3951
(Mail order.)

H. Celnick
2010 Walton Ave.
Bronx 10453
(212) 299-1326
(Mail order.)

Kershner Books
Box 51, Park Chester Sta.
Bronx 10462
(212) 829-5143
(Mail order.)

Nathan Simons Books
1816 Seminole Ave.
Bronx 10461
(212) 863-4328

Emil J. Bergmann
66-69 Fresh Pond Road

Brooklyn 11227
(212) 821-2713
(Mail order.)

Binkin's Book Center
54 Willoughby St.
Brooklyn 11201
(212) 855-7813
(Mail order.)

Black Sun Books
Box 459
Brooklyn 11202
(212) 858-1445
(Mail order.)

Bleeker Book Service
231 Berkeley Place
Brooklyn 11217
(212) 783-1651

The Book Post
Box 1814
Brooklyn 11201
(212) 875-1267
(Mail order.)

Boro Book Store
154 Montague St.
Brooklyn 11201
(212) 624-3439

Lillian Brussel
3736 Oceanic Ave.
Brooklyn 11224
(212) 449-5693
(Mail order.)

Central Book Company,
    Inc.

850 DeKalb Ave.
Brooklyn 11221
(212) 452-4700
(Mail order.)

J. Franklin, Bookseller
Box 74, Rugby Sta.
Brooklyn 11203
(No phone.)
(Mail order.)

Rose H. Gibel, Bookseller
107 Hoyt St.
Brooklyn 11217
(212) 852-2594

Frances Kenett
13 Cranberry St.
Brooklyn 11201
(212) 852-2424
(Mail order.)

S. Millman
Box 23, New Lots Sta.
Brooklyn 11208
(212) 649-0111

Richard C. Ramer, Old,
  Rare Scholarly Books
45 Martense St.
Brooklyn 11226
(212) 287-5942
(Mail order.)

H. C. Roseman
85 Livingston St., Suite 7K
Brooklyn 11201
(212) 834-8928

Jack Weinstein

5704 Farragut Road
Box 4, New Lots Sta.
Brooklyn 11208
(212) 251-5306

H. W. Giles, Old Rare
  Books
112 Genesee St.
Buffalo 14203
(716) 856-0405

Claude Held
Box 140
Buffalo 14225
(716) 634-4842
(Mail order.)

More's Old-Rare Books
169 Allen St.
Buffalo 14201
(716) 886-5800

Pan American Books
16 Farnham St., Box 161
Cazenovia 13035
(315) 655-9654

Hope Farm Press &
  Bookshop
Strong Road
Cornwallville 12418
(518) 239-4745

Berry Hill Book Shop
Box 118
Deansboro 13328
(315) 821-6188

Oceana Publications
75 Main St.
Dobbs Ferry 10522

(914) 696-1340

Anton Gud
41-22 Judge St.
Elmhurst 11373
(212) 898-2316
(Mail order.)

Tryon County Bookshop
Main St., Box 228
Fonda 12068
(518) 853-4234

Biblion, Inc.
Box 9
Forest Hills 11375
(212) 263-3910

Eric H. Ganley
108-19 64th Road
Forest Hills 11375
(212) 459-1119

Meadows Book Service
61-17 190th St., Rm. 207
Fresh Meadows 11365
(No phone.)
(Mail order.)

Adrian's
150 N. Brook St.
Geneva 14456
(315) 789-6667
(Mail order.)

Blanche E. Turner Books
8 Glendale Dr.
Glens Falls 12801
(518) 792-5454

North Shore Book Reserve
50 Allenwood Road
Great Neck 11023
(516) 467-8885
(Mail order.)

Beatrice C. Weinstock
14 Brook Bridge Road
Great Neck 11021
(516) 482-0904

Ye Towne Trading Post
573 Middle Neck Road
Great Neck 11023
(516) 487-1155

Owl Pen Books
Greenwich 12834
(518) 692-7039

Half Moon Books
Box 444
Guilderland 12084
(No phone.)
(Mail order.)

Long Island Book Center
191 Front St.
Hempstead 11550
(516) 483-6527

S. A. Roochvarg
140 Front St.
Hempstead 11550
(516) 485-5545

Barbara Falk Bookshop
117 E. Main
Huntington 11743
(516) 271-7133

I. V. Ekholm, Bookseller
201 Cliff Park Road
Ithaca 14850
(607) 273-4695

Caravan Maritime Books
87-06 168th Place
Jamaica 11432
(212) 526-1380

Paul A. Stroock
35 Middle Lane
Jericho 11753
(516) 433-9018

Austin Book Shop
82-60A Austin St., Box 36
Kew Gardens 11415
(212) 441-1199

Emil Offenbacker
84-50 Austin St., Box 96
Kew Gardens 11415
(212) 849-5834

Karl F. Weded, Inc.
Glenerie Lake Park
Kingston 12401
(914) 331-4749

Continental Bookshelf
Ferstler Road, Rte. 1
Kirkville 13082
(315) 656-9116
(Mail order.)

F. A. Bernett, Inc.
148 Larchmont Ave.
Larchmont 10538
(914) 834-3026

Harry Stevens Sons & Stiles
1A Albee Court
Larchmont 10538
(914) 834-7432

Lockrow's Book Store
2 Fiddler's Lane
Latham 12110
(518) 785-7046

Howard Frisch
Old Post Road, Box 75
Livingston 12541
(518) 851-7493

Richard A. Lowenstein
Geymer Drive, Rte. 4
Mahopac 10541
(914) 628-3325

Paul P. Appel
119 Library Lane
Mamaroneck 10543
(914) 698-8115

Victor Tanerlis
911 Stuart Ave.
Mamaroneck 10543
(914) 698-8950

Palenque Books
Milton 12547
(914) 795-5266
(Mail order.)

Norman Rush
10 High Tor Road
New City 10950
(914) 634-4511
(Mail order.)

Arno Book Farm, Inc.
320 Tenor Dr.
New Rochelle 10804
(No phone.)
(Mail order.)

The Bookery
209 North Ave., Box 1394
New Rochelle 10801
(914) 235-1411

Fordham Book Company
55 Church St., Box 6
New Rochelle 10801

Gordon's Books
291 Beechmont Dr.
New Rochelle 10804
(Mail order.)

Anchor Book Shop
114 4th Ave.
New York 10003
(212) 254-0312

Antiquarian Booksellers
  Center
630 5th Ave.
New York 10020
(212) 246-2564

Appelfield Gallery
1372 York Ave.
New York 10021
(212) 988-7835

Argosy Bookstores, Inc.
116 E. 59th St.
New York 10022
(212) 753-4455

Astor Place Magazine &
  Book Shop
37 E. 12th St.
New York 10003
(212) 260-2650

J. N. Bartfield Books, Inc.
45 W. 57th St.
New York 10019
(212) 753-1830

Benell Bookshop
Box 351, Cooper Sta.
New York 10003
(212) 662-7928

Biblo & Tannen, Booksellers
63 4th Ave.
New York 10003
(212) 475-1257

Book Ranger
105 Charles St.
New York 10014
(212) 924-4957

Books'N Things
34 E. 7th St.
New York 10003
(212) 533-2320

Abe Brayer
417 Grand St.
New York 10002
(212) 533-4872

A. Buschke
80 E. 11th St.
New York 10002
(212) 254-2555

Carnegie Book Shop, Inc.
140 E. 59th St.
New York 10022
(212) 755-4861

James F. Carr
227 E. 81st St.
New York 10028
(212) 535-8110

Chip's Bookshop
Box 123, Planetarium Sta.
New York 10024
(212) 362-9336

Colonial Out of Print Book
    Service
23 E. 4th St.
New York 10003
(212) 475-8354

Corner Book Shop
102 4th Ave.
New York 10003
(212) 253-7714

Dauber & Pine Bookshops,
    Inc.
66 5th Ave.
New York 10011
(212) 675-6340

Peter Decker
45 W. 57th St.
New York 10019
(212) 755-8945

Philip C. Duschnes
699 Madison Ave.
New York 10021
(212) 838-2635

K. Gregory
222 E. 71st St.
New York 10021
(212) 288-2119

Young Walter Griffin
11 E. 9th St.
New York 10003
(No phone.)

Abert Gutkin
1133 Broadway
New York 10010
(212) 243-3600

Lathrop C. Harper, Inc.
22 E. 40th St.
New York 10016
(212) 522-5115

Thomas F. Heller
308 E. 79th St.
New York 10021
(212) 737-4484

House of Books, Ltd.
667 Madison Ave., Suite 901
New York 10021
(212) 755-5998

House of El Dieff, Inc.
139 E. 63rd St.
New York 10021
(212) 838-4160

Ideal Bookstore
1125 Amsterdam Ave.
New York 10025
(212) 662-1909

Inman's Book Shop

50 E. 50th St.
New York 10022
(212) 755-2867

Walter J. Johnson, Inc.
111 5th Ave.
New York 10003
(212) 673-1120

James J. Kane Books
18 E. 33rd St.
New York 10016
(212) 532-4539

H. P. Kraus
16 E. 46th St.
New York 10017
(212) 687-4808

Lee & Lee, Booksellers
500 Broadway, Box 279
New York 10011
(212) 226-8135

R. H. Leffert
102 Charlton St.
New York 10014
(212) 924-5169

Martin's Bookshop
16 W. 4th St.
New York 10014
(212) 243-2886

Lawrence R. Maxwell
33 5th Ave.
New York 10003
(212) 477-8063

Isaac Mendoza Book
  Company

15 Ann St.
New York 10038
(212) 227-8777

Arthur H. Minters, Inc.
84 University Place
New York 10003
(212) 989-0593

Louis J. Nathanson
219 E. 85th St.
New York 10028
(212) 249-3235

Olana Gallery
305 E. 76th St.
New York 10021
(212) 861-3424

Pageant Book Company
59 4th Ave.
New York 10003
(212) 674-5296

Paragon Book Gallery, Ltd.
14 E. 38th St.
New York 10016
(212) 532-4920

Parnassus Book Shop
216 W. 89th St.
New York 10024
(212) 799-1144

H. B. Pedersen & Company
Box 116, Old Chelsea Sta.
New York 10011
(212) 929-2358

Phoenix Bookshop
18 Cornelia St.

New York 10014
(212) 675-2795

Pro Biblia
Box 212, Cooper Sta.
New York 10003
(No phone.)

Raven Book Shop
752 Broadway
New York 10003
(212) 254-1928

Reference Book Center
175 5th Ave.
New York 10010
(212) 677-2160

Leona Rostenberg Rare
  Books
Box 188, Gracie Sta.
New York 10028
(212) 831-6628

Ben Sackheim Books &
  Graphics
Box 578, Ansonia Sta.
New York 10023
(212) 874-2493

William H. Schab Gallery
37 W. 57th St.
New York 10019
(212) 758-0327

Walter Schatzki
153 E. 57th St.
New York 10022
(212) 693-4556

E. Schever, Inc.

112 E. 17th St.
New York 10003
(212) 533-7957

Justin G. Schiller, Ltd.
Box 1667, FDR Sta.
New York 10022
(212) 832-8231

Louis Schucman
100 Fifth Ave.
New York 10011
(212) 741-1087

Henry Schuman Rare
  Books, Ltd.
2211 Broadway
New York 10024
(212) 724-2393

Scientific Library Service
29 E. 10th St.
New York 10003
(212) 473-3826

Seven Gables Bookshop,
  Inc.
3 W. 46th St.
New York 10036
(212) 575-9257

S. R. Shapiro, Books for
  Libraries
29 E. 10th St.
New York 10003
(212) 673-0610

Milton Spahn Books
1370 St. Nicholas Ave.
New York 10033
(212) 568-9593

Christopher P. Stephens,
   Bookseller
75 Fort Washington Ave.,
   #34
New York 10032
(212) 568-2731

Stevens & Company Books,
   Inc.
162 E. 23rd St., Rm. 501
New York 10010
(212) 477-2930

Strand Book Store, Inc.
828 Broadway
New York 10003
(212) 473-1452

John H. Thorpe
8 W. 13th St.
New York 10011
(212) 675-1169

University Place Bookshop
821 Broadway, 9th Floor
New York 10003
(212) 254-5998

Vanity Fair Books
Box 116, Cooper Sta.
New York 10003
(212) 675-2826

Victoria Book Shop
16 W. 36th St.
New York 10018
(212) 947-7127

J. H. Villard, Inc.
175 5th Ave.
New York 10010

(212) 673-7340

Samuel Weiser, Inc.
734 Broadway
New York 10003
(212) 477-8453

Leo Weitz, Inc.
1377 Lexington Ave.
New York 10022
(212) 831-2213

E. Weyhe, Inc.
794 Lexington Ave.
New York 10021
(212) 838-5466

Ximenes Rare Books, Inc.
120 E. 85th St.
New York 10028
(212) 744-0226

Alfred F. Zambell, Scholarly
   & Rare Books
156 5th Ave.
New York 10010
(212) 734-2141

Irving Zucker Art Books
256 5th Ave.
New York 10001
(212) 679-6332

Antheil Booksellers
2177 Isabelle Court
North Bellmore 11710
(516) 826-2094
(Mail order.)

Deecee Books
32 Washington St.

Nyack 10960
(914) 358-3989

James R. Jackson
298 N. Rte. 9W
Nyack 10960
(914) 358-1874

Raymond H. Rarick
22 East St.
Oneonta 13820

Gen Rose
Biring Lane
Ossining 10562
(914) 941-0953
(Mail order.)

William Sallock
Pines Bridge Road
Ossining 10562
(914) 941-8363
(Mail order.)

Patchogue Book Shop
166 W. Main St.
Patchogue 11772
(516) 475-3520

Timothy Trace
Red Mill Road
Peekskill 10566
(914) 528-4074

Pyetell's Book Shop
333 5th Ave.
Pelham 10803
(914) 738-3861

Hotchkiss House, Inc.
18 Hearthstone Road

Pittsford 14534
(No phone.)

Tec-Books, Ltd.
41 Williams St.
Plattsburg 12901
(518) 561-2653

Kraut's Kollection
Harbor Dr.
Port Chester 10573
(914) 939-1946

Ira J. Friedman
90 S. Bayles
Port Washington 11050
(516) 767-3547

Orsay Books
86-32 Eliot Ave.
Rego Park 11374
(212) 651-6177

Charles H. Lockner
Box 66
Richmond Hill 11418
(212) 847-0278

Cheshire Cat
107 Thornton Road
Rochester 14617
(716) 342-2885

Genesee Book Shop
428 E. Main St.
Rochester 14604

Frank Opperman
326 Barrington St.
Rochester 14607
(716) 271-2561

(Mail order.)

James C. Hougate
Pattersonville Road
Rotterdam Junction 12150
(518) 887-5255

The Hennesseys
4th & Woodlawn
Saratoga Springs 12866
(518) 584-4921

Nathaniel Cowen
RFD 2, Box 28
Saugerties 12477
(914) 679-6475
(Mail order.)

Charles Benevento,
  Booksellers, Inc.
7 Phelps Place
Staten Island 10301
(212) 447-7876

Morris Heller
RFD 1, Box 48
Swan Lake 12783
(914) 583-5879

Richard M. Sylvester
4845 Velasko Road
Syracuse 13215
(315) 469-1413

William & Lois Pinkney,
  Antiquarian Books
241 Mullin St.
Watertown 13601
(315) 788-2121

Old Drover Inn

31 Jefferson St., Box 6
Westfield 14787
(716) 326-2587

Harry S. Friedman
50 Concord Ave.
White Plains 10602
(914) 946-4119

Henry Tripp, Scientific
  Books
92-06 Jamaica Ave.
Wood Haven 11421
(212) 441-3313

Sterling Book Inc.
Box 22
Woodmere 11598
(Mail order only.)

Ada McVickar Books
42 Park Ave.
Yonkers 10703
(914) 968-5223

NORTH CAROLINA

Book Mart
7 Biltmore Plaza, Box 5094
Asheville 28804
(704) 253-1692

Old Book Corner
137AE. Rosemary St.
Chapel Hill 27514
(919) 942-5178

Grandpa's House
Rte. 1, Box 208
Troy 27371
(919) 572-3484

NORTH DAKOTA

Howard O. Berg
317 7th St.
Devils Lake 58301
(701) 662-2343

Dakota Book Exchange
5 S. 8th St.
Fargo 58102
(701) 232-9843

Carl W. Swanson
207 E. 3rd St.
Velva 58790
(701) 338-2194

OHIO

The Bookseller
521 W. Exchange St.
Akron 44302
(216) 762-3101

Old Bookstore
210 E. Cuyahoga Falls Ave.
Akron 44310
(216) 253-5025

Parsons Bookstore
505 Lamson Ave.
Bedford 44146
(216) 232-2767

The Asphodel Book Shop
17192 Ravenna Road
Rte. 44
Burton 44021
(216) 834-4775

Robert G. Hayman
Adrian St.

Carey 43316
(419) 396-8104

Acres of Books, Inc.
633 Main St.
Cincinnati 45202
(513) 721-4214

Alrich, Inc.
7th & Central Aves.
Cincinnati 45202
(No phone.)

J. E. Nevil
722 Main St.
Cincinnati 45202
(513) 621-3316

Ohio Book Store
726 Main St.
Cincinnati 45202
(513) 621-5142

Peter Keisogloff Books
53 The Old Arcade
Cleveland 44114
(216) 621-3094

Paul H. North, Jr.
81 Bullitt Park Place
Columbus 43209
(614) 252-1826

L. J. Ryan
Box 243
Columbus 43216
(No phone.)
(Mail order.)

Carpenter's Village Book
Shop

340 N. White-Woman St.
Box 736
Coshocton 43812
(614) 622-9511

Morningside Bookshop
Box 336, Forest Park Sta.
Dayton 45405
(513) 836-1378

T. L. Hogue
1118 Garrison St.
Fremont 43420
(419) 332-8302

James H. Nece
258 S. State St.
Marion 43302
(614) 382-6709

Hilo Farm Antiques
9058 Little Mountain Road
Mentor 44060
(216) 255-9530
(Mail order.)

Irving M. Roth Antiques
89 Whittlesey Ave.
Norwalk 44857
(419) 663-1725

Lakeland Books
Rte. 3, Shell Beach Road
Thornville 43076
(614) 467-5774

Kendall G. Gaisser
1242 Broadway
Toledo 43609
(419) 243-7631

Great Lakes Book Store
347 Sumner St., Box 4083E
Toledo 43609
(419) 243-0932

Wayfarer Books, Older &
  Otherwise
3014 Hopewell Place
Toledo 43606
(419) 536-4050
(Mail order.)

Robert S. Rochester
634 Albin Ave.
Washington Court House
  43160
(614) 335-3388
(Mail order.)

Joseph F. Schutz
50 Stanton Ave.
Youngstown 44512
(216) 782-1794
(Mail order.)

OKLAHOMA

McGraths
1525 Irving St.
Muskogee 74401
(918) 687-4094

A Points Northe
21½ N. Harvey
Oklahoma City 73102
(405) 232-1066

Aladdin Book Shoppe
524 Broadway
Oklahoma City 73102

(405) 232-8072

Miller's Old Book Shop
211 S. Boulder
Tulsa 74103
(918) 585-1955

Terry's Old Bookstore
6 N. Main St.
Tulsa 74103
(918) 587-0236

Tulsa Book Specialist
2344 S. Gary Place
Tulsa 74114
(918) 939-5577

OREGON

Book Nook
1020 N.W. Summitt Ave.
Portland 97210
(503) 222-5453
(Mail order.)

Fransen's Books & Prints
1017 S.W. Morrison St.
Portland 97205
(503) 227-5339

Green Dolphin Bookshop
215 S.W. Ankeny
Portland 97204
(503) 224-3060

Old Oregon Book Store
610 S.W. 12th Ave.
Portland 97205
(503) 227-2742

William D. Thompson

Box 1741
Portland 97207
(No phone.)

Books-On-Wheels
Box 758
Selma 97538

PENNSYLVANIA

Ken Hottle
Box 714
Allentown 18105
(215) 433-3812

C. B. Yohe
4870 Criss Road
Bethel Park 15102
(412) 835-4279

Sam Laidacker
3 E. 5th St., Box 416
Bloomsburg 17815
(717) 784-4912

Susquehanna House
John S. Laidacker
203 Main St.
Catawissa 17820
(717) 356-7711

Mitchell's Book Shop
296 N. Main St.
Doylestown 18901
(215) 348-4875

The Odd Shop
226 S. 19th St.
Harrisburg 17104
(717) 238-6441

Benjamin Scholl
2045 Green St.
Harrisburg 17102
(717) 234-6525

S. S. Stoctay, Ph.D.
Box 5054
Harrisburg 17110
(717) 238-6441

Laurel Book Service
33 W. 3rd St.
Hazleton 18201
(717) 454-5821

Seven Seas Bookshop
714 Suter St.
Johnstown 15905
(814) 288-4441

Conestoga Book Service
60 Howard Ave.
Lancaster 17602
(No phone.)

Geoffrey Steele, Inc.
Lumberville 18933
(215) 297-5187

D. A. Bulen
301 Randolph St.
Meadville 16335
(814) 332-0181

House of Old Books
Main & Manheim Sts.
Mount Joy 17552
(717) 653-4328

Graedon Book Shop
Rte. 1

New Hope 18938
(215) 794-8351

Jeff Wilson, Bookseller
3529 Rhoads Ave.
Box 33
Newtown Square 19073
(215) 353-1140

William H. Allen, Bookseller
2031 Walnut St.
Philadelphia 19103
(215) 563-3398

G. H. Arrow Company
S.E. Corner 4th & Brown
  Sts.
Philadelphia 19123
(215) 922-3211

Bernard Conwell Carlitz
1901 Chestnut St.
Philadelphia 19103
(215) 563-6608

George S. MacManus
  Company
1317 Irving St.
Philadelphia 19107
(215) 735-4456

Mercury Projects
Box 2212
Philadelphia 19103
(No phone.)

Charles J. Miller
41 S. 19th St.
Philadelphia 19103
(215) 568-5437

William H. Schafer, Books
  & Prints
1524 S. 28th St.
Philadelphia 19146
(215) 465-1451

Schuylkill Book & Curio
  Shop
873 Belmont Ave.
Philadelphia 19104
(215) 473-4769

Charles Sessler, Inc.
1308 Walnut St.
Philadelphia 19107
(215) 735-1086

M. Stepanuk Books
2409 W. Perot St.
Philadelphia 19130
(215) 769-2383

Vanity Fair
5512 Wayne Ave.
Philadelphia 19144
(215) 844-8844

Walnut Book Store
900 Walnut St.
Philadelphia 19107
(215) 923-1436

Book Door Service
Box 5158
Pittsburgh 15206
(412) 781-1066

Book Search Service
135 Sewickley-Oakmont
  Road
Pittsburgh 15237

(412) 364-6440

Schoyer's Books
1404 S. Negley Ave.
Pittsburgh 15217
(412) 521-8464

Frank W. Skleder Books
240 Forbes Ave.
Pittsburgh 15222
(412) 261-1890

Olga Snyder
1107 Federal St.
Pittsburgh 15212
(412) 231-6564

The Americanist
1525 Shenkel Road
Pottstown 19464
(215) 323-5289

Franklin M. Roshon
Buchert Road, RD 4
Pottstown 19464
(215) 323-6047

Hoffman Research Services
Box 342
Rillton 15678
(412) 863-2367

Fifty King
332 Lackawanna Ave.
Scranton 18503
(717) 347-2145

Lock Stock & Barrel Shop
328 N. Washington Ave.
Scranton 18503
(717) 344-5561

Universal Books, Ltd.
116 E. Spruce St.
Titusville 16353
(814) 827-6049

Petroleum Americana
Box 504
Warren 16365
(814) 723-9000

Baldwins Book Barn
865 Lenape Road
West Chester 19380
(215) 696-0816

Hale House
Box 181
Wynnewood 19096
(No phone.)

Miller's Used Book Shop
459 W. Market St.
York 17404
(717) 843-7216

RHODE ISLAND

Patrick T. Conley Books
1100 Pontiac Ave.
Cranston 02920
(401) 944-3367

Frank J. Williams,
Bookseller
183 Knollwood Ave.
Cranston 02910
(401) 944-7285

Corner Book Shop
416 Spring St.
Newport 02840

(401) 846-8406

Don E. Burnett, American
  Historical Books
34 Lake Dr.
North Kingstown 02852
(401) 884-5397

Dana's Old Corner Book
  Store
44½ Weybosset St.
Providence 02903
(401) 421-2057

Dick's Book Shop
44 Richmond St.
Providence 02903
(401) 421-6791

(Out-of-print.)

S. Clyde King
Box 2036, Edgewood Sta.
Providence 02905
(401) 781-0837

Lincoln Book Shop, Inc.
905 Westminster St.
Providence 02903
(401) 331-0932

Tyson Books
51 Empire St.
Providence 02903
(401) 421-3939

SOUTH CAROLINA

Acme Books
Capitol Sta., Box 11996
Columbia 29211
(803) 782-5767

Noah's Ark Book Attic
Stony Point, Rte. 2
Greenwood 29646
(803) 451-3013

The Attic, Inc.
Box 449
Hodges 29653
(803) 451-3013

Hampton Books
Rte. 1, Box 76
Newberry 29108
(803) 276-6870

Kitemang Books
229 Mohawk Dr.
Spartanburg 29301
(803) 576-3338

TENNESSEE

M. V. Denny
306 Central Ave.
Clinton 37716
(615) 457-1535

F. M. Hill Books
Box 1037
Kingsport 37662
(615) 247-8704

Elder's Bookstore
2115 Elliston Place
Nashville 37203
(615) 327-1867

Raleigh Ashley Bookseller
540 Lake St., Box 255
Tiptonville 38079
(901) 253-6678

TEXAS

The Jenkins Company
6929 S. Interregional Hwy.
Box 2085
Austin 78767
(512) 444-6616

Betty Smedley Rare Books
2509 Harris Blvd., Box 78703
Austin 78703
(512) 477-5013

A. B. Fenner Books
601 N. Hwy. 288
Clute 77531
(713) 265-2216

Murphey's Book Bin
Box 6575
Corpus Christi 78411
(512) 884-7060

The Aldredge Book Store
2506 Cedar Springs
Dallas 75201
(214) 748-2043

Book Broker
2002 W. Illinois St.
Dallas 75224
(214) 331-8054

Harper's Book Shop
2540 Elm St.
Dallas 75226
(214) 747-0144

Texas Bookman
3310 Knox St., Box 30033
Dallas 75230
(214) 521-5740

Wilson Bookshop
3005 Fairmount
Dallas 75201
(214) 747-5804

Frontier Book Company
Box 805
Fort Davis 79734
(915) 426-3359

Beverly Bond Books
3210B Norfolk
Houston 77006
(713) 524-6536

Bookman
2243 San Felipe Road
Houston 77019
(713) 523-1357

Braes-Link Book Shop
8417 Stella Link
Houston 77025
(713) 668-2232

Colleen's Books & Things
6880 Telephone Road
Houston 77017
(713) 641-1753

Kendrick Book Store
2429 Rice Blvd.
Houston 77005
(713) 528-3388

Conway Barker
1231 Sunset Lane
La Marque 77568
(713) 935-2810
(Autographs.)

Gloria Krakowski Book
  Service
518 N. Main St.
McAllen 78501
(512) 686-3377

McCarley Book Company
Box 668
Mineral Wells 76067
(817) 325-3851

Gail Klemm Books
Box 1327
Richardson 75080
(214) 239-0010

Fletcher's Books, Anson
  Jones Press
Box 65
Salado 76571
(817) 947-5414

Book Mart
3127 Broadway
San Antonio 78209
(512) 828-4885

Brock's Book Store
312 E. Commerce St.
San Antonio 78205
(512) 226-5992

Joshua David Bowen
124 E St.
Summit 78212
(512) 734-3330

W. M. Morrison Books
Box 3277
Waco 76701
(817) 754-6235

Waco Book Store
610 Washington Ave.
Waco 76701
(817) 754-9164

Wayne's Books
4502 Callfield Road
Wichita Falls 76308
(817) 692-0483

UTAH

Omar Khayyam's Rubaiyat
121 E. 3rd S.
Salt Lake City 84111
(801) 355-7844

Ye Old Book Shoppe
10 N. State St.
Salt Lake City 84111
(801) 355-0761

VERMONT

Ken Leach, Bookscout
Box 78
Brattleboro 05301
(802) 257-7918

Charles E. Tuttle Company,
  Inc.
26-30 S. Main St.
Drawer F
Rutland 05701
(802) 773-8930

VIRGINIA

Guilford Books
Box 635
Arlington 22216

(No phone.)

Virginia Book Company
Berryville 22611
(703) 955-1428

The Forest Bookshop
Rte. 1, Box 50B
Charlottesville 22901
(804) 293-5179

Quizzicum Book Store
6860 Lee Hwy.
Falls Church 22213
(703) 534-2631

Leamington Book Shop
623 Caroline St.
Fredericksburg 22401

C. J. Carrier Company
851 Stuart St., Box 114
Harrisonburg 22801
(701) 434-3535

Lost Generation Bookshop
6858 Elm St.
McLean 22101
(703) 356-1977

Way Books
Box 8
Mount Solon 22843
(703) 350-2448

Wards Corner Book Shop,
  Inc.
7519 Granby St.
Norfolk 23505
(804) 489-1312

Lois Ginsberg Books &
    Prints
Box 1502
Petersburg 23803
(804) 733-3217

Bargain Books of
Portsmouth
3134 High St.
Portsmouth 23707
(804) 399-5801

Collector's Old Book Shop
26 N. 7th St.
Richmond 23219
(804) 644-2097

O. H. Powers, Jr.
621 18th St., Box 4398
Roanoke 24015

John Sharp, Bookseller
Drawer EE
Williamsburg 23185

WASHINGTON
Rip's Book Service
5th & Park Ave.
Bremerton 98310
(206) 377-3617

Wester Books
Box 341
Ellensburg 98926
(No phone.)

McDuffies Books
Box 97
Lopez 98261

Hopfengarten Gallery &
    Bookshop
Box 335
Mabton 98935
(509) 894-4763

Browser's Bookshop
522 S. Washington St.
Olympia 98501
(206) 357-7462

Beatty Book Store
1925 3rd Ave.
Seattle 98101
(206) 624-2366

Benford Publishing
    Corporation
1101 N. Northlake Way
Seattle 98103
(206) 632-3600

Comstock's Bindery &
    Bookshop
7903 Rainier Ave., S.
Seattle 98118
(206) 725-9531

John Knaide
1919 2nd Ave.
Seattle 98101
(206) 624-9996

Ottenberg Books
724 Pike St.
Seattle 98101
(206) 682-5363

Rayner's Old Book Store
920 3rd Ave.
Seattle 98104

(206) 622-0357

Ralph H. Sacks, Bookseller
8512 15th St., N.E.
Seattle 98115
(206) 525-0647

Seattle Bookfinders
Box 7471 Bitterlake Sta.
Seattle 98133
(No phone.)

John W. Shleppey Rare
  Books
4530 Sheridan, W.
Seattle 98199
(206) 284-4188

Shorey Book Store
815 3rd Ave.
Seattle 98104
(206) 624-0221

George H. Tweney Rare
  Books
16660 Marine View Drive,
  S.W.
Seattle 98166
(206) 243-8243

Clark's Old Book Store
W. 318 Sprague Ave.
Spokane 99204
(509) 624-1846

Jack L. Frederic Books
E. 1217 Empire Ave.
Spokane 99207
(509) 483-4839

The Old Book Home

3217 Cora
Box 7777, Rosewood Sta.
Spokane 99208
(509) 327-2884

Carl's Book Store
945 Broadway
Tacoma 98402
(206) 272-8827

Fox Book Company
1140 Broadway
Tacoma 98402
(206) 627-2223

WEST VIRGINIA

Eric Lundberg
Augusta 26704
(304) 496-5286

J. B. F. Yoak, Jr.
5401 Virginia Ave., S.E.
Charleston 25304
(304) 925-9793

Heal's West Virginia
  Bookstore
607 Duff Ave.
Clarksburg 26301
(304) 622-0851

Emily Driscoll
203 W. German St.
Box 834
Sheperdstown 25443
(304) 876-2202

WISCONSIN

Lantern Bookshop

942 Wisconsin Ave.
Beloit 53511
(608) 362-4740

Biological Book Service
215 Forest St.
Madison 53705
(608) 238-3255

Owens' Rare Books
6221 S. Highlands Ave.
Madison 53705
(608) 238-7709

Paul's Book Store
670 State St.
Madison 53703
(608) 257-2968

Speckled Dog Book
    Company
5402 Whitcomb Dr.
Madison 53711
(608) 271-1675

Mary & Fred Blair
    Bookfinders
3236 N. 15th St.
Milwaukee 53206
(414) 264-6339

Raymond Dworczyk Rare
    Books
2114 W. Rogers St.
Milwaukee 53204
(414) 383-2659

Richard Loreck
3031 N. Prospect Ave.
Milwaukee 53211
(414) 962-6231

Matte Book Shop
3551 S. Pine Ave.
Milwaukee 53207
(414) 744-1583

Renaissance Book Shop
221 N. Water St.
Milwaukee 53202
(414) 271-6850

BOOKS: SPECIALTY

Dealers and Collectors

ARIZONA

(C) John T. Hamilton, III
P.O. Box 6765
Tucson 85733

(Wants Western business
directories.)

ARKANSAS

(D) Bookfinders
Rte. 2
Eureka Springs 72632

(Wants Arthur
Rackham's *Book of
Pictures, Peter Pan, The
Wind in the Willows,
The Tempest,* and other
titles.)

CALIFORNIA

(D) Jack London Bookstore
& Museum
Box 337
Glen Ellen 95442

(Jack London books,
magazines, memorabilia.
Also Western
Americana.)

(D) Doris Harris,
Autographs
6381 Hollywood Blvd.
Los Angeles 90028

(213) 465-7900
(Autographs only, in all
fields. Letters and
manuscripts.)

(C) Schmidtmann
Rte. 1, Box 371
Mentone 92359
(712) 794-1211

(Any books on Nevada;
also pamphlets.)

(C) Gary R. Toomer
1743 Halley St.
San Diego 92154
(714) 423-0385

(Shirley Temple books,
magazines.)

(D) Robert Kuhn Antiques
and Coins
720 Geary St.
San Francisco 94109
(415) 441-7737

(Buys autographs, signed
photos.)

(D) John Oakhurst
2206 40th Ave.
Santa Cruz 95062

(California books, maps,
etc.)

(C) L. H. Selman

761 Chestnut St.
Suite 10
Santa Cruz 95060

(Out-of-print books and pamphlets on cacti and succulents.)

(C) Collector
Box 1224
Sun Valley 91352

(Dog books, all kinds.)

CONNECTICUT

(D) Jacqueline C. B. Levine,
Books for Collectors
60 Urban St.
Stamford 06905
(203) 323-1726

(Wants limited editions; books about books; books on the sea and ships; Derrydale Press books.)

FLORIDA

(C) C. Guarino
Box 115
Marco 33957

(Old geography textbooks, pre-1890; also, early books about America.)

GEORGIA

(D) Paige One
3216 Clairmont Road
Atlanta 30329

(*Doll's Houses* by Lathem. *English Dollhouses of the 18th and 19th Century* by Greene. Books under 1½' high.)

ILLINOIS

(C) Louis D. Melnick
530 Michigan
Evanston 60202

(Old American Bibles with family records, any condition. Send earliest and latest dates along with family name.)

(C) James G. Stevenson
161 Thacker
Hoffman Estates 60194
(312) 882-0421

(Boy Scouts of America books published before 1948; fiction and nonfiction, including handbooks.)

(C) William Gowen
923 South Take
Mundelein 60060

(Tom Swift books, 1910–35. Must have dust jackets.)

IOWA

(D) Kettle Books (Broker)
RR 1
Akron 51001

(Histories, local, towns from Iowa, Nebraska, Kansas, South Dakota.)

(D) McBlain Books
Box 971
Des Moines 50304

(Books, pamphlets on Africa; black America and Latin America, pre-1950; sheet music and documents by black authors.)

KENTUCKY

(C) Carl Howell, Jr.
31 Public Square
Hodgenville 42748

(Books on Abraham Lincoln.)

(C) Don Grayson
2600 Meadow Dr.
Louisville 40220

(Books, historical material on Kentucky.)

(D) Old Pine Tower Antiques
Box 218
Pewee Valley 40056

(Wants *Little Colonel* and Mary Ware books; Annie Fellows Johnson's works.)

MARYLAND

(C) Jerome Shachet

3205 Mayfair Road
Baltimore 21207

(Old books on boxing, boxing magazines, scrapbooks; *Police Gazettes,* pre-1920.)

MASSACHUSETTS

(D) Paul Richards
49 Meadow Lane,
Box 62
Bridgewater 02324
(617) 697-8086

(Autographs.)

(D) Kenneth W. Rendell, Inc.
62 Bristol Road
Somerville 02144
(617) 776-3872

(Autographs.)

MINNESOTA

(C) Alden Miller
3212 34th Ave., S.
Minneapolis 55406

(Histories of Chicago and Northwestern railroads, 1836–1976.)

NEW JERSEY

(C) Collector
136 Parkview Terr.
Lincroft 07738

(New Jersey histories. Also, Mormon and early West.)

NEW YORK

(C) Jack Arone
377 Ashford
Dobbs Ferry 10522
(Railroad guidebooks.)

(C) Grace Friar
12 Grafton St.
Greenlawn 11740
(516) 757-7724
(Books wanted on
occult, witchcraft,
psychic, Eastern
religion, health food,
and related subjects.)

(C) Jonathan White
286 Corbin Place
New York 11235
(Science-fiction books;
fantasy, mystery, etc.
Wants sf "fanzines.")

(C) F. Rowe
175 Brewster Road
Scarsdale 10583
(Children's books,
Twilight Town circa
1910.)

(C) Daniel Jacoby
383 Andrews Road, E.
Williston 11596
(Railroad books.)

(D) Doak
45 Allen Dr.
Woodstock 12498
(Any books, pamphlets

on radio pre-1930.)

OHIO

(C) Bill Curry
435 Rockwood Ave.
Chesapeake 45619
(All first editions of Jesse
Stuart's books.)

(C) Dale E. Thomas
5397 E. 132nd St.
Cleveland 44125
(First editions of Horatio
Alger; reprints. State
publisher.)

(C) Michael Martina
Box 1302
Warren 44482
(Ohio, Illinois, Indiana,
Kentucky, Tennessee
histories.)

PENNSYLVANIA

(C) Franklin
Box 17
Buckingham 18912
(Arthur Conan Doyle
books. Also, *Strand*
magazines.)

(C) D. H. Ernst, Books
RR 1, Box 124
Selinsgrove 17870
(Pennsylvania histories;
books by Shoemaker,
Stover, Singmaster.)

(D) Reiner Books
Swengel 17880

(Wants books published by the American Tract Society, Presbyterian Board of Publishers, Baptist Publishers Board; Carlton and Porter titles by John Bunyan; old Protestant and Reformation titles.)

SOUTH DAKOTA

(C) Jim Aplan
Box 474
Onida 57564

(Anything on Captain Jack Crawford, the post scout; anything on old Utica, N.Y., 1840–70; gunsmith, Morgan James, cowboy, Indian, General Custer, fur trade, Black Hills, South Dakota.)

TENNESSEE

(C) F. M. Hill
Box 1037
Kingsport 37662

(Books, maps, pamphlets related to Tennessee and other Southern states.)

TEXAS

(C) Ron Pearson
10620 Creekmere Dr.

Dallas 75218
(214) 321-9717

(Books published by National Geographic Society.)

(D) Packsaddle Books
1890 Del Rio Blvd.
Eagle Pass 78852

(Texas books, maps, etc.)

(C) Richard Howe
12335 Rip Van Winkle
Houston 77024

(Books on pianos and music boxes.)

(C) Colonel E. T. Noyes
438 Oakleaf Dr.
San Antonio 78209

(First editions of Washington Irving's works, specifically: Volume 1, *History of New York,* 1809; *Astorio,* 1836; *The Adventures of Captain Bonneville,* 1837; Parts II and IV of the *Sketch Book,* 1819–20.)

UTAH

(D) Utah Coin and Antique Shop
75 W. 3rd St., S.
Salt Lake City 84101

(Books, pamphlets about

the Mormons or the
West.)

VIRGINIA

(C) Vincent A. Bertolini
    214 Midtown Bldg.
    Norfolk 23505
    (Volumes of *The
    Horseless Age.*)

WISCONSIN

(D) The Canine Collection
    P.O. Box 308
    Big Bend 53103
    (Dog books, all types.)

CANADA

(C) Williams
    Box 4126
    Calgary, Alberta
    (Canada and Arctic
    books, pamphlets, maps,
    and prints.)

BOTTLES, FLASKS, JARS, and INSULATORS

Collectors

ALABAMA

Don Tucker
Box 5
Eldridge 35554
(Wants good bitters bottles
for less than $100.)

CALIFORNIA

Gary Piper
106 Wilson St.
Albany 94710
(Poison bottles wanted;
Bimal preferred.)

Ed McCann
3970 Kansas
San Diego 92104
(714) 295-6028
(Wants early California
medicine: Bitterwich,
Moonplant, Wakelee's
Citrate of Magnesia,
Murray's Magic Oil, etc.
Also, trade cards, tokens,
etc.)

Randy Haumann
415 Amherst St.
San Francisco 94134
(415) 239-7567 (evenings)
(Wants San Francisco and
Napa sodas. Colored

umbrella inks and pot lids
with animals.)

John Compton
3448 Annadale Place
San Jose 95121
(408) 274-6975
(Western whiskey collector
wants amber fifths:
Cutter-Mooreman, Cutter
Hardy, Blakes-Miller,
Stewart, mint or near-mint
condition.)

Gary Frederick
1124 Magnolia St.
South Pasadena 91030
(213) 799-3385
(Wants pop bottles, crown
top embossed or enamel
label, 1920–60.)

Scott Gordon
2278 Shady Brook Dr.
Thousand Oaks 91362
(Wants mint-condition
colored, iron pontil soda
embossed "Somerset,
Pennsylvania," or any
colored pontiled bottle
embossed "Somerset." Also
amber, green, or cobalt
Hutchinson's with
Somerset.)

John Alexander
200 Tulsa Lane

Watsonville 95076

(Wants Phoenix bourbon
and Gilt Edge Whiskey
bottles.)

CONNECTICUT

Harold Krevolin
35 North Ridge Road
Old Greenwich 06870
(203) 637-1484

(Wants older figurals, clear,
frosted, colored, milk glass.)

FLORIDA

Jim Scrogins
414 Orange Ave.
Jacksonville 32211

(Wants White House
Vinegar bottles. All sizes.
All types.)

GEORGIA

Bob Basford
1020 Tanglewood Trail,
Rte. 3
Woodstock 30188
(404) 926-2607

(Wants bottles and jars
embossed with the name of
a candy, or the word
"candy" or "confection,"
etc.)

IDAHO

G. Kadlec, M.D.
560 Shoup Ave.

West Twin Falls 83301

(Wants back-bar bottles with
glass labels or enamel
writing. Also, flasks with
glass labels.)

ILLINOIS

R. E. Ridder
Box 184
Elsah 62028

(Wants Illinois blob sodas,
especially colored and
pontiled. Also harder-to-find
Hutches.)

R. M. Pennell
211 W. Hickory St.
Hinsdale 60521
(312) 887-0466

(Wants Chicago beers.)

Kenneth Sosnowski
119 E. Lahon
Parkridge 60068
(312) 823-1287

(Wants old and unusual milk
bottles and jars. Product jars
related to milk and cream.)

INDIANA

R. E. Pliske
P.O. Box 1222
LaPorte 46350

(Wants Dr. Jaynes bottles,
especially hair tonic,
liniment, square tonic,
vermifuge, Carminative

Balsam. Also old veterinary bottles.)

MARYLAND

Alfred Cahall
Rte. 3, Box 533
Easton 21601

(Wants mint-condition pontil Robert Turlingtons. State color, size, and price. Also would like to hear from Eastern Shore of Maryland collectors or diggers who have small collections to sell.)

MICHIGAN

Richard Havelka
3535 Dexter Road
Ann Arbor 48103

(Wants labeled ink bottles, especially wants half pint and sample cobalt Carters' Cathedrals as well as ink-go-withs such as wooden ink carongs, sanders, ink sand, trade cards, tins, and cardboard signs.)

Robert L. Daly
1480 Dyemeadow Lane
Flint 48504
(313) 732-3555

(Will pay upward of $1,000 for old bottles marked "BITTERS," log-cabin shape, marked "North Bend/Tippecanoe." Also

wants historical whiskey flasks and other early American bottles.)

George Charles Loik
20141 Webster
Mt. Clemens 48043
(313) 791-6992

(Wants Detroit soda and mineral waters, aqua to puce, pontiled or not, before 1900. Detroit medicines, crocks, and jugs.)

E. Eberle
3200 N. Main
Royal Oak 48073

(Wants Hayner and Altschul whiskey bottles.)

Ruth Miller
605 Lexington
Royal Oak 48073

(Wants whiskey bottles, labels, trays, etc., with name "Eberle, Springfield, Ohio.")

MISSISSIPPI

Bo Cribbs
509 Dunton Road
Clinton 39056

(Wants glassworks bottles. Must have glassworks embossed. Also sodas, whiskeys, and flasks.)

MONTANA

Ed Massey

P.O. Box 722
Libby 59923

(Wants bitters codds, Hutchinsons, owls, poisons, and other embossed bottles. No screw tops.)

NEVADA

W. V. Wright
220 S. Bruce
Las Vegas 89101

(Wants Nevada embossed bottles.)

NEW JERSEY

H. Thompson
43 Cozy Corner
Avenel 07001

(Wants fire-extinguisher grenades: Hazelton, Kalamazoo, Harkness, American, Acme, Healy.)

Larry Kline
321 Fayette St.
Bridgeton 08302

(Wants beers and sodas.)

Ronald Bernstein
1480 Rte. 46, Apt. 313A
Parsippany 07054

(Wants glass candy containers.)

NEW YORK

Mrs. Raymond Thomas

78 Morris St.
Amityville 11701

(Wants nursing bottles and pap boats, mint condition. Describe, price, and sketch.)

Jim Whetzel
609 Saw Mill Road
Box 36
Ardsley 10502

(Top prices paid for mint-condition historical flasks, barrels, cabins, or other figural bitters, poisons, open pontil medicines, tea kettle inks, and pontiled colognes. State price wanted.)

David Pupo
31 Bowen Road
Churchville 14428

(Wants photographic bottles, labeled or embossed "Kodak," "Eastman," "E. Anthony," "Defender Photo Supply," "Gennet," "Rexo," "Phoenix," "Ansco," "Scovill," "Seed," "Hammer," "Agfa," "Walker," "Burke and James," "Hauf.")

Joe Quinlan
Dansville 14437

(Wants blob top John Pragel Beer from Dansville.)

Vince Martonis
41 Chatsworth

Kenmore 14217

(Wants Dr. M. M. Fenner, Fredonia, N.Y., bottles and trade cards.)

Mrs. Pat Sebastian
9 South Magnolia Ave.
Pearl River 10965

(Wants holy water bottles, Avon snail and mouse, Coca-Cola bottles and items, dolls old or current, and Cliquot Club Eskimo doll to go with her bottles.)

Burton Spiller
169 Greystone Lane
Rochester 14618

(Figural bitters bottles wanted. Colored historical flasks, milk-glass figurals, fancy Bininger and whiskey bottles, plus trays and related items.)

NORTH CAROLINA

Bill Ricketts
Box 9605
Asheville 28805
(704) 298-6348

(Wants Coca-Cola, Pepsi, Dr. Pepper, and other soft-drink bottles.)

David Wilson
Box 622
Columbus 28722
(704) 894-8642

(Wants North Carolina bottles in good condition.)

NORTH DAKOTA

Wilbert Adolf
Box 67
Alexander 58831

(Will buy embossed drugstore bottles from North Dakota towns.)

OHIO

Don Spangler
4557 Ridgebury
Dayton 45440

(Wants expanded ribbed bottles, dishes, pans, tumblers, etc., made by early Ohio and Midwestern glass houses.)

PENNSYLVANIA

Frank A. Perna
RR 1, Box 77
New Alexandria 15670

(Wants Latrobe, Pennsylvania, bottles, crocks, and miscellaneous, including H. J. Miller.)

Jerry Pickel
RR 4
Red Lion 17356
(717) 244-4160

(Wants Hutchinson sodas in show condition from any of

the following states: Florida, Montana, Vermont, Utah, Nebraska, and Georgia. Also colored yellow-green, emerald green, amber, and cobalt Hutchinsons.)

Mark Kickerson
RR 1, Box 123
Shinglehouse 16748

(Wants Pennsylvania flasks, such as Cunninghams and Ihmsen; also colored quart whiskeys from Pennsylvania. Will trade old knives for old bottles.)

RHODE ISLAND

Al Polselli
11 Cooper Dr.
Lincoln 02885

(Squat bottles wanted. Will buy Dutch or English squats. Also want Cathedral pickle jars and pepper-sauce bottles.)

SOUTH CAROLINA

J. L. Jones
Box 142
Greer 29651

(Hutchinson soda bottles wanted, especially territorials.)

TEXAS

Kim Kokles

6018 Northaven
Dallas 75230
(214) 361-7004

(Wants bitters: Drakes Plantation, emerald green, lime green; Queen yellow, chocolate; old stomach bitters (Bryant's); American Life Bitters.)

Peggy Bryant
846 W. 43rd St.
Houston 77018

(Wants embossed Texas whiskeys, jugs, sodas.)

Bob & Beka Mebane
701 Castano Ave.
San Antonio 78209
(512) 824-4529

(Wants American historical flasks, rare and unusual colors. Also rare ink bottles. Pottery Railroad pig bottles.)

UTAH

Bob Conrad
1197 W. 10600, S.
Riverton 89065

(Wants Warners Cures remedies.)

VERMONT

Bob Churinske
RFD 2
8 Bromur St.
Barre 05641

(Wants sparkling mint, pontiled scroll flasks. All sizes and colors.)

WASHINGTON

Pete Hendricks
5112 S. Fountain
Seattle 98178

(Wants Washington Territory bottles. Any Drakes Plantation Bitters; Washington sodas, Seattle whiskeys and beers.)

WISCONSIN

George Hansen
RR 1, Box 455-D
Burlington 53105

(Wants label under glass and enameled back-bar whiskeys.)

Wayne Kroll
RR 2
Fort Atkinson 53538

(Wants Milwaukee branch office beer bottles: Schlitz, Pabst, Miller, Blatz Best.)

Charlie Lange
4157 N. 79th St.
Milwaukee 53222

(Wants Schlitz, old small bottles, and other Milwaukee breweries which include the names of their agents, bottlers, branches. Also unusual Schlitz blobs

and related items.)

Joe Wheeler
RR 1
Plainfield 54966

(Wants Wisconsin beer bottles.)

Dealers

ARIZONA

Old West Bottle Company
P.O. Box 1172
Tucson 85701

COLORADO

Metal Detector Sales
5125 Alameda
Denver 80219

FLORIDA

Ye Old Bottle Shoppe
Box 1378
Bartow 33830

The Outrigger Shop
4594 Overseas Hwy.
Marathon 33050

INDIANA

Dave's Old Bottles
720 N. Jackson St.
Crown Point 46307

Schmitt House Bottle

Diggers
113 W. Chestnut St.
Jeffersonville 47130
(812) 282-7842

MAINE

Hobbs Farm
Ingerson Road
Ashby 01431

Old Jail Bottle & Antique
   Shop
Portland St.
North Berwick 03906
(207) 676-4459

NEW MEXICO

Krol's Rock City
5 Miles E. Hwy. 26
Deming 88030

NORTH CAROLINA

J. H. Stevens
704 W. Main St.
Elizabeth City 27909

OREGON

Martin's Bottles
1740 Spring
Medford 97501

PENNSYLVANIA

Kauffman's Ol Bottles
   N'Stuff
RR 4, Box 246
Manheim 17545

WASHINGTON

That Log Cabin Place
U.S. Hwy. 2
General Delivery
Gold Bar 98251

ENGLAND

Bull's Brow Farm
Ditchling Common
Hassocks
Sussex, BN68Tn, England

CLOCKS, LAMPS, PRIMITIVES, CAMERAS, TELEPHONES, TYPEWRITERS, ODDITIES

Clock Dealers

ALABAMA

Parkway Upholstering &
  Refinishing
2708 Dauphin Is. Pkwy.
Mobile 36605
(205) 476-2310
(Specialty clocks.)

Spring Hill Jewelry
3496 Springhill Ave.
Mobile 36608
(205) 344-9779

ARIZONA

Antique Clock Mart
5665 E. 22nd St.
Tucson 85711
(602) 747-5674

CALIFORNIA

Corinthian Studios
521 Sutter
San Francisco 94102
(415) 362-0717

FLORIDA

Seabreeze Antique Shop
222 Seabreeze Blvd.
Daytona Beach 32018

GEORGIA

Clock Gallery
2794 Piedmont Road, N.E.
Atlanta 30305
(404) 262-3441

ILLINOIS

It's About Time
375 Park
Glencoe 60022
(312) 835-2012
(Clock restoration.)

INDIANA

Antique Gallery
4303 S. Hanna
Fort Wayne 46806
(219) 744-2561
(Specialty clocks.)

Ye Old Clock Shop
6020 Crawfordsville Road
Speedway 46224
(317) 244-5657

MARYLAND

Nelson R. Coleman, III,
  Ltd.
2539 N. Charles St.
Baltimore 21218

MASSACHUSETTS

Neil Gray
Newton 02158
(617) 244-5632

The Clock Mill
389 Belmont Ave.
Springfield 01108
(413) 739-2226

MISSOURI

Braun Galleries
10315 Clayton Road
St. Louis 63131
(314) 991-1798

MONTANA

The Time Shop
1524 10th Ave., S.
Great Falls 59404
(406) 761-5695
(Old World clocks.)

NEBRASKA

City Clock Company, Inc.
210 Gateway N.
Lincoln 68504
(402) 466-8148
(Repairs and sells.)

Miller Jewelry
6127 Havelock
Lincoln 68505
(402) 464-7929

NEW JERSEY

Fera's Antique Shop
199 Washington St.
Newark 07102
(201) 622-3596

Easton Jewelers
6719 Atlantic Ave.
Ventnor City 08406
(609) 823-3751

NEW YORK

Antique Clocks
33 Poplar St.
Massapequa 11758
(516) 799-5460

WYOMING

Kindel Antiques
205 S. 4th St.
Basin 82410
(307) 568-2232

Lamps and Lighting Fixture Dealers

ALABAMA

House of Lamps
1112 Telegraph Road
Prichard 36610
(205) 457-7326
(Buys antique lamps and
shades, all kinds.)

CALIFORNIA

The Lamplighter
3020 Adams Ave.
San Diego 92116
(714) 282-0877

Pat McFadden
2803 Harbor
Ventura 93003
(Buys brass lighting fixtures,
electric or gas sconces, desk
lamps, bases, glass shades in
sets, art glass, etc.)

KANSAS

Mary Corvell Antiques
1213 S. Washington St.
Wellington 67152
(316) 326-2347
(Lamp specialist.)

MISSOURI

Village Antiques
1215 S. Big Bend Blvd.
St. Louis 63117

Lamp Collectors

MICHIGAN

Joe Makalak
150 S. Berkshire
Bloomfield Hills 48013
(313) 338-8180
(Tiffany lamp bases wanted.)

NEW JERSEY

Ed Malakoff
276 Princeton Dr.
River Edge 07661
(201) 487-1989
(Will pay top prices for
Puffies or painted Pairpoint
scenes.)

NEW YORK

E. S. Michaels
P.O. Box 403
Whitestone 11357
(Wants Tiffany, Pairpoint,
Handel lamps.)

OHIO

Shaw
630 N. Wayne St.
Kenton 12639
(Wants dated lamps and old
lighting devices.)

WASHINGTON

Linda Adams
605 Stewart St.
Seattle 98101
(Wants early figural
Christmas-tree lights.)

Primitives Dealers

ALABAMA

Atchinson Antiques

53 S. Warren
Mobile 36602
(205) 432-8423

Happy House Oldtiques &
   Gifts
2009 1st Ave.
N. Irondale 35210
(205) 956-3123

ARIZONA

The Buggy Stop
3201 E. Bell Road
Phoenix 85032
(602) 971-5030

Fry's Antiques
6821 N. 16th St.
Phoenix 85016
(602) 277-0426

Red House Antiques
914 E. Camelback Road
Phoenix 85014
(602) 265-7795

CALIFORNIA

Shirl-Wil Antiques
1385 N. Magnolia
El Cajon 92020
(714) 442-5557

The Owl and the Crow
729 W. Washington
San Diego 92103
(714) 296-4468

Copper & Things
371 N. Robertson

Los Angeles 90048
(213) 276-8800

Old Wagon Wheel Antiques
1125 Clement
San Francisco 94118
(415) 752-2117

COLORADO

Bee's Antiques
4166 Tennyson
Denver 80236
(303) 458-5010

CONNECTICUT

Larry Shapiro
Box 101
Rocky Hill 06067
(203) 563-1348

ILLINOIS

Rudy's Relics
532 Eden Park
Rantoul 61866
(217) 892-2554

INDIANA

Rustic Relics
110 S. Line
Columbia City 46725
(219) 244-7246

The Wood & Stone
   Antiques
1116 Pearl St.
Columbus 47201
(812) 376-8337

Country Cousin Antiques
110 W. King St.
Garrett 46738
(219) 357-5587

Myers Antiques
8914 Southeastern Ave.
Indianapolis 46239
(317) 862-5012

Shaker Table Antiques
P.O. Box 23
Prairieton 47870
(Primitives and Shaker
items.)

KANSAS

White Eagle Antiques
1215 Franklin
Riverside 66605

MASSACHUSETTS

Brimfield Antiques
Main Street
Brimfield 01010
(413) 245-3350

NORTH CAROLINA

The Nostalgia Store
103 Cherry St.
Black Mountain 28711
(704) 669-6093

Camera Dealers

FLORIDA

Frank D. Guarino
P.O. Box 89
Debary 32712
(305) 688-8174
(All antique photographic
items.)

ILLINOIS

Ford's Enchanted Cottage
567 S. Greenleaf St.
Waukegan 60085
(312) 623-0653
(All types of cameras.)

Camera Collectors

CALIFORNIA

Tontz
4043 Nora
Covina 91722
(213) 338-9976 (nights)
(Old cameras.)

TENNESSEE

Barrett Ogden
1490 Merrycrest
Memphis 38111
(Old cameras.)

Old-Telephone Dealers

CALIFORNIA

Billard's Old Telephones
21710 Regnart Road
Cupertino 95014

FLORIDA AND
NEW YORK

Leon Dworetsky
33 Poplar St.
Massapequa, N.Y. 11758
Also at: 9056 Runnymeade
  Road
Jacksonville, Fla. 32217

Old-Typewriter Dealers

NEW YORK

Paul Lippman
175 W. 13th St.
New York 10011
(Typewriters prior to 1920.)

Julian Marwell
317 W. 89th St.
New York 10024
(Typewriters prior to 1910.)

Dealers and Collectors of Oddities

ALABAMA
(C) Owen

P.O. Box 6144
Homewood Sta.
Birmingham 35209
(Wants early safety
razors, preferably with
cases.)

CALIFORNIA

(C) Herb Shearer
    904 LaPuente Dr.
    Bakersville 93309
    (Collects razor-blade
    banks.)

IDAHO

(C) Anne MacLeod
    1330 Ponderosa Dr.
    Moscow 83843
    (Wants decorative fans,
    suitable for framing.)

ILLINOIS

(D) Jerry Bayless
    802 E. Wood St.
    Decatur 62521
    (217) 429-5474
    (Wants old washing
    machines.)

IOWA

(C) Clifford White
    2417 Middle Road
    Keokuk 52632
    (319) 524-8521
    (Wants penny pencils

made about 1920.
Round, unfinished
wood, not sharpened;
with pointed erasers.)

MICHIGAN

(C) William Porter
908 Pierce
Birmingham 48009
(313) 647-3876

(Wants Mission Oak
furniture, circa 1900–16,
made at Gustav Stickley's
"CRAFTSMAN"
workshops in Eastwood
[Syracuse], New York.
Look for paper label, red
decal, or burned-in mark
of old-fashioned joiner's
compass with motto "Als
ik kan" inside and script
"STICKLEY" under-
neath. Also wants
Roycroft furniture with
carved in mark of circle
with "R" inside and
double cross above. Will
travel 2,000 miles to get
or pay shipping for
farther distance.)

NEW JERSEY

(C) Dan Keogh
42 Saratoga Dr.
Oakland 07436
(201) 337-6595

(Wants airplane models
used for identification
training by U.S. Armed
Forces.)

NEW YORK

(C) Robery Doyle
94 Main St.
Fishkill 12524

(Wants straight razors,
fancy or unusual.)

(C) Winston
143 E. 60th St.
New York 10022

(Wants old fountain
pens.)

NORTH CAROLINA

(D) Whitfield's Antiques
2128 Leeds Lane
Winston Salem 27103

(Wants carrousel horses
and animals.)

OHIO

(D) Mike Gorski
1770 Dover Road
Westlake 44145
(216) 871-6071

(Wants old slot
machines; any kind or
condition.)

WISCONSIN

(C) John P. Snow
4539 N. Bartlett Ave.
Shorewood 53211

(Wants duck-hunting
stamps. Unsigned with
original gum, $5 each;
signed or stuck to
license, $1 each.)

COINS and STAMPS

Dealers

ALABAMA

Century Coins and Stamps
221 Century Plaza
Birmingham 35211
(205) 591-5100

Dyar Honeycutt
Box 1337
Gadsden 35902

Action Stamp & Coin Shop,
  Inc.
1825 29th Ave.
Homewood 35209
(205) 870-7932

ALASKA

Stamp & Coin Cache
436 W. 5th Ave.
Anchorage 99501
(907) 272-6232

Far North Stamps
Davis Ave., Pinewood Park
Juneau 99801
(907) 586-2689

ARIZONA

A-1 Coin Exchange
4768 N. Central Ave.
Phoenix 85012
(602) 279-5958

Lee's Stamp & Coin Shop,
  Inc.
4604 N. 7th St.
Phoenix 85013
(602) 265-0293

Morad's Coins
5751 N. 31st Dr.
Phoenix 85017

North American Coin &
  Currency, Ltd.
Suite G-2, National Bank
  Plaza
100 W. Washington St.
Phoenix 85003
(602) 257-0873

American Philatelic
  Brokerage
7225 N. Oracle Road
Tucson 85704
(602) 297-3456

A.P.S. Loid's S.P.A.
P.O. Box 5844
Tucson 85703
(Stamps.)

Arizona Stamp & Coin
4668 Speedway Blvd.
Tucson 85712
(602) 327-0675

The Copper Man
Box 17676
Tucson 85731

Antiquarian Coin & Book
  Shop
4246 N. Scottsdale Road
Scottsdale 85251

ARKANSAS

M & M Coin Exchange,
  Inc.
P.O. Box 546
7 W. Main Plaza
Jacksonville 72076
(501) 982-2495

Arkansas Coin Exchange
4513 John F. Kennedy
North Little Rock 72116

CALIFORNIA

Foster's Coin & Stamp
  Company
2189 Bancroft Way
Berkeley 94704

Escondido Coin Shop
N. Broadway
Escondido 91731
(714) 745-1613

Robert L. Hughes, Inc.
6920 Hollywood Blvd.
Hollywood 90028
(800) 421-0588 or
(213) 462-3261

Jonathon's Coins
525 W. Manchester
Inglewood 90301

Bick International

509 N. Fairfax
Los Angeles 90036
(213) 651-1842
(Stamps.)

Bowers & Ruddy Galleries,
  Inc. (A Subsidiary of
  General Mills)
6922 Hollywood Blvd.
Los Angeles 90028
(213) 466-4595

California Coin & Stamp
  Galleries
448 S. Hill St., Suite 1017
Los Angeles 90013

C & T Coins
Box 66531
Los Angeles 90066

Stamps in the Attic
323 1st St.
Los Angeles 94022
(415) 941-7717

Superior Stamp & Coin
  Company, Inc.
517 W. 7th St.
Los Angeles 90014
(213) 627-2621

Alexander Stamp & Coin
  Shop
6740 Magnolia
Riverside 92506
(714) 684-9930

Marshall Stamps
P.O. Box V
Rolling Hills Estates 90274

Henry's Stamp Shop
311 Mission Valley
  Center, W.
San Diego 92109
(714) 295-1575

Ricardo S. Martinez
  Company
P.O. Box 5228
San Diego 92105

Captain Tuttle
5549 Las Alturas
San Diego 92114

Coin Gallery of San
  Francisco
62 Post St.
San Francisco 94104
(415) 421-2832

William Hall Coins
2001 Union St.
San Francisco 94123
(415) 563-5300

Robert Kuhn Antiques &
  Coins
720 Geary
San Francisco 94109
(415) 474-6981

Camino Coin Company
5 37th Ave.
San Mateo 94403
(415) 341-7991

Joel Rettew
Rare Coin Galleries, Inc.
3750 B. South Bristol
Santa Ana 92704

Goldmunzen International
12 Figueroa St.
Santa Barbara 93101
(805) 965-7523

Jack Beymer
647 N. Coddingtontown
Santa Rosa 95401

COLORADO

L & L Coins
5801 W. 44th Ave.
Denver 80212

CONNECTICUT

Madison Coin & Stamp
  Company
891 Boston Post Road
Madison 06443
(203) 245-7319

John Dean Coin Company,
  Inc.
1250 Boston Post Road
Milford 06460
(203) 874-2612

Sam Sloat, Inc.
136 Main St.
Westport 06880
(203) 226-4279

DELAWARE

Delaware Stamp & Coin
  Company
810 Orange St.
Wilmington 19801
(302) 655-4797

DISTRICT OF COLUMBIA

Deak & Company
1800 K Street, N.W.
Washington 20006
(202) 872-1233

FLORIDA

Robert L. Steinberg
P.O. Box 7255
Fort Lauderdale 33304

Ben's Coin & Gun Shop
1023 Ridgewood Ave.
Holly Hill 32017
(904) 255-0564

Arlington Stamp & Coin
  Company
1332 University Blvd., N.
Jacksonville 32211
(904) 743-1776

Edgewood Coin Shop
934 S. Edgewood Ave.
Jacksonville 32205
(904) 389-0013

Sunshine Stamps & Coins,
  Inc.
420 Julia
Jacksonville 32233
(904) 355-4111

Graham Rayner & Associate
P.O. Box 256
Jensen Beach 33457
(305) 878-2247

World Numis
Box 868

Maitland 32751

Hy Bedrin
520 N.W. 165th Road
Miami 33169

Ricardo Del Campo
225 S.E. 1st Ave.
Miami 33131
(305) 373-6895
(Stamps.)

Sidney W. Smith & Sons
2510 Biscayne Blvd.
Miami 33137
(305) 573-1200

Florida Rare Coins
531 N.E. 124th St.
North Miami 33161
(305) 895-2220

Decker's Coins & Stamps
2134 W. Colonial Dr.
Orlando 32804
(305) 841-3614

Collector's Shop, Inc.
708 Ridgewood Ave.
Port Orange 32019
(904) 761-0592

Flying Eagle Coin Shop
187 Masters Drive
St. Augustine 32084
(904) 824-5064

Seminole Coin Center
107 W. 1st St.
Sanford 32771
(305) 323-4352

Tom McAfee
Tom's Coins
124 E. Morse Blvd.
P.O. Box 1256
Winter Park 32789
(305) 647-8338

GEORGIA

Georgia Stamp & Coin
  Company, Inc.
129 Carnegie Way, N.W.
Atlanta 30303
(404) 524-2676

Lenox Stamps & Coins
3393 Peachtree Road, N.E.
Atlanta 30319
(404) 261-4521

Mableton Coin Company
5185 Bankhead
Mableton 30059
(404) 941-3579

Regal Coin Exchange
3605 Waters Ave.
Savannah 31404
(912) 352-4935

HAWAII

Ala Moana Stamp & Coin
  Company
1236 Ala Moana Blvd.
Honolulu 96814
(808) 947-3711

Collector's Art
1461 S. King St.
Honolulu 96814

(808) 947-4414

IDAHO

Idaho Stamp & Coin Shop
3506 Rose Hill
Boise 83705

Security Silver Exchange,
  Inc.
216 N. 8th St.
Boise 83706
(208) 336-0908
(Coins.)

ILLINOIS

Admiral Coin & Stamp Mart
4136 Harlem Norridge
Chicago 60656
(312) 456-5100

Jake's Coin & Stamp Shop
5521 W. Belmont St.
Chicago 60641
(312) 725-1344

Marshall Field & Company
111 N. State St.
Chicago 60603
(312) 781-4281
(Stamps.)

Rare Coin Company of
  America
31 N. Clark St.
Chicago 60602
(312) 346-3443

Sandler Coin & Stamp

Company
3938 N. Pulaski
Chicago 60641
(312) 777-0644

U.S. Stamps & Covers
Room 1820
36 S. State St.
Chicago 60604
(312) 782-0231

Jess Peters, Inc.
P.O. Box 123
Decatur 62525
(217) 428-2074

Chandler's Inc.
630 Davis St.
Evanston 60204
(312) 475-7200
(Stamps.)

Blackhawk Coins
1505 15th St.
Moline 61265

B & J Coin Shop
3123 S. Dirksen Parkway
Capitol City Shopping
  Center
Springfield 62703
(Stamps, too.)

INDIANA

Brass Bell Antiques
1332 Taylor St.
Fort Wayne 46804
(219) 743-1867
(Coins.)

Russell's Coins & Stamps
514 W. Jefferson
Fort Wayne 46802
(219) 743-5933

Circle Coin Shop
217 E. 54th St.
Indianapolis 46220
(317) 251-0522

IOWA

Hickman & Oakes
Drawer 1456
Iowa City 52240

KANSAS

Joe Flynn's & Sons Rare
  Coins, Inc.
P.O. Box 3140
Kansas City 66103
(913) 236-7171

Covenant House
P.O. Box 6102
Shawnee Mission 66205

House of Stuart, Ltd.
326 Delaware
Tonganoxie 66086
(913) 831-1684

KENTUCKY

Dellmuth's Antique Shop
958 Baxter Ave.
Louisville 40204
(606) 584-8842
(Coins.)

217

LOUISIANA

Lazard Coin & Stamps
3146 Calhoun
New Orleans 70125
(504) 861-2581

MAINE

J. M. Blood, Inc., Foreign
  Covers and Stamps
380 High St.
Holyoke 01040

Coin & Stamp Shop
652 Congress
Portland 04101
(207) 774-7271

Hall Stamp Company
477 Congress
Portland 04111
(207) 772-9017

Valley Coin Shop
695 Washington St.
South Attleboro 02703

T.J.C. Stamp & Coin
  Company
1 Silver Street
Waterville 04901
(207) 873-2329

MARYLAND

Golden Eagle Coin
  Exchange
9119 Riggs Road
Adelphi 20783
(301) 439-1444

Mathew Bennett
31 G.W. Chesapeake
P.O. Box 5432G
Baltimore 21204
(Stamps.)

The Numismatic Gallery,
  Inc.
600 Reisterstown Road
Pikesville 21208
(301) 653-2828

Julian Leidman
8439 Georgia Ave.
Silver Spring 20910
(301) 585-8467

Maryland Coin Exchange
10753 Colesville Road
Silver Spring 20910
(301) 593-2419

MASSACHUSETTS

American Gold Exchange
44 Bromfield St.
Boston 02108
(617) 482-2524
(Coins.)

Cash Coin Exchange
  Center, Inc.
40 Court St.
Government Center
Boston 02108
(617) 227-0099

Michael R. Kirzner
44 Bromfield St.
Boston 02108

(617) 482-6498
(Stamps and coins.)

Silver & Gold Redeeming
  Corporation of America
1865 Massachusetts Ave.
Cambridge 02138
(617) 661-8048

New England Rare Coin
  Galleries
1661 Worcester Road
Suite 101
Framingham 01701
(617) 879-7711

Adrien J. Lapointe
4 Front St.
Worcester 01608
(617) 752-1739
(Stamps and coins.)

MICHIGAN

Gregg Mellon
Box 35281, High Park Br.
Detroit 48203
(Coins.)

Mercury Coin & Stamp
  Company
P.O. Box 54-D
Royal Oak 48068

MINNESOTA

Bob's Coins
St. James 56081
(507) 375-3869

MISSOURI

Ace Coin & Antiques
419 N. Main
Kansas City 64152
(816) 833-1824

Heart of America Stamp &
  Coin Company
1729 Stewart
Kansas City 64104
(816) 371-7779

Ed Ross Stamps
Box 8573
Kansas City 64114

Westridge Coins
Box 9326
Kansas City 64133

W. G. Alexander
115 N. Euclid Ave.
St. Louis 63108
(314) 535-8890
(Coins.)

Famous Barr Company
721 Olive
St. Louis 63101
(314) 421-5704
(Coins.)

MONTANA

Montana Coin & Stamp
  Company
2818 3rd Ave., N.
Billings 59101
(406) 252-6223

NEW HAMPSHIRE

Dover Coin Center
10 2nd St., Suite B
Dover 03820

NEW JERSEY

M & R Gallery
Box 298
Hawthorne 07506

Fera's Antique Shop
199 Washington St.
Newark 07102
(201) 622-3596
(Coins.)

East Coast Numismatic
  Exchange, Inc.
3258 Hwy. 516
Old Bridge 06857

A & S Stamps & Coins
Woodbridge Shopping
  Center
Woodbridge 07095
(201) 636-2120

NEW YORK

Marlen Stamps & Coins,
  Ltd.
214-24 73rd St.
Bayside 11364
(212) 479-7785

Astoria
107-A Middleneck Road
Great Neck 11021
(516) 482-9244

(Coins.)

Max Hirschhorn
255 Broadway, Dept. 5
Lynbrook 11563
(516) 593-3353

Harmer Rooke Numismatics
3 East 57th St.
New York 10022

Stacks
123 W. 57th St.
New York 10019
(212) 582-2580
(Coins.)

J & J Coins
P.O. Box 144
Utica 13503

Northshore Numismatics
653 Old Country Road
Westbury 11590

PENNSYLVANIA

Ye Olde Stamp & Coin
Shop
P.O. Drawer E
Engleville 19408
(215) 265-4458

Panther Valley Coin
  Exchange
153 W. Railroad St.
Nesquehoning 18240
(717) 454-1846

Harry J. Forman, Inc.
Box 5756

220

Philadelphia 19120
(215) 244-4412
(Coins.)

Three Rivers Coin Galleries
P.O. Box 52495
Pittsburgh 15206

TENNESSEE

Chattanooga Coin
109 E. 7th St.
P.O. Box 1028
Chattanooga 37401
(615) 267-3847

C & R Treasure Chest
2957 Austin Peay
Memphis 38128
(901) 388-6170

TEXAS

Southwest Rare Coin
Galleries
Post Oak Bank Bldg.
2200 S. Post Oak Road
Houston 77027
(713) 621-7210

VIRGINIA

Norview Coin Shop
42 Southern Shopping
Center
Norfolk 23505
(804) 853-8118

Nick's Coin Shop
121 E. Main St.
Richmond 23219

(804) 648-8127

WASHINGTON

Washington Numismatic
Gallery
12618 B Kingsgate Way,
N.E.
Kirkland 98033

WISCONSIN

Mark Ferguson
P.O. Box 2584
Oshkosh 54901
(414) 231-7529
(Coins.)

Stamps-Only Dealers

CALIFORNIA

Brewart Stamps
405 W. Katella
Anaheim 92802
(714) 533-0400

United States Stamps
Company, Inc.
368 Bush St.
San Francisco 94104

Marlin Larson
217 Country Garden Lane
San Marcos 92069

Continental Stamp
Company
20909 B. Ventura
Woodland Hills 91364

COLORADO

Boulder Stamps
375 Dellevue Drive
Boulder 80302

Bruin Stamp Company
Box 3111
Boulder 80303

Christopher Swinbank
1200 Pearl St.
Boulder 80302
(303) 443-1750

CONNECTICUT

Berkshire Stamp Galleries
Box 337
Thomaston 06787

FLORIDA

Tropical Stamp Store
P.O. Box 6261
Fort Lauderdale 33310

Mission Stamp Service
P.O. Box 88
North Miami 33161

Jay Richards
P.O. Box 323
North Miami 33161

W & J Rose
P.O. Box 20378
St. Petersburg 33742

GEORGIA

Dunwoody Stamp Company
P.O. Box 88548
Dunwoody 30338

ILLINOIS

Liberty Stamp Shop, Inc.
314-16 S. Dearborn
Chicago 60604

James V. Rasdale
36 S. State St.
Chicago 60603

IOWA

E & F Stamps
16 E. Southridge Road
Marshalltown 50159

MASSACHUSETTS

Simmy's Stamp Company,
   Inc.
148 State St.
Boston 02109

Norman C. Hinds, Jr.
P.O. Box 451
Wakefield 01880

MICHIGAN

R. L. Ducharme
P.O. Box 1601
Grand Rapids 49501

MISSOURI

Town & Country Stamps,
Ltd.
Box 1352K
St. Louis 63138

NEW HAMPSHIRE

D. M. Stamp Company
P.O. Box 163
Concord 03301

NEW JERSEY

Maritius Stamps
P.O. Box 33
Cranford 08016

M & R Gallery
Box 298
Hawthorne 07506

Hull Stamp Company
Hillsdale 07642
(201) 666-1230

Dowd Company, Inc.
44 Wynnewood Road
Livingston 07039

East Coast Numismatic
Exchange, Inc.
3258 Hwy. 516
Old Bridge 06857

William A. Fox
263 White Oak Ridge Road
Short Hills 07078
(201) 467-2366

Greg Manning Company,
Inc.
76 S. Orange Ave.
South Orange 07079
(800) 631-1245

Richard H. Dresel
P.O. Box 628
West Englewood Sta.
Teaneck 07666

McAlonan
41-21 54th St.
Woodside 11377

NEW MEXICO

Intercity Stamp Company
Box 98
Santa Fe 87501

NEW YORK

Jefferson Stamp Company,
Inc.
44 Pondfilled Road
Bronxville 10708
(914) 793-6079

David L. Gilbert, Inc.
1744 East 17th St.
Brooklyn 11229

Robert J. Kaszovitz
P.O. Box 6
Brooklyn 11204
(212) 438-8280

Stampscope, Inc.
P.O. Box 505
Dewitt 13214

L. S. Holding
P.O. Box 166
Howard Beach 11414
(212) 345-7317

Global Philatelic Agency,
  Ltd.
P.O. Box, Drawer A C
Katonah 10536
(914) 248-7500

Herrick Stamp Company
P.O. Box 219
Lawrence 11559

Ronald Frank Company,
  Inc.
Lincolndale 10540
(914) 248-7500

International Philatelic
  Corporation
P.O. Box 826
Lynbrook 11543
(516) 678-6157

Metro Stamp Company,
  Inc.
7520 Metropolitan Ave.
Middle Village 11379

Cherrystone Stamp Center,
  Inc.
132 W. 34th St.
New York 10001
(212) 239-4926

Embassy Stamp Company
55 W. 42nd St.
New York 10036

Harmer-Rooke
3 E. 57th St.
New York 10022
(800) 221-7276

Outlet Company
247 W. 42nd St.
New York 10036
(212) 279-4678

Alfred Rubis
P.O. Box 202, Ansonia Sta.
New York 10023

Union Stamp Company
147 W. 42nd St.
New York 10036
(212) 279-7325

Eberling Stamp Company
105 Franklin Ave.
Staten Island 10301

Country Stamp Center
Mamaroneck Ave.
White Plains 10601

OHIO

J & D Stamps
P.O. Box 39291
Cincinnati 45239

Queen City Stamp
  Company
1015 Central Trust Tower
Cincinnati 45202

World, Inc.
11725 Royalton Road
Cleveland 44133

OREGON

Roadrunner Stamp
  Company
P.O. Box 11407
Portland 97211

PENNSYLVANIA

Stuart Printz
P.O. Box 3146
Allentown 18106

Robert L. Myers
Box 154
Coopersburg 18036

Danam Stamp Company
3150 Township Line
Drexel Hill 19026

Earl P. L. Apfelbaum, Inc.
1819 J. F. Kennedy Blvd.
Philadelphia 19103

The Stamp Window
P.O. Box 57
Richboro 18954

Lambert W. Gerber
Tamaqua 18252

WISCONSIN

Jay Smith
2114 Van Hise Ave.
Madison 53705

Robert E. Hofmeister
6596 N. Bourbon St.
Milwaukee 53224

CANADA

Kirk & Kelly Stamps
328 Malaga Road
Oshawa, Ontario L 1 J 1 N 7

Vanlee Stamp Exchange
39 Kingsway
Vancouver, B.C. V 5T-3H 7

ENGLAND

Rushstamps
Dept. B
Lyndhurst
Hants, England

225

COMIC BOOKS, MAGAZINES,
and CATALOGUES

Dealers and Collectors

CALIFORNIA

(C) Schulman
Box 212
Downey 90241
(Old magazines, sheet
music, postcards, comics
catalogues.)

(D) Icart Vendor
3146 Purdue Ave.
Los Angeles 90066
(Old magazines with
illustrations/prints by
Parrish, Mucha,
Bradley, Remington,
Rockwell, Leyendecker,
Flagg. Also, World War
I posters.)

(C) Freyor
362 Coral View
Monterey Park 91754
(*Weird Tales, Thrill
Book, Tales of Magic
and Mystery.* Any
ghost-story magazines.)

(D) Howard Old Books
Box 82661
San Diego 92138
(Lighting-fixture
manufacturing
catalogues, 1920–30, any
condition. Also,

homing-pigeon books.)

(D) The Magazine
839 Larkin St.
San Francisco 94109
(415) 441-7737
(Wants old magazines,
posters, collectible
erotica.)

(C) E. Flynn
Box 4111
Thousand Oaks 91350
(All back issues of
Acquire magazine.)

(C) Bob Finch
23451 Carlow Road
Torrence 90505
(213) 378-2771
(Thousand-dollar reward
for first issue of *National
Geographic,* October
1888, in good condition.
Also, other issues
through 1915. Any other
Geographic advertising,
brochures, etc.)

COLORADO

(D) *Morning Star-Salina
Star*
Boulder 80302

(Wants old wood and
stove catalogues.)

(D) The Shadow Box &
Record Exchange
1201 E. 13th Ave.
Denver 80218
(303) 831-9893

(Wants fantasy,
science-fiction
paperbacks, new and old
comics, posters, prints,
portfolios.)

(C) Jack Shapiro
3201 S. Monroe
Denver 80202

(Magazines with covers
by artist Coles Phillips.)

CONNECTICUT

(C) John Garity
Noank 06340

(All comics, *Mads,
Playboys,* old *Look* and
Life magazines. State
price.)

DISTRICT OF COLUMBIA

(D) Comic Strip
3326 M Street, N.W.
Washington 20007
(202) 338-2626
(Comics wanted.)

(D) Economy Books
1909 Eye Street, N.W.
Washington 20006

(202) 659-5668
(Wants comics, old
magazines, juveniles.)

FLORIDA

(C) Jack Good
Box 4462
Fort Lauderdale 33304
(305) 564-7390

(Old *Life* magazines
with Marilyn Monroe on
cover: April 7, 1952; May
25, 1953; November 9,
1959; August 15, 1960;
August 7, 1964;
September 8, 1972.)

(C) David P. Folds, Jr.
1061 Dimini Lane
Riviera Beach 33404
(305) 842-3712

(Buys Norman Rockwell
*Saturday Evening Post,
Literary Digest,* old *Life,*
and other Rockwell
covers; also Rockwell
oddities.)

ILLINOIS

(D) Kelly's Comics, Books,
Art
913 W. Cullom Ave.
Chicago 60613

IOWA

(D) Broken Kettle Book
Service

RR 1
Akron 51001
(Sales catalogues and manuals for steam engines, gasoline engines, windmills, guns, musical instruments, pre-1930. Pre-1940 tractor and general farm-machine catalogues.)

(C) Nancy E. Kayser
RR 3
Webster City 50595
(Sale catalogues, sale posters, brochures, anything pertaining to Aberdeen-Angus cattle between 1880 and 1930.)

MAINE

(C) Ray MacDougall
RR2, Box 278
Wells 04090
(Wants *National Geographics* 1888–1912.)

MARYLAND

(C) Walters
1242 Riverbay Road
Rte. 6
Annapolis 21401
(Old fishing-tackle catalogues.)

(D) Steve Geppi
612¹/₂ Edmondson Ave.
Baltimore 21228
(301) 788-8222
(Wants comic books, also pulp collections: 1 or 10,000.)

NEW HAMPSHIRE

(D) Salem Books
Box 393
Salem 03079
(Wants family genealogies, town histories, city directories.)

NEW YORK

(D) Rogofsky
Box F 1102
Flushing 11354
(*Doc Savage, G-8, Operator #5, Shadow, Spider, Dusty Ayres, Wu Fang,* etc., magazines. Paying to $200 each.)

(C) E. M. Barker
28 Prospect Ave.
Ilion 13357
(*Harper's Weekly, Leslie's, Gleason's, Ballou's,* and other illustrated weeklies. Any weekly, pre-1892. *American Heritage* softcover issues, pre-1953. *American Food and Drink,* pre-1900.)

(C) Jack Hunt
Box 194
Kenmore 14217
(Wants comics; pre-1964
Playboys.)

(D) Buster Brown Historical
Society of Comics and
Marketing
119 E. 36th St.
New York 10016
(Buster Brown items.)

(C) Kenneth Galente
150 W. 55th St.
New York 10019
(212) 879-4036
(Movie magazines,
twenties to forties.)

(C) Collector
Box 240
Eltingville Sta.
Staten Island 10312
(*Liberty, Bluebook,* and
Leatherneck magazines.
World War I regimental
histories, early aviation,
Marines.)

NORTH CAROLINA

(C) Steve Hall
116 Highland Ave.
Boone 28606
(704) 264-5763
(Wants Johnson Smith
novelty catalogues, any
date.)

OHIO

(D) Joe Tricarichi
2520 Ashurst
Cleveland 44118
(Comic books, 1923–63.)

(C) Don Van Orman
24557 Mitchell Dr.
North Olmstead 44070
(Catalogues, almanacs,
brochures, maps,
postcards, Early
Americana.)

(D) Dawnat
7024 Jerry Dr.
West Chester 45069
(*Playboy, Penthouse,*
other men's magazines,
coin books, auction
catalogues.)

PENNSYLVANIA

(C) W. L. Zeigler
New Oxford 17350
(Wants old poultry books
and magazines.)

(C) W. P. Ellis
145 Ivywood
Radnor 19087
(Eastman Kodak
catalogues, ads,
pamphlets. Collector
pays highest prices.)

(C) Eckert
Box 557

Trevose 19047

(Wants World War II periodicals and service journals: *Yank, Stars and Stripes, Leatherneck, Air Force,* etc.)

SOUTH CAROLINA

(C) R. J. Sayers
Box 6345
Columbia 29206

(Wants all Boy Scout related publications prior to 1950.)

TENNESSEE

(C) F. M. Hill
Box 1037
Kingsport 38662

(Periodicals, pamphlets related to Tennessee and other Southern states.)

(D) Hillcrest
RR 2, F 162
Spring City 37381

(Old catalogues wanted for resale.)

TEXAS

(D) Walt's Emporium
Box 19406
Dallas 75219

(Radio, telegraph, phone manuals, books, catalogues, magazines before 1939 for resale.

Any literature on self-winding-clock company, Western Union clocks.)

(D) Jefferson Miles
Box 7623
Fort Worth 76111

(Old comic books, pulps.)

(C) Tom Bartlett
8523 Ferris
Houston 77096

(Comic books wanted, 1935–65.)

(D) Wheeler's
P.O. Box 20027
Houston 77025

(Wants collections and runs of seventeenth- and eighteenth-century magazines and papers; also, anything on geese.)

VIRGINIA

(C) Joe Oleksiewkz
430 E. Nelson Ave.
Alexandria 22310
(703) 836-0329

(*TV Guides* before 1970. Dell's *Who's Who* magazine annuals of the 1950s.)

(D) Archambault
995 S. Main St.
Harrisonburg 22801

(703) 434-2316

(Will pay $10 each for all pre-1932 *Black Masks* in good condition. Buys all types of pulps and comics.)

(C) R. W. Clifton
Box 6027
Richmond 23222

(World War I pictorials, early motorcycle magazines, long runs of American newspapers pre-1945.)

(C) OAJ
2204 Haviland Dr.
Richmond 23229

(Comic books 1930–64.)

WISCONSIN

(C) Bruce Rayeske
816 Columbia Ave., S.
Milwaukee 53172

(Cash for gun catalogues before 1940.)

(D) Continental Hobby House
P.O. Box 193
Sheboygan 53081

(Top prices paid for *Harper's Weekly, Puck* magazines, old toy and railroad catalogues. Any old catalogues containing full-page pictures.)

CANADA

(C) Mitch
760 Ash Ave.
Winnipeg, Manitoba

(Comic books 1900–1958.)

FIREARMS, KNIVES, and MILITARY ITEMS

Firearm Dealers

ALABAMA

Cousin Joe's Levy Loan
  Company
2116 2nd Ave., N.
Birmingham 35208
(205) 251-3381

Confederate Ordnance Gun
  Shop
305 A Glenwood
Mobile 36606
(205) 473-3731

Eddie's Pawn & Gun Shop
555 S. Wilson Ave.
Prichard 36610
(205) 457-7268

ALASKA

Great Northern Guns
P.O. Box 8-644
2920 Tudor Road
Anchorage 99502

Kobuk Pawn & Barber Shop
124 Noble St.
Fairbanks 99701
(907) 452-6367

ARIZONA

Gem Jewelers & Loan
  Company
599 N. Central Ave.

Phoenix 85004
(602) 259-3293

Gunsmoke Sports Center
2526 E. Indian School Road
Phoenix 85016
(602) 955-0930

Jewel Box
601 N. Central Ave.
Phoenix 85004
(602) 252-5777

Stop 'N Swap
1520 E. Washington
Phoenix 85034

CALIFORNIA

Gun Corner
10837 San Pablo Ave.
El Cerrito 94530
(415) 529-1941

Hollywood Collateral Loan
  Association
1612 Vine St.
Hollywood 90028
(213) 464-7175

Dal's Antiques & Trading
  Post
15617 Hawthorne Blvd.
Lawndale 90260
(213) 675-1692

Eagle's Nest
3715 W. Sunset

Los Angeles 90026
(213) 665-9103

Chuck and Rita's
5515 Lankershim
North Hollywood 91602
(213) 761-2201

Tiny's Guns and Leather
   Shop
507 Industrial Place
Palm Springs 92262
(714) 325-1068

Treasure Island Stamps,
   Coins & Guns
122 Town & Country
   Village
Palo Alto 92668
(415) 326-7678

Ski's Swap Shop
3530 University Ave.
San Diego 92104
(714) 281-1247

Robert Kuhn Antiques
720 Geary
San Francisco 94109
(415) 474-6981

San Francisco Gun
   Exchange
124 2nd St.
San Francisco 94105
(415) 982-6097

Collector Shop
935 Manor
San Leandro 94579
(415) 352-2203

A. Ames Guns
1200 Pico
Santa Monica 90406

COLORADO

Cinderella Shop
631 15th St.
Denver 80202
(303) 825-6442

Lakewood Gunbrokers, Inc.
1470 Carr
Denver 80215
(303) 233-3484

CONNECTICUT

Silver City Sporting Arms
182 Campbell Ave.
West Haven 06516
(203) 932-4717

DELAWARE

Gardner's Gun Shop
1609 E. Newport Pike
Wilmington 19808
(302) 994-5515

FLORIDA

Middle Pawn Shop
327 2nd Ave.
Daytona Beach 32017
(904) 252-9163

Pyles Antiques
738 Main St.
Daytona Beach 32018
(904) 252-1765

The Gun Place, Inc.
802 S.E. 17th St.
Fort Lauderdale 33316
(305) 523-4246

Ben's Coin & Gun Shop
1023 Ridgewood Ave.
Holly Hill 32017
(904) 255-0564

Simms & Associates
4524 Verona Ave.
Jacksonville 32210
(904) 387-1996

Westside Gun & Pawn
    Outlet
5022 Normandy Blvd.
Jacksonville 32205
(904) 781-8136

Smallest Gun Shop
12233 N.W. 7th Ave.
Miami 33168
(305) 685-0208

Central Florida Arms &
    Pawn Company
1812 Orange Blossom Trail
Orlando 32804
(305) 843-7222

Crossroads Sports
Hwy. 17-92 & 436
Zayre Plaza
Orlando 32809
(305) 834-4867

Prager's Gun Shop
1707 N. Mills Ave.
Orlando 32803

(305) 896-2026

Collectors Shop, Inc.
708 Ridgewood Ave.
Port Orange 32019
(904) 761-0592

GEORGIA

Widener Arms, Inc.
3030 Milledgeville Road
Augusta 30904
(404) 736-1433

The Antique Armory
2525 Main St.
East Point 30344
(404) 761-1739

The Gun Room
2468 Spring, S.E.
Smyrna 30080
(404) 432-2324

IDAHO

Purcell's
1011 Main St.
Boise 83702
(208) 344-7636

ILLINOIS

1st Mark Antique Weapons
1435 N. Wells
Chicago 60610
(312) 944-9212

Sundeen Gun Store
10444 S. Cicero
Oak Lawn 60453

(312) 423-5522

IOWA

Holm Gun Sales & Service
1524 Clark
Des Moines 50314
(515) 244-8029

KENTUCKY

The Blue Max, Inc.
135 W. Market
Louisville 40202
(502) 583-9911

Dellmuth's Antique Shop
938 Baxter Ave.
Louisville 40204
(502) 584-8842

LOUISIANA

Mames H. Cohen
319 Royal St.
New Orleans 70130

MAINE

Al Martin's Locksmith Shop
661 Congress
Portland 04101
(207) 772-0912

MARYLAND

Valley Gun Shop
617 York Road
Baltimore 21204
(301) 823-2707

Globe & Anchor Militaria
  Shop
1720 E. Joppa Road
Joppa 21085
(301) 661-2655

Bobbs Trading Company
3310 Rhode Island Ave.
Mount Rainier 20822
(301) 779-0322

MASSACHUSETTS

Bedelle, Inc.
50 School St.
Boston 02143
(617) 227-8925

Cline's Gun Room &
  Antiques
876 Pleasant St.
Canton 02021
(617) 828-1679

Bay State Arms Company
Rte. 30
Southboro 01772
(617) 485-9717

MISSOURI

Hart Mayer's
7445 Broadway
Kansas City 64114
(816) 523-7655

W. G. Alexander
115 N. Euclid Ave.
St. Louis 63108
(314) 535-8890

Farmers Wayside Stores,
Inc.
Villa Ridge
St. Louis 63089
(314) 742-4435

MONTANA

John's Rifle Shop
1865 Harrison Ave.
Butte 59701
(406) 723-8179

Montana Outfitters
115 7th, S.
Great Falls 59405
(406) 761-3350

NEBRASKA

Acher Arms
3295 A St.
Lincoln 68522
(402) 475-8371

Arms & Ammo
1101 S. 60th St.
Omaha 68506
(402) 553-5951

Snuff Box Antiques
847 N. 68th St.
Omaha 68132
(402) 558-0500

NEVADA

Fort Carson Antique Guns,
Inc.
320 N. Carson St.
Carson City 89701

(702) 882-2440

NEW HAMPSHIRE

Brentwood Auction Gallery
Rte. 125
Brentwood 03833

Cozy Corner Antiques
Epping Road
Raymond 03077
(603) 895-2875

NEW JERSEY

The Antique Place
10 West St.
Englewood 07631
(201) 567-9493

Roehrs Gun Shop
21 Park St.
Harrington Park 07640
(201) 768-1000

Gene's Gun Room, Inc.
16 Elmwood Ave.
Irvington 07111
(201) 371-1098

Roy & Tess Allaria
217 Grand Ave.
Leonia 07605
(201) 944-0775

Atlantic Arsenal Firearms
1020 Main St.
Pleasantville 08232
(609) 641-3315

NEW MEXICO

The Gold Mine
4322 Central Ave., S.E.
Albuquerque 87108
(505) 268-0140

NEW YORK

Armour & Arms
1052 Wright
Valley Stream 14888
(516) 825-8390

WYOMING

Buckhorn Shop
Indian Hills Center
Cheyenne 82001
(307) 638-3729

Firearms Collectors

ARIZONA

Dale Sandige
2914 N. 40th St.
Phoenix 85018

(Wants cannons.)

CALIFORNIA

Arthur Yates
P.O. Box 1980
Costa Mesa 92626
(714) 639-1966

(Wants Japanese swords and suba.)

T. Hayaski

3825 Woolwind Dr.
Los Angeles 90063
(Wants Japanese swords, guns, parts.)

Shelley & Norma
2106A 57th Ave.
Sacramento 95822
(Wants military medals, badges, patches, insignias and daggers, any country.)

FLORIDA

Guarino
Box 89
De Bary 32713
(Wants Civil War Swords, drums, carbines.)

GEORGIA

Gerald Shaw
2217 Beech St.
Savannah 31404
(Wants pocket knives, new and old.)

ILLINOIS

Monek
950 E. Westminster
Lake Forest 60045
(Weapon canes wanted.)

MISSOURI

J. D. Marcus
Box 317

Savannah 64485
(816) 324-4375
(Wants case knives, razors.)

NEW YORK

Kenneth D. Smith, Jr.
1 Chase Manhattan Plaza
New York 10005
(World War I aviation
items.)

Collector
Box 240
Eltingville Sta.
Staten Island 10312
(Wants American medals,
insignia, wings, military
photos, aviation items.)

PENNSYLVANIA

Dale Biever
54 Douglas St.
Boyertown 19512
(Wants World War I
uniforms.)

John A. Tellefsen
P.O. Box 242
Breemall 19008
(Wants pocket knives in
unusual shapes: shoes, legs,
guns, bats, etc.)

Sara Lee Sales
Box 4286
Pittsburgh 15203
(Wants Nazi war relics.)

TENNESSEE

John Heflin
Rte. 1, Box 601
Brentwood 37027
(Anything relating to the
Civil War.)

VIRGINIA

Joseph Murphy
5001 Seminary Road
Alexandria 22311
(Colt and C. & B. guns.)

GLASS AND CHINA

Collectors

ALABAMA

I. S. Hazel
1211 Selma St.
Mobile 36604
(205) 432-5401
(VERIYS wanted.)

Lois Stroud
Rte. 3, Box 274
Phoenix City 36837
(Wants child's Blue Willow
sets.)

ARKANSAS

Dan Loudermilk
610 S. Leslie
Stuttgart 72160
(Wants Royal Bayreuth
figurals, bird and strawberry
pattern glass, and
Northwood custard glass.)

Mrs. J. R. Cullam, Jr.
Box 294
Wilson 72345
(Wants Minton china,
Montrose pattern. Any
pieces.)

CALIFORNIA

H. Lutrin
19682 Hesperian Blvd.
Hayward 94541
(415) 483-8333
(Wants R. Lalique glass,
Longway pottery, art glass
and shades. Send photo and
price.)

Mario Pancino
Box 345
La Canada 91011
(Wants Mettlach or
Musterschutz steins; also old
German military steins.)

Trudy Lee
2116 Lomina
Long Beach 90815
(Wants Daisy and Button
pressed glass. Must have
original magenta color; no
clear.)

Mrs. Dorene Paoluccio
624 Sycamore
Modesto 95354
(Any pieces of Tea Leaf
china. Will correspond with
other collector of this.)

Collector
853 Castro St.
Mountain View 94040
(Mettlack steins wanted.)

Collector
P.O. Box 7878
Riverside 92503

(Wants juicers: Sunkist,
Valencia Fry, Fleur de Lis,
or similar. Quote price.)

S. Price
4453 Florida
San Diego 92116
(Buys anything in Pratt
Ware.)

Alan Schneider
4314 California St.
San Francisco 94118
(Wants old stained-glass,
beveled, jeweled windows.
Will buy collections.)

L. H. Selman
407 Cliff St., Suite 10
Santa Cruz 95060
(Paperweights wanted. Old
and new; single items or
collections.)

Kiyce
Box 394
South Pasadena 91030
(Calendar plates wanted.)

E. Flynn
Box 4111
Thousand Oaks 91359
(805) 495-0386
(Wants collector's plates.)

M. L. Opfer
Box 4367
Whittier 90607
(213) 968-2931
(Wants R. S. Prussia, scenic,

portrait, and Melon Boy
pieces.)

Linda Wynn
1510 Siesta
Valinda 91746
(Wants citrus reamers, all
china, ceramic, or silver.)

CONNECTICUT

Richard Hatscher
3 Sand Hill Road
Bethel 06801
(203) 743-1468
(Wants Carnival glass, any
color, any pattern, any
quantity.)

J. Wernick
304 Seymour Ave.
Derby 06418
(203) 735-2050
(Wants articles of black
amethyst, glass with sterling
overlay.)

B. Sheppard
115 Ridgewood Ave.
Hamden 06517
(Wants marbles: Sulfides,
Swirls, and old ones.)

S. Block
Box 51
Trumbull 06611
(Wants Copeland Spode,
Spode Tower dinnerware,
small blown perfume vials.)

DISTRICT OF COLUMBIA

Jon Heiden
131 Kentucky Ave., S.E.
Washington 20003

(Wants art-glass shades and lamp bases by Tiffany, Steuben, etc.)

Oscar Merber
2700 Virginia Ave., N.W.
Washington 20037

(Wants art glass: French and American signed pieces. Send photos.)

FLORIDA

Collector
P.O. Box 173
Stuart 33494

(Buys American glass cup-plates.)

ILLINOIS

Collector
Box DD
1006 S. Michigan Ave.
Chicago 60605

(Wants EAPG wine glasses.)

J. Wilson
2648 N. Kilpatrick
Chicago 60639

(Wants Carnival glass tumblers, mugs, plates, hatpin holders, etc. Also, frokicking-bears pattern wanted in clear or colored glass.)

D. Shiaras
Rte. 3, Box 66
Grand Detour 61021
(815) 652-4278

(Wants Mettlack and Musterschutz steins. Needs the following numbers to complete collection: 2049; 2324; 2718 through 2730; 2828; 2829; 2894 and 2917.)

Paul Jankauer
9323 N. Kedvale
Skokie 60076
(312) 675-7233

(Will buy your Carnival-glass collection or odd pieces.)

INDIANA

Rue Dee Marker
P.O. Box 292
Fremen 46506
(219) 546-2632

(Wants Hummels. Highest prices paid for plaques 165, 168, 180. Also for figures.)

Mrs. Frank Gilkison
508 Brentwood Lane
Muncie 47304

(Wants Spode Copeland china Christmas tree, coffee mugs in mint condition.)

Robert E. Bender
515 W. Cedar St.
Zionsville 46077

(Coin glass wanted.)

IOWA

Collector
2440 Arlington
Davenport 52803
(Railroad dining-car china
wanted.)

KANSAS

Maude House
1009 Freeman St.
Kansas City 66112
(913) 299-6385
(Wants Christmas plates,
1968–74.)

MARYLAND

George C. Humphrey
4932 Prince George Ave.
Beltsville 20705
(301) 937-7899
(Wants John Rogers statuary
in any condition.)

Ricketts
1046 Marion St.
Laurel 20810
(Wants reamers, glass,
ceramic, silverplate, or
anything unusual.)

Roes
13 Charles Road
North Linthicum 21090
(Wants beer steins.)

William Crowl
12069 Nebel Street
Rockville 20850
(Wants 1876 [centennial]
china, mugs, plates,
pitchers, bowls, cups, and
saucers.)

Berkley
2011 Hermitage
Wheaton 20902
(Wants collector's plates.)

MASSACHUSETTS

Paul Dunigan
60 Van Greenby
Lowell 01853
(617) 453-0393
(Wants Royal Doulton china
picturing autos.)

Renee
P.O. Box 274
Winthrop 02152
(Wants English Cameo
glass.)

MICHIGAN

Diana Peters
3217 McClure St.
Flint 48506
(313) 743-0284
(Advanced collector wants
superior Cameo items:
Galle, Daum Nancy, etc.
Such as Marquetry, Mold
Blown, good scenics. Will
also buy other Cameo of

other makers. Write or call collect.)

Bauman
703 Parkdale
Rochester 48063
(Wants goat figurines.)

Tom Michael
28200 Florence
St. Clair Shores 48081
(313) 773-7559
(Wants art-glass shades, Tiffany jewels, prisms, raw glass.)

J. R. Jervis
Box 357
Sawyer 49125
(Wants agate marbles.)

MINNESOTA

Don Guttormson
Spring Grove 55316
(Wants custard glass and ruby glass souvenir pieces.)

MISSOURI

Mrs. Charles B. Wheeler
804 E. 109th St.
Kansas City 64131
(Wants white and gold Haviland china.)

Louis Dorn
4 Stoneybrook
Ladue 63124

(Royal Doulton toby jugs, mugs, ash trays, lighters, pitchers, Flambé wanted.)

Geiser
Rte. 1, Box 426
Rolla 65401
(Wants English cups and saucers.)

Reba Newell
2931 Persimmon
St. Charles 65201
(Buys Albany ribbed spiral glass, blue or vaseline.)

MONTANA

M. H. Layne
817 5th Ave., N.
Great Falls 59401
(Wants Westmoreland pressed Waterford goblets, stemmed sherbets.)

NEBRASKA

Dwayne McCullough
Box 62
Grant 69140
(Wants any and all pieces of Alrea pattern of Noritake china.)

NEW JERSEY

Vaccaro
514 Page Ave.
Allenhurst 07711

(Tiffany items wanted.)

William Dowling
P.O. Box 174
Newton 07860

(Wants Noritake cups and
saucers, Modesta and
Garfield.)

NEW YORK

Ruth Van Kuren
Clarence Center 14032

(Anything marked "Buffalo
Pottery.")

Shamulka
111 Lincoln Ave.
Endicott 13760

(Wants Fry Foval [pearl art
glass], Steuben, Sinclaire,
Hawkes; any quantity.)

Barbara Hoyt
14 Jerome Dr.
Glen Cove 11542

(Royal Doulton character
jugs wanted, all sizes.)

J. Salvatore
317 Clifton Pkwy.
Hamburg 14075

(Wants finely decorated
pieces of Nippon. Send
color photo.)

John E. Bilane
74 Trinity Place, Rm. 1005
New York 10006
(212) 248-7086

(Wants American glass
cup-plates, lacy salts. Perfect
condition preferred.)

Larry Martin
P.O. Box 296
New York 10956

(Wedgwood wanted, single
piece or entire collection.)

Steve Newman
c/o Paris Poulbot
24 West 55th St.
New York 10019
(212) 489-1345

(Wants signed Tiffany,
Galle, Daum Nancy, and A.
Walter in mint condition.)

Richard B. Schull
P.O. Box 125
Radio City Sta.
New York 10019

(Wants railroad china,
especially demitasse cups
and saucers.)

Collector
P.O. Box 85
North Syracuse 13212

(Wants Royal Ivy [crackle],
pitcher and tumblers,
mottled cranberry or
vaseline.)

Edith Esposito
735 Bryant Ave.
Roslyn Harbor 11576
(516) 484-2427

(Wants all unusual citrus

juicers and creamers: glass, red, black, blue, etc. Also, juicers made from ceramic, porcelain; clowns, animals, etc.)

Joseph Golembewski
124 Conklin Ave.
Syracuse 13206
(Wants art glass, damaged Tiffany, Steuben, Quesal.)

Burton Handelsman
18 Hotel Dr.
White Plains 10605
(914) 428-4480
(Wants occupational shaving mugs, old barber racks.)

OHIO

H. Francis
Box 42053
Cincinnati 45242
(Wants old toothpick holders. Send description.)

Robert L. Miller
112 Woodland Dr.
Eaton 45320
(513) 456-3725 (home)
(Hummels wanted.)

Mrs. John Crider
218 N. Broadway
Spencerville 45887
(Wants covered animal dishes and figural items in milk glass and all colors.)

Blair Museum of Lithophanes
2032 Robinwood
Toledo 43620
(Wants Lithophanes [porcelain transparencies], any shape or size.)

OKLAHOMA

Collector
P.O. Box 3085
Bartlesville 74003
(Wants mugs.)

Vincent
W. Star, Rte. 87
Boise City 73933
(Wants Shelley English bone china, Pompadour pattern #13516.)

H. Collier
Box 51214
Tulsa 74151
(Royal Doulton tobies wanted, all sizes.)

OREGON

D. Russell
P.O. Box 515
Bandon 97411
(Antique glass crystal, ceramic owls wanted.)

A. Decker
P.O. Box 696
La Grande 97850

(Pattern glass wanted.
Goblets, any piece in jumbo
Dragon, Classic Beaver
Band, Monkey, Log Cabin,
etc. Any children's glass
dishes or those portraying
birds and animals.)

Scott Arden
20457 Hwy. 126
Noti 97461

(Railroad china wanted. Up
to $100 for rare service
plates.)

Janice Elder
975 S.E. Sandy
Portland 97214

(Wants damaged, cracked,
imperfect art glass; French
and English cameo, Tiffany,
Steuben, and other
iridescent glass.)

PENNSYLVANIA

Lewis
7 Banbury
Pittsburgh 15202

(Wants leaded stained-glass
windows, any condition.)

E. Kirkwood
441 Ivyland Road
Warminster 18974
(215) 348-9695

(Wants porcelains, portrait
urns, and plates; art glass.)

Janet Potter

RD 2, Box 88
West Grove 19390

(Wants three-piece sets of
Stangl baby dishes.)

Adrienne Giuffre
538 Montgomery School
  Lane
Wynnewood 19096

(Wants Venetian glass;
ribbon or hand-painted on
goblets, plates, etc.)

SOUTH DAKOTA

R. H. Meyer
Box 69
Belle Fourche 57717
(605) 892-4394

(Cut-glass lamp shades and
bases wanted.)

TENNESSEE

Caplinger
500 Bowling
Nashville 37205

(Wants Tennessee pattern
glass.)

TEXAS

Alice Britt
Rte. 2, Box 215
Cameron 76520

(Wants bird with straw in
beak, clear or colored glass;
especially syrup pitchers.)

Donald B. Miller

7312 Briley Dr.
Fort Worth 76118
(Wants cut-glass salt and
peppers, with sterling tops.)

Bill Luttrell
3205 N. Shepherd St.
Houston 77018
(Wants Libbey glass, Nash
era, 1933. Modern American
series, 1940.)

M. Sanders
P.O. Box 953
Mexia 76667
(Buys bird and strawberry
pattern glass.)

Bob and Beka Mebane
701 Castaha Ave.
San Antonio 78209
(512) 824-4529
(Rare American historical
and pictorial flasks in glass
or pottery.)

Fleet
3013 Club Lake Dr.
Tyler 75701
(Old crock jugs with writing
on them wanted. Also,
miniature jugs.)

VIRGINIA

Wren
1616 Stoneybrook Dr.
Richmond 23233
(Wants Shelley English bone

china; Primrose pattern
#13430, scalloped edges.)

WISCONSIN

Starr
5873 Riverside Dr.
Greendale 53129
(Buys Royal Doulton
character jugs.)

Richard Bucht
Land O'Lakes 64640
(Beer and soda glasses
wanted.)

Dealers

ALABAMA

Lill's 3 L's Antiques
1744 Main St.
Daphne 36526
(205) 626-0939

Atchinson Al Antiques
52 S. Warren
Mobile 36602

Haviland House Antiques,
   Plantation Antique
   Galleries
3750 Government Blvd.
Mobile 36609

ARIZONA

Belfords
Box 649

Stuttgart 72160

CALIFORNIA

James Grant
P.O. Box 252
Freedom 95019

Lila Leavitt Antiques
976 Lighthouse Ave.
Pacific Grove 93950

Carole Cohen Antiques
105 Summit Ave.
Redlands 92373
(714) 792-8807

E. Steinmeyer
2994 Miguel St.
Riverside 92506

China Matching Service,
  Specializing in Lenox
Mary Dexter
P.O. Box 17643
San Diego 92117

Robert Bersani
949 Valencia St.
San Francisco 94111
(415) 647-9011

Shadow Hills Antiques
P.O. Box 911
Tustin 92680
(714) 544-7055

Debbie Webb Limited
7400 Blewett Ave.
Van Nuys 91409

COLORADO

Cinderella Antique Shop
631 15th St.
Denver 80202
(303) 825-6442

FLORIDA

Little White House Antiques
5025 S. Ridgewood Ave.
Allandale 32023
(904) 767-4040

Seabreeze Antique Shop
222 Seabreeze Blvd.
Daytona Beach 32018
(904) 252-2071

Lockwood's Antiques
1472 Guave Ave.
Melbourne 32935

Charold & Company, Ltd.
64 S. Palm
Sarasota 33577

Keene's Korner Kottage
400 S. Orlando Ave.
Winter Park 32789
(305) 644-4461

GEORGIA

Tom's Treasure House,
  Cutglass Specialist
1288 Oakdale Road, N.E.
Atlanta 30307
(404) 378-7976

Vip Antiques
Box 52601

Atlanta 30355

Temptations—
  Upstairs-Downstairs
230 W. Bay St.
Savannah 31401
(912) 233-5500

ILLINOIS

Straw Flower, Inc.
206 S. Main St.
Findlay 62534
(217) 756-8623

Treasure-Trove Antiques
18148 Martin St.
Homewood 60430
(312) 798-9794

IOWA

The Lion's Den Antiques
RR 1
Ogden 50212
(515) 275-4011

Maxine's Hen House
Rte. 1
Oskaloosa 52577
(515) 672-2922

INDIANA

Teague's Antiques
Rte. 2, Box 101
Bloomfield 47832

Kennedy Antiques
Box 459
Elwood 46034

Angie's Antiques
110 E. Main St.
P.O. Box 108
Markleville 46056
(317) 533-2028

KENTUCKY

Barbara W. Hite, Haviland
  Matching
120 Wildwood Lane
Anchorage 40223

LOUISIANA

John J. Langskov
1403 Parkway Ave.
Cedar Falls 50613

MAINE

Clipper Ship Antiques &
  Guest House
46 N. Main St., Rte. 1
Ogunquit
(207) 646-9735

MARYLAND

Anna Lois Webber
P.O. Box 4104
Chevy Chase 20015
(301) 656-1860

Kensington Arts & Antiques
P.O. Box 423
Kensington 20795
(301) 949-2041

Burnt Mills Antiques
P.O. Box 702

Silver Spring 20901

My Grandfather's Shop,
  Ltd.
940 Sligo Ave.
Silver Spring 20910
(Limited plates.)

MASSACHUSETTS

Edmund G. Colson
32 Brooksweld Road
Canton 02021
(617) 828-4339

Windsong Antiques
243 Bank St.
Harwich, Cape Cod 02645

The Brown Jug
Main St. at Jarves
Sandwich, Cape Cod 02563

MICHIGAN

Plantation Galleries
6400 Davison Road
Davison 48423

Allen's Antiques
3421 Greenfield Road
Dearborn 48120

Temple Antiques
6721 Greenfield Road
Dearborn 48120

MINNESOTA

Hanson Antiques
6945 Park Ave.

Minneapolis 55423
(612) 869-5774

MISSOURI

Husted's Antiques
915 N. Osteopathy Ave.
Kirksville 63501
(816) 665-2392

NEBRASKA

Mrs. H. H. Brown, Antiques
102 S. Elder St.
North Platte 69101
(308) 532-0280

NEW JERSEY

Summit Glass Showcase
465 Springfield Ave.
Summit 07901
(201) 277-0365

NEW YORK

Exquisite Antiques, Ltd.
2938 Merrick Road
Bellmore 11710
(516) 781-7305

Mary Galletti Antiques
154–14 Northern Blvd.
Flushing 11354
(212) 762-5685; (212)
358-5923 (after 5 P.M.)

The Carrousel
Box 736
Huntington 11743
(516) 423-1757 (by

appointment only)

The Wicker's Antiques
Millbrook 12545
(914) 677-3906 (by
appointment only)

Maude B. Feld, Antiques of
  Distinction
790 Madison Ave.
Suite 605
New York 10021
(212) 988-9830

Macklowe Gallery
1088 Madison Ave.
New York 10028
(212) 561-3383

Philip & Shirley Gordon,
  Antiques
41 Prospect Ave.
Plattsburgh 12901
(518) 561-3383

Paula Ellman
63-57 Fitchett St.
Rego Park 11374
(212) 672-6641

Lyon's Den
P.O. Box 565
Riverhead 11901
(516) 727-0699

The Glass Corner
P.O. Box 7130
Rochester 14616
(716) 225-2387

Cara's Corner Antiques

18 Sheridan Road
Scarsdale 10583
(Mail order only.)

Lilyan's Collectiques
79 Cunningham Ave.
Uniondale 11553
(516) 483-6211

From the Cutter's Wheel
P.O. Box 285
Webster 14580
(716) 671-3760 (evenings)
(Mail order or appointment.)

NORTH CAROLINA

William Moore Davis
Rte. 1, Box 478
Smyrna 28579
(919) 729-2391 (after 7 P.M.)

Theodota
Box 842
Southern Pines 28387

OHIO

Vel's Place
195 W. Schreyer Place
Columbus 43214
(614) 263-8460

Seven Acres
5840 Horning Road
Dent 44240
(216) 687-2224

Allan J. Hodges Antiques
12700 Lake Ave., 902

Lakewood 44107

Haviland Matching Service
Mrs. B. E. Brock,
   Brockhaven Antiques
3700 Grand Ave.
Middletown 45042
(513) 422-3036

National Heisey Glass
   Museum
Box 27, 6th & Church St.
Newark 43055
(614) 345-2932 or (614)
344-2377
(Will buy Heisey items.
Home of Heisey Collectors
of America.)

Old Towne Colonial Corner
6692 Crenshaw Dr.
Parma Heights 44130
(216) 886-4333

OKLAHOMA

Sharp's 1860 Antiques
1860 E. 15th St.
Tulsa 74104
(918) 939-1121

PENNSYLVANIA

Matt's Attic
Box 882
Clearfield 16830

Adelaide L. Geyer
1035 Landis Lane
Hatfield 19440

The Toll House Antiques
3350 Brookdale Dr.
Pittsburgh 15241

Castleton China
   Replacement Center
RD 6, Box 152
New Castle 16101
(Buys Castleton china. State
price wanted. No offer
made.)

Franklin Badger
RD 5, Box 99A
Towanda 18848
(717) 265-5626

TENNESSEE

Allison Antiques
4005 Franklin Road
Nashville 37201
(615) 383-6039

TEXAS

The Collector's House of
   Antiques
3900 Montrose Blvd.
Houston 77006
(713) 526-6296

VIRGINIA

Mrs. R. H. Elliot
Rte. 4, Box 392
Gretna 24557
(804) 324-4928

WISCONSIN

White River House
400 W. Chestnut St.
Burlington 53105
(414) 763-8042

Christophersen's
334 W. Fillmore
Eau Claire 54701

Grace Graves, Haviland
  China Matching Service
3959 N. Harcourt Place
Milwaukee 63211
(414) 964-9180

Beatrice Meredith Antiques
3841 N. 66th St.
Milwaukee 53216
(414) 461-6387
(Mail order only.)

Attic Antiques
4101 E. 2nd St.
Superior 54880
(715) 398-7051

MEMORABILIA

Dealers

CALIFORNIA

Collector's Item Shop
1317 Gilman
Berkeley 94706
(Specialty political items.)

Railroad Relics
11210 Lavender
Fountain Valley 92708
(714) 531-0195
(Dining car, express
company, telegraph items.)

FLORIDA

State Street Antiques
P.O. Box 991
DeLand 32720
(904) 734-8595
(Firefighting memorabilia,
nautical items.
Masculine-oriented
antiques.)

MASSACHUSETTS

Golddiggers of 1933
143 Pearl St.
Cambridge 02138
(617) 868-1933
(Memorabilia from the
twenties and thirties.)

Collectors

CALIFORNIA

Donald Ackerman
P.O. Box 64352
Los Angeles 90064
(Wants harness horse items,
tin buttons, posters, Currier
and Ives.)

Orth
1436 Killarney
Los Angeles 90065
(Wants World's Fair
materials.)

Richard Short
P.O. Box 1038
San Bernardino 92402
(Wants Rudolph Valentino
materials.)

FLORIDA

Garcia
8963 S.E. 34th St.
Miami 33165
(Wants Shirley Temple
items.)

GEORGIA

Herb Bridges
Sharpsburg 30277

(Wants *Gone With the Wind* items.)

ILLINOIS

John Sullivan
3748 N. Damen
Chicago 60618
(Wants baseball and football memorabilia.)

S. Cleft
1712 Redwood
Hanover Park 60103
(Wants railroad lanterns, locks, keys, hardware, etc.)

E. G. Pez
Box 133
Taylor Springs 62089
(Wants baseball memorabilia.)

INDIANA

The Potawatomi Museum
Rte. 3, Box 303
Angola 46703

KENTUCKY

Lois Shearer
2901 Tremont Dr.
Louisville 40205
(Wants Shirley Temple items.)

LOUISIANA

Joseph Russell

1315 Simon
Carroll 51401
(Wants auto memorabilia, gearshift knobs, motor meters, dial tire gauges, ornate radiator caps, etc.)

MAINE

Carl Terison
Cumberland 04021
(Wants *Superman* items.)

MASSACHUSETTS

Michael Drukman
60-10 Middlesex Road
Waltham 02154
(Wants firefighting memorabilia.)

MICHIGAN

Edwin Puls
185 Linden Road
Birmingham 35203
(Wants Presidential campaign buttons, ribbons, tokens.)

Edward Budnick
10368 Lanark
Detroit 48224
(Wants old baseball items.)

Wayne David Lun
3754 Philip
Detroit 48215
(Wants early firefighting

items.)

Franklin Vandyck
850 Harway St.
Kalamazoo 49001
(Wants circus paper
items—posters, route cards,
programs, etc.—new and
old.)

MINNESOTA

J. Frehlig
2523 Upton Ave.
North Minneapolis 55411
(Wants Boy Scout items.)

NEW JERSEY

Vaccaro
514 Page Ave.
Allenhurst 07711
(Wants old automobile
emblems, screw hubs, etc.)

Anne Hamyak
700 S. Main St.
Manville 08835
(Wants Orphan Annie
items.)

Norman B. Buckman
31 Surf Ave.
Ocean Grove 07756
(Wants memorabilia of
Ocean Grove, a
world-famous Victorian
seaside resort; anything
relating to visits by
Presidents, others.)

Ivan Horvath
Box 331
Summit 07901
(Wants Elvis Presley
memorabilia.)

NEW YORK

Jack Arone
377 Ashford
Dobbs Ferry 10522
(Wants railroad items and
timetables pre-1935, trolley
and steamboat timetables,
brochures, booklets, guides,
calendars, signs, etc.)

Lt. Col. Gill
Elnora 12065
(Wants Irving Berlin
memorabilia.)

Will Jordon
435 W. 57th St.
New York 10019
(Wants anything to do with
mimics, imitators, or
impersonators.)

Anna Labbate
P.O. Box 1233
New York 10008
(Wants Elvis Presley items.)

Nelson
111 W. 82nd St., Apt. 3C
New York 10024
(Wants Betty Boop items.)

S. Roman

53 W. 16th St.
New York 10011
(Wants antique Christmas
ornaments.)

Frederick M. Lavin
1 Firtop Drive
Orchard Park 14127
(Wants Pan American
Exposition [Buffalo, N.Y.
1901] souvenirs and related
materials.)

NORTH CAROLINA

John Fitter
111 Georgetown Road
Hendersonville 28739
(Wants financial Americana,
any items relating to
American business.)

OHIO

Rossen
1111-33 Public Square
Cleveland 44113
(Wants World Fair items
from Columbian Exposition
[1893], Pan-Am [1901], St.
Louis [1904], Chicago
[1933].)

OREGON

Scott Arden
20457 Hwy. 126
Natl 97461
(Wants all kinds of railroad
items.)

PENNSYLVANIA

Marshall Ackerman
2250 Lehigh Pkwy., N.
Allentown 18103
(215) 433-3723
(Wants anything relating to
William McKinley, also any
Presidential inauguration
material.)

Roesler
378 Miller
Luzerne 18709
(Wants chess memorabilia.)

Miscellaneous Man
New Freedom 17349
(Wants circus, travel, and
other posters, pre-1950.)

SOUTH CAROLINA

B. Sayers
P.O. Box 6345
Columbia 29206
(Wants Boy Scout
memorabilia.)

TENNESSEE

W. Porter Ware
Sewanee 37375
(Wants Jenny Lind
memorabilia.)

TEXAS

Chandler
Box 20664

Houston 77205
(Wants Beatles items.)

WASHINGTON

Loraine Burdick
5 Court Place
Puyallup 98371
(Wants old movie materials,
Shirley Temple paper dolls.)

Linda Adams
605 Stewart St.
Seattle 98101
(Wants political-campaign
items: glassware, postcards,
ribbons, medals, etc.)

MUSICAL ITEMS

Dealers and Collectors

ARIZONA

(D) Jewel Box
601 N. Central Ave.
Phoenix 85004
(602) 252-5777
(Musical instruments
wanted.)

CALIFORNIA

(D) Ken Blazier
2937 Elda St.
Duarte 91010
(RCA Victor dog
coin-operated
phonographs.)

(C) George Collings
Box 4511
Fresno 93728
(Records.)

(D) Dal's Antiques—Trading
Post
15617 Hawthorne Blvd.
Lawndale 90260
(Records.)

(D) A-C-H Bookshop
1916 W. 7th St.
Los Angeles 90057
(Records.)

(C) Robert Greenlaw

307 N. Rampart St.
Rm. 412
Los Angeles 90026
(Sheet music.)

(D) Pacific Books
4762 Melrose Ave.
Los Angeles 90029
(213) 666-8465
(Records.)

(D) Lark in the Morning
Box 1176
Mendocino 95460
(707) 964-5569
(Musical instruments.)

(D) Joyce Book Shop
1116 Franklin St.
Oakland 94697
(415) 452-2571
(Records.)

(D) Antiquarian Shop
524 Bryant
Palo Alto 94301
(415) 328-4414
(Wants music boxes.)

(C) Reader
18300 Locust Ave.
Patterson 95363
(Disc phonographs.)

(D) The Green Apple
506 Clement St.
San Francisco 94118
(415) 387-4918
(Records.)

(D) Jack's Record Cellar
P.O. Box 14068
San Francisco 94114
(Records.)

COLORADO

(C) Louis Hill
1230 Martin Dr.
Colorado Springs 80915
(Records.)

(D) Antique Appraisers &
Buyers
14701 Montview Blvd.
Denver 80220
(303) 366-5592
(Show-biz music.)

(D) Nostalgia Shop
2431 S. University Blvd.
Denver 80201
(303) 778-6566
(78-rpm records.)

(D) The Shadow Box &
Record Exchange
1201 E. 13th Ave.
Denver 80218
(303) 831-9893
(Fire department
trumpets wanted.)

FLORIDA

(D) Alexander's Antiques
1115 Tucker Ave.
Orlando 32807
(305) 273-7220
(Pianos wanted.)

GEORGIA

(D) Stuff 'n Such Antiques
125 W. Congress St.
Savannah 31401
(912) 232-9736
(Mechanical music.)

ILLINOIS

(D) The Fret Shop Musical
Museum
5210 S. Harper
Chicago 60615
(312) 667-6310
(Musical items.)

(C) Julia C. Dean
1404 N. Loomis
Naperville 60540
(312) 355-8079
(Wants old sheet music.)

(C) McNeill
1117 S. Taylor St.
Oak Park 60304
(Buys sheet music.)

INDIANA

(D) Golden Memories
Records, Inc.

P.O. Box 217
Mooresville 46158
(317) 831-5307
(Records.)

KENTUCKY

(D) Sexton's Antiques
213 E. Market St.
Louisville 40202
(502) 584-5080
(Wants old music boxes.)

LOUISIANA

(D) Danny's Dungeon
1813 Magazine
New Orleans 70130
(504) 522-3042
(Buys old radios.)

MAINE

(D) Paul C. Burgess,
Vintage Records
Box 12-A
Friendship 04547
(Buys and sells 78-rpm
records, jazz, blues,
personality, C & W,
Pioneer, cylinders.

(D) The Barn
Gray Road
Portland 04102
(207) 892-0776
(Old records.)

MARYLAND

(D) Montgomery's Antiques
& Collectibles
2080 University Blvd., E.
Langley Park 20783
(301) 431-0313
(Old records.)

(C) Allen Sutton
108 Knob Hill Court
Tomonium 21093
(Records.)

MASSACHUSETTS

(D) Collector's Den
2020 Massachusetts Ave.
Cambridge 02138
(617) 776-6293
(Music boxes.)

(D) Golddiggers of 1933
143 Pearl St.
Cambridge 02138
(617) 868-1933
(Sheet music, records
from the twenties
through the forties.)

(D) The Music Emporium,
Inc.
1768 Massachusetts Ave.
Cambridge 02138
(617) 661-2099
(Wants antique musical
stringed instruments.)

(C) A. L. Gillespie
94 Boxford Road

261

Rowler 01969
(78-rpm records.)

(D) Sound Track
P.O. Box 3895
Springfield 01101
(Records.)

MICHIGAN

(D) Arnold's Archives
1106 Eastwood, S.E.
East Grand Rapids 49506
(Records.)

(D) Homespun Music
775 W. Main St.
Kalamazoo 49007
(616) 381-5669
(Wants antique
instruments: guitars,
banjos, mandolins,
violins, etc. Also, old
advertising signs and
display items related to
musical stringed
instruments.)

MINNESOTA

(D) Alden Miller
3212 34th Ave., S.
Minneapolis 55406
(Pipe-organ
memorabilia.)

MISSOURI

(D) Braun Galleries
10315 Clayton Road

St. Louis 63131
(Buys antique music
boxes.)

NEW JERSEY

(D) T. M. Thibault
P.O. Box 42
Cedar Brook 08018
(609) 561-7761
(Records, all speeds, and
sheet music.)

(D) Mr. Records
P.O. Box 764
Hillside 07205
(Records.)

(C) John C. Sicignana
29 Columbia Ave.
Nutley 07110
(Records.)

NEW YORK

(C) P. Charosh
60 Clarkson Ave.
Brooklyn 11226
(Wants Berliner, Climax,
Zonophones, Monarch,
and Deluxe Victor.)

(D) Musical Notes
12 Crafton St.
Greenlawn 11740
(516) 757-7724
(Buys and sells sheet
music, piano rolls,
records, automatic

instruments, music boxes.)

(C) Tim Brooks
1940 80th St.
Jackson Heights 11370

(Collector of early history of phonograph industry; record and phonograph catalogues.)

(D) David Reiss
P.O. Box 916-D
Ansonia Stn.
New York 10023

(Records.)

(D) Orhews Music Shop
14 W. 45th St.
New York 10036

(Wants antique musical instruments.)

(D) List Communications
P.O. Box 916-D
Ansonia Stn.
New York 10023

(Records.)

OHIO

(C) Paul Scriven
238 W. State St.
Niles 44446

(Buys 16″ radio transcriptions and recordings.)

OKLAHOMA

(C) Jan Garris
P.O. Box 20114
Oklahoma City 73120

(Buys records.)

PENNSYLVANIA

(C) M. Schnebly
622 S. Allison St.
Green Castle 17225

(Wants Vesta Victoria Grand Prize records.)

(C) Norman P. Gentiue
2121 Pine St.
Philadelphia 19103

(Wanted: old recordings of radio broadcasts by dance orchestras in the 1920s and 1930s, especially the 1929 Old Gold programs over CBS stations by Paul Whiteman and his orchestra; programs from Roseland Ballroom in 1928 over WHN by Jean Goldkette and his orchestra; programs from Yoeng's Chinese-American Restaurant in New York City in 1929–30 and '31 by Paul Tremaine and his orchestra. Prices negotiable.)

(C) Frederick P. Williams
8313 Shawnee Street

Philadelphia 19118
(Records.)

TEXAS

(C) H. Kornblit
902 Frostwood, Suite 176
Houston 77024
(713) 464-8332

(Wants antique flutes
and older flute music of
all kinds.)

(D) Leigh Brown, Collecting
Records
434 Avant
San Antonio 78210
(512) 534-3740

(Wants all kinds of
records, 1900–1970; 78s,
45s, LP's. Buys
"worthwhile" collections;
sells occasionally.)

(D) Docks
Box 13685
San Antonio 78213

(Buys jazz, blues, rock,
country records, 1920
through 1950s.)

VIRGINIA

(D) Comix Record Shop
211 King St.
Alexandria 23202
(703) 549-0749

(C) Joseph Murphy
5001 Seminary Road

Alexandria 22311
(Musical instruments.)

(D) Sandwine Antiques
1235 N. Irving St.
Arlington 22201
(703) 528-9229

(Wants gramophones.)

WASHINGTON

(C) Collector
Box 724
Redmond 98052

(Transcriptions of old
radio shows.)

(C) Darrell Lehman
12322 28th St., N.W.
Seattle 98125
(206) 364-7944

(Victor Talking Machine
Company materials:
record catalogues,
needle envelopes/tins,
advertising memorabilia,
parts of machines, fiber
needle cutters, posters,
etc.)

WISCONSIN

(C) Gary Alderman
P.O. Box 9164
Madison 53715

(Jazz LPs of the forties,
fifties, sixties.)

WYOMING

(D) Laramie Banjo Shop
310 S. 7th St.
Laramie 82070
(307) 745-7167

(Buys stringed
instruments.)

CANADA

(C) Earl Mathewson
141 4th St.
Toronto, Ontario

(Records wanted; also,
Edison discs.)

VINTAGE-CLOTHING MARKETS

ARIZONA

Eve Doyer
1626 N. 46th St.
Phoenix 60081

(Wants antique clothing for men, women, and children for years 1850 to 1926. Also, accessories, costume jewelry, etc. State prices, colors, condition.)

CALIFORNIA

Ritsy Rags
1610 G St.
Arcata 95521
(707) 822-5820

(Vintage clothing wanted, from twenties, thirties, and forties. Ladies' floral, lace, velvet, satin, beaded, embroidered, sequined, etc. Dresses, blouses, Oriental items, capes, gowns. Gents' panama and pin-striped suits, tails, vest, western and Hawaiian shirts, hats, etc.)

J. C. Patch & Company
1474 University Ave.
Berkeley 94702
(415) 548-9010

(Buys antique clothing and accessories.)

Jean Stewart
72 Wood Lane

Fairfax 94930

(Wants antique clothing, early 1900s. White lace dresses and blouses. Authentic folk costumes and embroideries. European and Oriental clothing wanted, too.)

Bizarre Bazaar
5634 College Ave.
Oakland 94618
(415) 655-2909

(Wants clothing from the twenties, thirties, forties.)

Rich-Lee Antiques
3549 University
San Diego 92104
(714) 280-5540

(Antique clothing and accessories wanted.)

Made in England
1913 Fillmore St.
San Francisco 94115
(415) 929-1442

(English clothing from the thirties and forties.)

COLORADO

Antique Appraisers & Buyers
14704 Montview Blvd.
Denver 80220
(303) 366-5592

(Wants show-biz clothing.)

Nostalgia Shop
2431 S. University Blvd.
Denver 80210
(303) 778-6566

(Buys pre-1945 clothing.)

Vintage 76
1881 S. Broadway
Denver 80202
(303) 777-3854

(Buys antique clothing and
accessories, 1900–1940s.)

DISTRICT OF COLUMBIA

Deja Vu
1675 Wisconsin Ave., N.W.
Washington 20007
(202) 965-1988

(Vintage clothing wanted.)

FLORIDA

Edge City
1017 Park St.
Jacksonville 32204
(904) 353-9423

(Antique clothing wanted:
turn-of-the-century
petticoats, nightgowns, lace
dresses, blouses, shawls, etc.
Also, light clothing from the
twenties and thirties, such as
pajamas, kimonos, lounging
outfits.)

Grace's Thrift Shops
2518 N.E. 2nd Ave.
Miami 33137
(305) 573-1907

(Buys furs, costumes, ornate
clothing.)

Twentieth Century, Ltd.
3417 Main Hwy.
Miami 33133

(Nostalgia clothing wanted.)

Pantomine Park
110 Park Ave., S.
Winter Park 32789
(305) 628-4044

(Wants antique clothing.)

ILLINOIS

Follies
6981 N. Sheridan
Chicago 60626
(312) 761-3020

(Old-fashioned [before 1955]
accessories and clothing.)

INDIANA

Barbara Maddux
111 N. Dunn St.
Bloomington 47401

(Wants antique clothes
[pre-1945] for retail. Must be
in wearable condition.
Men's, women's, and
accessories. State condition,
description, vintage.)

Ballards Antique Costumes
6349 N. Guilford St.
Indianapolis 46220

(Wants old [pre-1944]
clothing for men and

women. Not only silks but white cottons in dresses, nightgowns, waists, corset covers.)

MISSOURI

Pastimes
18 E. 39th St.
Kansas City 64111
(816) 753-9335
(Vintage clothes and soft goods wanted.)

Alternate Ultra Antiques
398 N. Euclid Ave.
St. Louis 63108
(314) 361-4870
(Buys vintage clothes.)

NEBRASKA

Second Chance
415 S. 11th St.
Omaha 68102
(402) 346-4930
(Pre-1950 clothing wanted.)

NEW MEXICO

(C) Collector
2734 Burton, S.E.
Albuquerque 87106
(Wants men's clothing: colored or pin-striped suits, wide lapels, medium size; smoking jackets. Hawaiian shirts, tails, hats, hand-painted ties.)

Demchuck
419 Dallas St., N.E.
Albuquerque 87108
(Wants pre-1928 ladies' clothing materials, laces. Highest prices paid. Also, wants 1930s smocked dresses, chiffon, velvet clothing, and shawls.)

NEW YORK

The Thrif-tee Owl
2970 Merrick Road
Bellmore 11710
(516) 826-3522
(Wanted: clothing from the twenties and thirties and forties; furs, hats, and jewelry, too.)

Best of Everything, Limited
242 E. 77th St.
New York 10022
(212) 734-2492
(Clothing and accessories of the 1920s–50s.)

Nedra Antiques Furniture & Clothing
1566 2nd Ave.
New York 10022
(212) 737-8747
(Clothing of the twenties through the forties.)

Nostalgia Alley Antiques
174 E. 82nd St.
New York 10022
(Vintage clothing.)

PAPER: POSTCARDS, VALENTINES, PAPER DOLLS, ETC.

Paper Dealers

CALIFORNIA

Wilber Worth
8844 W. Olympic Blvd.
Beverly Hills 90211
(Send SASE for free
brochure.)

Greg Cox
P.O. Box 2134
McKinleyville 95521

CONNECTICUT

Lyon Hobby Mart
Box 63
Hartford 06101

The Nuhns
Box 562
West Haven 06516

FLORIDA

Dorothy Wilkison
P.O. Box 251
Bradenton 33505

Gordon McHenry, The
  Paper of America
Box 14463
Gainesville 32604

ILLINOIS

Spaulding Antiques
6428 W. Gunison
Chicago 60656
(Postcards.)

Ackert Enterprises
521 S. 7th St.
DeKalb 60115

MAINE

Stevens
154 Church St.
Duxbury 02332

MASSACHUSETTS

Sally S. Carver
179 South St.
Brookline 02167

Boxell
Box 224
Holden 01520

MICHIGAN

Jack Custer
22547 Edison
Dearborn 48124

NEW YORK

Yesterday's Children's

Postcards
P.O. Box 2693
Buffalo 14226

Nelson
Box 306
Chappaqua 10514

OHIO

Rustco
P.O. Box 742
Lima 45802

Ruth Murphy
8186 Westmoor Road
Mentor 44060

OREGON

Jacelyn Decker
732 Walnut St.
Albany 97321

PENNSYLVANIA

Louise Heiser
325 Ridge Ave.
McSherrytown 17344

Jean Woodcock
New Milford 18834
(Paper dolls, 1900–53; any
kind or quality.)

TEXAS

Lillian Brown
434 Avant
San Antonio 78210

WISCONSIN

Alby's
400 W. Chestnut
Burlington 53105

WEST GERMANY

Willi Bernhard
200 Hamburg 73
Wiesennedder 2

Clyde F. Perry
Schwansee Street 64
8 Munich 90

Paper Collectors

ALABAMA

Steve Davis
P.O. Box 26192
Birmingham 35226
(Wants Birmingham
items—pre-1930 street-scene
postcards.)

CALIFORNIA

Ed Herney
1409 5th St.
Berkeley 94710
(415) 527-4558
(Wants postcards,
scrapbooks.)

Ken Prag
Box 431
Hawthorne 90250
(Wants all stock certificates,

270

bonds, express-company paper, railroad passes.)

Peggy Hecker
5010 Cadet
San Diego 92117

(Wants old Whitestone, N.Y., postcards and stereoviews.)

COLORADO

Jack Shapiro
3201 S. Monroe St.
Denver 80210

(Wants to buy or trade old U.S. or Cuban cigar bands.)

Mrs. Pat Roberts
20 Ames St.
Lakewood 80226
(303) 233-1609

(Wants horses on postcards.)

CONNECTICUT

James Bernier
40 Grandview Ave.
Watertown 06795

(Wants posters, calendars by Peters Cartridge Co.)

FLORIDA

Holmes Carey
P.O. Box 89
De Bary 32713

(Wants old insurance policies [pre-1900] with illustrations on face.)

ILLINOIS

Mark & Lois Jacabos
702 N. Wells
Chicago 60607

(Wants Americana collectibles: political memorabilia, postcards, etc.)

Ed Pesco
Box 133
Taylor Springs 62089

(Wants baseball, football, and non-sport cards from gum, candy, etc., pre-1960.)

MISSOURI

George Crawford
311 Sunset Dr.
Clinton 49236

(Wants Indianapolis 500 postcards, programs, etc.)

Dorothy Barnett
10084 Affton Place
St. Louis 63123
(314) 638-9016

(Wants pre-1920 Santa, children, pretty girls, holiday postcards.)

NEW YORK

Bevie
P.O. Box 141
Cedarhurst 11516

(Wants old posters.)

Brownie Gill

Clifton Park 12065
(Wants woven silk cards.)

Lt. Col. Gill
Elnora 12065
(Wants woven silk
postcards.)

Joe Schwartz
Box 4568
Grand Central Sta.
New York 10017
(Wants Canadian picture
postcards, used and unused.)

Collector
Box 17022
Rochester 14617
(Wants paper items,
brochures, salesbooks, from
the twenties and thirties.)

OHIO

R. E. Baer
P.O. Box 206
Groveport 43125
(Wants woven silk
postcards.)

Mary Young
1040 Greenridge
Kettering 45429
(Wants paper dolls,
children's coloring books
from 1930s, 1940s.)

C. R. Smith
88 Maureen Dr.
Newark 43055

(614) 522-3075
(Wants Ohio postcards:
towns, depots, streets, fire
engines, etc.)

Jack Snyder
244 Waggoner
Toledo 43612
(Wants old telegrams, phone
bills.)

PENNSYLVANIA

Miscellaneous Man
New Freedom 17349
(Wants original posters of
almost any type prior to
1950.)

George Driebe
203 N. 9th St.
Stroudsburg 18360
(Wants posters, calendars by
Peters, Remington,
Winchester-Marlin, and
other powder or gun
companies.)

TEXAS

Arnold
2234 South Blvd.
Houston 77098
(Wants original movie
posters: Bogart, Gable, etc.)

WASHINGTON

E. Charles Worth
814 N.W. 73

Seattle 98117
(Wants steamship menus.)

W. LaPoe
11986 Lakeside Place, N.E.
Seattle 98125

WISCONSIN

Esther Bolhagen
Rte. 2, Box 36013
Wautoma 54982

(Wants nonstandard or
unusual U.S. decks of
playing cards, pre-1930.)

CRAFTS

Sewing Collectors

Collector
Box 6722
Tucson, Ariz. 85733

(Wants patchwork quilts
pre-1940; also, early pictorial
hooked rugs.)

Andrea Clarke
8625 35th Ave., S.W.
Seattle, Wash. 98126

(Wants tatting shuttles.)

Sewing Dealers

CALIFORNIA

Cinnamon Toast
3585 Sacraments
San Francisco 94118

(Buys exceptional quilts.)

MAINE

H.O.M.E. Inc.
Box 408
Orland 04472

(The H.O.M.E. stores are
located at the Rural Life
Center on U.S. Rte. 1,
Orland; 26 State St., Bangor;
and summer store on Main
St., Bar Harbor. All crafts,
from caps to quilts, bird
feeders to toys, are on
consignment and made
exclusively by Maine people.
For further information call
[207] 469-7961.)

NEVADA

Hobbycraft
1020 S. Wells
Reno 89502

NEW JERSEY

Crafts Plus
267 Fort Lee Road
Leonia 07605

NEW YORK

Mission Crafts
Box 565
Hughesville 12537

America Hurrah Antiques
316 E. 70th St.
New York 10021
(212) 535-1930

(Buys patchwork quilts,
hooked rugs.)

Mrs. Barbara S. Janos
353 E. 83rd St., Apt. 9B
New York 10028

(Buys pieced quilts,
pre-1940. Also, American
samplers, pre-1850.)

Heirloom Thimbles
Sewing Corner
Box 420
Whitestone 11357

PENNSYLVANIA

Creative Hands Co., Inc.
P.O. Box 11602
Pittsburgh 15234

WEST VIRGINIA

East River Mountain
  Craftshop
Bluefield 24701

Shops That Sell Crafts
on Consignment

ARIZONA

Family Arts Exchange
5807 N. 7th St.
Phoenix 85014

Women's Exchange Special
  Ties of Tucson
4215 N. Campbell
Tucson 85719

CONNECTICUT

Greenwich Exchange for
  Woman's Work, Inc.
28 Sherwood Place
Greenwich 06830

Litchfield Exchange for
  Woman's Work, Inc.

Cobble Court
Litchfield 06759

Heritage Village Woman's
  Exchange
Southbury 06488

Fairfield Woman's
  Exchange, Inc.
332 Pequot Road
Southport 06490

Stamford Woman's
  Exchange
45 Prospect St.
Stamford 06901

The Woman's Exchange
993A Farmington Ave.
West Hartford 06107

DISTRICT OF COLUMBIA

Appalachian Spring
1655 Wisconsin Ave., N.W.
Washington 20007

GEORGIA

Unique Corner Woman's
  Exchange of Athens
Taylor-Grady House
634 Prince Ave.
Athens 30601

INDIANA

The Hen House
4816 Tippecanoe Dr.
Evansville 47715

The Little Turtle Woman's
  Exchange
Time Corner Shopping
  Center
Fort Wayne 46804

MAINE

The Woman's Exchange
36 Exchange St.
Portland 04111

MASSACHUSETTS

Dedham Woman's
  Exchange, Inc.
445 Washington St.
Dedham 02026

The Old Town Hall
  Exchange
Lincoln Center 01773

The Hay Scales Exchange,
  Inc.
2 Johnson St.
North Andover Center
  01085

MARYLAND

Woman's Industrial
  Exchange
Baltimore 21201

NEW JERSEY

The Hunterdon Exchange
155 Main St.
Flemington 08822

The Depot
217 1st St.
Hohokus 07423

Woman's Exchange of
  Monmouth County
32 Church St.
Little Silver 07739

Newark Exchange for
  Woman's Work
32 Halsey St.
Newark 07102

The Village Exchange
De Forest & Woodland Ave.
Summit 07901

NEW YORK

Craftsmen Unlimited, Inc.
16 Main St.
Bedford Hills 10507

Woman's Exchange of
  Brooklyn, Inc.
76 Montague St.
Brooklyn 11201

New York Exchange for
  Woman's Work, Inc.
541 Madison Ave.
New York 10022

The Elder Craftsmen
  Showcase
850 Lexington Ave.
New York 10021

Scarsdale Woman's
  Exchange, Inc.

33 Harwood Court
Scarsdale 10583

NORTH CAROLINA

The Country Store
113 W. Franklin St.
Chapel Hill 27514

Sandhills Woman's
Exchange
Pinehurst 28374

OHIO

The Sassy Cat
88 N. Main St.
Chagrin Falls 44022

The Woman's Exchange
3507 Michigan Ave.
Cincinnati 45208

PENNSYLVANIA

The Old York Road
Woman's Exchange
429 Johnson St.
Jenkintown 19046

Chestnut Hill Community
Center
8419 Germantown Ave.
Philadelphia 19118

Ladies Depository
Association of Philadelphia
109 S. 18th St.
Philadelphia 19103

Woman's Industrial

Exchange
541 Penn Ave.
Pittsburgh 15222

Woman's Exchange of the
Neighborhood League
185 E. Lancaster Ave.
Wayne 19087

The Woman's Exchange of
West Chester
10 S. Church St.
West Chester 19380

The Woman's Exchange of
Reading, Inc.
720 Penn Ave.
West Reading 19602

The Woman's Exchange of
Yardley
47 W. Afton Ave.
Yardley 19077

TENNESSEE

The Woman's Exchange of
Memphis, Inc.
88 Racine St.
Memphis 38111

TEXAS

St. Michael's Woman's
Exchange
5 Highland Park Village
Dallas 75205

SILVER, GOLD, PEWTER, and
JEWELRY BUYERS
(no code indicates dealer)

ALABAMA

Gold Reclaiming Company
601 Bel Air Blvd., Suite 402
Mobile 36606
(205) 476-4297

(Buys gold and diamonds.)

Money Tree
206 Hemley Ave.
Mobile 36607
(205) 471-2622

(Buys scrap gold and silver.)

Spring Hill Jewelry
3496 Springhill Ave.
Mobile 36608
(205) 344-9779

(Wants antique jewelry,
watches.)

ALASKA

Alaska Trading Post
240 W. 5th Ave.
Anchorage 99501
(907) 277-0332

(Buys gold and diamonds.)

G. & H. Enterprises Coin
  Shop
New Polaris Bldg.
Box 2832
Fairbanks 99707
(907) 452-6461

(Buys gold, silver, and
(ivory.)

ARIZONA

A Trading Post Sales
9316 N. Central
Phoenix 85020
(602) 943-6366

(Antique jewelry wanted.)

David Adler
6815 N. 2nd St.
Phoenix 85012
(602) 264-9146

(Wants good antique silver.)

Arizona Coin Exchange
David McHenry
P.O. Box 22146
Phoenix 85028
(602) 971-1285

(Buys scrap silver and gold.)

Dress Well Shoppe
6008 N. 16th St.
Phoenix 85028
(602) 264-5720

(Buys Indian jewelry.)

Millie's Antiques
712 N. Central Ave.
Phoenix 85004
(602) 254-5697

(Buys silver pieces.)

Ye Olde Curiosity Shoppe
7245 1st Ave.
Scottsdale 85256
(602) 947-3062
(Wants antique jewelry.)

ARKANSAS

National Pawn Shop
100 E. Washington
North Little Rock 72114
(501) 372-9707
(Buys old gold and jewelry.)

CALIFORNIA

Antic Mews
1410 Solano Ave.
Albany 94706
(415) 525-8142
(Wants antique beads.)

Precious Metals Trading &
  Refining Company
3201 W. Mission Road
Alhambra 91803
(213) 570-1828
(Scrap metals wanted.)

Hugo F. Forster &
Company
170 Glenn Way
Belmont 94002
(415) 593-1042
(Buys gold, silver, platinum,
tableware, jeweler's scrap,
industrial scrap, dental gold.

Send registered mail to P.O.
Box 812, Belmont 94002.)

David Orgell
320 N. Rodeo Dr.
Beverly Hills 90035
(213) 272-4550
(Buys fine silver, art objects.)

Hollywood Collateral Loan
  Association
1612 Vine St.
Hollywood 90028
(213) 464-7175
(Buys diamonds, jewelry,
and silver.)

Lila's Antiques
3559 Mount Diablo Blvd.
Lafayette 94549
(415) 284-9017
(Specialist in jewelry and
silver.)

Dal's Antiques & Trading
  Post
15617 Hawthorne Blvd.
Lawndale 90260
(213) 675-1692
(Buys jewelry, silver, and
gold.)

Antique World
331 1st St.
Los Altos 94022
(Antique jewelry wanted.)

Abbey Antique Buyers
8230 W. 3rd St.
Los Angeles 90048

(213) 653-4870

(Buys gold, silver, diamonds, jewelry.)

ABCO Antiques
133 S. Vermont
Los Angeles 90004
(213) 388-7177

(Buys silver, jewelry, and ivory.)

Continental Coin
5627 Sepulveda Blvd.
Los Angeles 90045
(213) 781-4232

(Wants scrap gold.)

Continental Jewelers &
  Refiners
36 W. 3rd St.
Los Angeles 90013
(213) 624-5456

(Buys gold, silver, platinum, diamonds, jewelry, and watches.)

Don Quixote Antiques
5011 Hollywood Blvd.
Los Angeles 90027
(213) 666-1167

(Buys antique jewelry.)

American Coin & Stamp
  Company
12164 Ventura Blvd.
North Hollywood 91604
(213) 877-3139

(Buys gold, silver, and platinum.)

Riskin Gem Shop Jewelers
1946 Broadway
Oakland 94612
(415) 832-7193

(Buys diamonds, antique jewelry, old gold.)

Dave's Jewelry Loan
110 E. Andreas
Palm Springs 92262
(714) 324-4411

(Buys or trades jewelry, old gold and silver.)

Thomas Broadwin
550 Hamilton Ave.
Palo Alto 94301
(415) 324-1874

(Buys old gold, silver jewelry, and diamonds, any condition or quantity.)

Electronic Watch Repair
  Company
1043 7th St.
San Diego 92101
(714) 234-7866

(Buys antique jewelry, diamonds, watches, and old gold.)

Ski's Swap Shop
3530 University Ave.
San Diego 92104

(Buys antique jewelry.)

Treasure Trove
3538 University
San Diego 92104
(714) 283-7139

(Buys antique jewelry,
pocket watches.)

Blackwell Antiques
563 Sutter St.
San Francisco 94102
(415) 433-4886

(Buys jewelry.)

Corinthian Studios
521 Sutter St.
San Francisco 94102
(415) 363-0717

(Buys antique jewelry.)

The Jewel Case
245 Powell
San Francisco 94102
(413) 781-1140

(Buys diamonds, old gold
jewelry, any condition.)

Maxferd Jewelry Company
972 Market St.
San Francisco 94108
(415) 885-1634

(Buys any silver or gold.)

Sylvar Antiques & Fine Arts
1216 Polk St.
San Francisco 94109
(415) 776-0300

(Buys silver items and
flatware; also ivory.)

J. & R. Antique & Coin
Shop
15261 Hesperian Blvd.
San Leandro 94578
(415) 278-4160

(Specializing in old watches.
Buys jewelry and scrap gold
and silver.)

W. B. Precious Metals &
  Diamonds
3150 El Camino Road
Santa Clara 93109
(415) 296-5400

(Buys silver, gold, platinum,
any form and quantity.)

COLORADO

Azure Antiques & Sales
1305 Delaware
Denver 80204

(Buys old jewelry.)

William Crow Jewelry, Inc.
910 16th St.
Denver 80202
(303) 292-2350

(Buys antique jewelry.)

Pacific Jewelry & Loan
  Company
537 15th St.
Denver 80202
(303) 255-7122

(Buys antique jewelry.)

Turn of the Century
  Antiques
1421 S. Broadway
Denver 80203
(303) 722-8700

(Antique jewelry. Also buys
scrap gold, silver, and
platinum.)

DELAWARE

George W. Thomas
Middletown 19709
(302) 378-2414

(Buys pewter.)

(C) Carl Doubet, Jr.
9th and Orange Sts.
Wilmington 19801
(302) 655-3303

(Buys silver, gold, and
diamonds.)

DISTRICT OF COLUMBIA

Georgetown Silver Shoppe
1261 Wisconsin Ave., N.W.
Washington 20007
(202) 337-0011

(Buys old silver.)

Rose Brothers Antiques
3317 Connecticut Ave.,
N.W.
Washington 20008
(202) 363-3681

(Buys antique jewelry.)

Shaw & Sussinger Jewelry
1613 Eye Street, N.W.
Washington 20006
(202) 331-1020

(Buys antique and estate
jewelry.)

Tiny Jewel Box
1143 Connecticut Ave.,
N.W.
Washington 20036

(202) 393-2747

(Antique jewelry, silver, art
objects. Buys estates.)

FLORIDA

Little White House Antiques
5025 S. Ridgewood Ave.
Allandale 32023
(904) 767-4040

(Buys silver pieces.)

Banker's Antiques
252 S. Beach St.
Daytona Beach 32014
(904) 258-6182

(Wants old jewelry, silver
and gold.)

Middle Pawn Shop
327 2nd Ave.
Daytona Beach 32017
(904) 252-9163

(Buys gold and silver.)

Seabreeze Antique Shop
222 Seabreeze Blvd.
Daytona Beach 32018
(904) 252-2071

(Wants old jewelry, gold,
silver, brass figurines.)

(C) Hamilton
269 Tropic Dr.
Fort Lauderdale 32018

(Unusual sterling-
souvenir spoons wanted.
Describe fully
and state price in first
letter.)

Antique Merchandise Mart,
Inc.
235 S. Maitland Ave.
Maitland 32751
(305) 644-1222

(Buys antique jewelry,
silver.)

Ajax Steel & Alloys
Corporation
3333 N.W. River Dr.
Miami 33139
(305) 633-0465

(Buys scrap gold, silver,
platinum, mercury, and
other precious metals.)

Cash Inn House of Instant
Money
1829 N.W. 79th St.
Miami 33126
(305) 693-2274

(Buys antique jewelry.)

M. Geiger Rare Coins &
Stamps
139 N.E. 1st St.
Miami 33132

(Buys antique jewelry and
old watches.)

Gerstel's
Seybold Arcade, No. 137
Miami 33132
(305) 379-5095

(Buys antique jewelry and
precious metals.)

(C) Silver
P.O. Box 011423

Flagler Sta.
Miami 33101

(Wants silver flatware,
holloware, and jewelry;
one piece or collection.

S. Davis & Company
1252 Lincoln Road
Miami Beach 33139
(305) 673-0785

(Buys old gold and silver.)

Bentley Investments, Inc.
8990 Biscayne Blvd.
Miami Shores 33138
(305) 751-3607

(Buys gold jewelry, scrap
silver and gold.)

American Refining &
Smelting
835 N. Federal Hwy.
Orlando 32805
(305) 763-2001

(Buys jewelry, diamonds,
sterling-silver flatware, coins,
and scrap gold.)

Thompson Antiques
814 W. Colonial Dr.
Orlando 32804
(305) 849-0395

(Specializes in antique
jewelry. Wants old gold
jewelry.)

Keene's Korner Kottage
400 S. Orlando Ave.
Winter Park 32789
(305) 644-4461

(Buys jewelry, copper, pewter, and brass.)

GEORGIA

American Eagle Antiques, Inc.
2181 Peachtree Road, N.E.
Atlanta 30309
(404) 355-4310

(Wants antique jewelry and silver.)

Atlanta Coin & Stamp Company
1574 Piedmont Ave., N.E.
Atlanta 30324
(404) 875-6530

(Buys scrap gold, silver, old sterling flatware, old jewelry.)

Rare Coins, Inc.
3500 Peachtree Road, N.E.
Atlanta 30326
(404) 231-1394

(Buys 14K gold jewelry.)

Mableton Coin Company
5185 Bankhead
Mableton 30059
(404) 941-3579

(Buys scrap silver and gold.)

HAWAII

Collector's Art
1461 S. King
Honolulu 96814
(808) 947-4414

(Buys antique jewelry, coins, and silver.)

Consignment Center
1145 S. King St.
Oahu, Honolulu 96814
(808) 521-3834

(Buys antique jewelry.)

Gem Loans
2171 C. Kalakau Ave.
Oahu, Honolulu 96825
(808) 923-8155

IDAHO

Security Silver Exchange, Inc.
216 N. 8th St.
Boise 83706
(208) 336-0908

(Buys gold and silver.)

Silver & Gold Exchange of Idaho
1134 N. Orchard, Suite 5
Boise 83704
(208) 376-1110

Buys any amount of silver and gold.)

ILLINOIS

Able Diamond & Jewelry Buyers
5 S. Wabash, Suite 1007
Chicago 60603
(312) 323-7054

(Buys diamonds, gold, platinum jewelry.)

Admiral Coin & Stamp Mart
4136 Harlem Norridge
Chicago 60656
(312) 456-5100

(Buys pocket watches, old gold jewelry.)

M. C. Anderson Gold
  Company
5 N. Wabash
Chicago 60602
(312) 726-1600

(Buys old gold, silver and platinum.)

Chicago Coin Corporation
406 S. Michigan Ave.
Chicago 60605
(312) 431-1605

(Buys scrap gold, silver, and jewelry.)

Fischer's Antique Shop
2569 N. Clark St.
Chicago 60614
(312) 525-4999

(Buys antique jewelry and broken gold, silver, and platinum.)

The Old Jewelry Shop
Marshall Field Annex Bldg.,
  Rm. 842
25 E. Washington St.
Chicago 60602
(312) 263-6764

(Buys antique jewelry exclusively.)

Rose Industries

29 E. Madison St., Rm. 506
Chicago 60602
(312) 726-1031

(Buys old gold, silver, platinum, coins, broken jewelry, eyeglasses, watches, silverware.)

Spaulding Antiques
6428 W. Gunison St.
Chicago 60656
(312) 867-7119

(Buys jewelry, sterling silver. Specializes in complete estates.)

JRS Antiques, Ltd.
600 Green Bay
Winnetka 60093
(312) 446-0470

(Wants jewelry and silver.)

INDIANA

Gard Gallery
396 S. Lake St.
Gary 46403
(219) 938-6860

(Wants antique jewelry.)

Things Unlimited
Antique Flea Market
24th & Meridian
Indianapolis 46222
(317) 923-0938

(Buys antique silver and gold pieces.)

KANSAS

Sunflower
Lorraine 67459
(Wants sterling-silver
souvenir spoons.)

Georgetown Rare Coin &
  Stamp Company
9345 W. 74th St.
Merriam 66204
(913) 384-3005
(Buys scrap silver and gold
and jewelry.)

Dale's Jewelry
1515½ Seward St.
Topeka 66616
(913) 354-7929
(Buys scrap metals.)

(C) Mary Zulaica
    P.O. Box 8063
    Topeka 66608
    (Wants antique jewelry.)

KENTUCKY

(C) E. G. Monroe
    Dept. of Art
    Western Kentucky
    University
    Bowling Green 42101
    (Wants items in coin
    silver other than large
    dinner forks, Fiddle
    Thread pattern made by
    Hyde and Goodrich,
    New Orleans, 1810.)

Drexler Treasure Isle Coins
  & Stamps
1433 Bardstown Road
Louisville 40205
(502) 459-0185
(Buys diamonds, old gold
and silver jewelry.)

Jacob Henry, Coin & Stamp
  Dealer
1504 Bardstown Road
Louisville 40205
(502) 458-6787
(Buys old gold and antique
jewelry.)

LOUISIANA

De Sylva-Dyer Antique
  Jewelry
619 Royal St.
New Orleans 70130
(504) 525-2727
(Buys antique jewelry.)

Gulf States Coin Exchange
126 Royal St.
New Orleans 70130
(504) 581-4601
(Buys silver and gold
jewelry.)

Moliere's Antique Shop
612 Chartres
New Orleans 70130
(504) 525-9497
(Buys antique jewelry.)

Marsha Oliver, Ltd.
3951 Magazine

New Orleans 70115
(504) 897-6670
(Buys antique jewelry.)

The Queen Flea
3441 Magazine
New Orleans 70115
(504) 891-0481
(Buys antique silver.)

MAINE

Gem Antiques
25 Longwood Terr.
Portland 04102
(Buys antique jewelry.)

MARYLAND

Art Gold and Silver Plating
  Company
1009 W. Baltimore St.
Baltimore 21201
(301) 685-6532
(Buys scrap silver, gold, and
platinum.)

Walter Reed Antique Shop
8118 Woodmont Ave.
Bethesda 20015
(301) 652-2727
(Buys antique jewelry.)

Bended Jewelry Center
1501 Reisterstown Road
Pikesville 21208
(301) 653-9000
(Buys silver, jewelry, ivories,
bronzes.)

MASSACHUSETTS

Brodney Gallery of Fine Arts
811 Boylston
Boston 02116
(617) 536-0500
(Wants antique jewelry.)

Church Company
364 Boylston
Boston 02147
(617) 267-6800
(Buys antique jewelry and
silver.)

Fireston & Parson
Ritz Carlton Hotel
Boston 02117
(617) 266-1858
(Buys antique silver.)

Independent Gold & Silver
27 School St.
Boston 02143
(617) 742-0635
(Buys all forms of scrap
precious metals.)

Joseph T. Place & Son, Inc.
333 Washington St.
Boston 02121
(617) 523-1143
(Buys old silver, both
sterling and plated.)

Simpson Jewelry
24 Bromfield
Boston 02108
(617) 542-1680
(Buys antique jewelry.)

Washington Antiques
8 Cypress St.
Brookline 02147
(617) 566-9474

(Buys old jewelry, clocks,
silver, brass, and coins.)

Collector's Den
2020 Massachusetts Ave.
Cambridge 02138
(617) 776-6293

(Buys scrap gold, silver, and
platinum.)

Grace & Sossen Antique
   Jewelry
860 Massachusetts Ave.
Cambridge 02138
(617) 661-3318

(Buys antique jewelry.)

Monkey Business Fun
   Antiques
844 Massachusetts Ave.
Cambridge 02138
(617) 354-9284

Jewelry and pocket
watches.)

Silver & Gold Redeeming
   Corporation of America
1865 Massachusetts Ave.
Cambridge 02138
(617) 661-8048

(Buys gold and silver scrap.)

Harvco Alloys
386 Watertown
Newton 02172
(617) 965-2692

(Buys scrap gold, silver, and
platinum.)

Acapulco Gold & Silver
87 Electric Ave.
Somerville 02143

(Buys scrap silver and gold.)

MISSOURI

Ace Coins & Antiques
419 N. Main St.
Kansas City 64152
(816) 833-1824

(Buys scrap gold, silver, all
precious metals. Also,
pocket watches.)

W. G. Alexander
115 N. Euclid Ave.
St. Louis 63108
(314) 535-8890

(Buys jewelry.)

Famous Barr Company
721 Olive St.
St. Louis 63101
(314) 421-5704

(Buys all types of jewelry.)

Hauser & Miller Company
4011 Forest Park Ave.
St. Louis 63108
(314) 531-3071

(Buys gold and all forms of
precious-metal scrap.)

Selkirk
4166 Olive St.
St. Louis 63108

(314) 533-1700
(Jewelry, silver, jade wanted.)

Village Antiques
1215 S. Big Bend Blvd.
St. Louis 63101
(314) 421-5704
(Buys old jewelry.)

MONTANA

Montana Coin & Stamp
  Company
2818 3rd Ave., N.
Billings 59101
(406) 252-6223
(Buys scrap silver and gold.)

NEBRASKA

Miller Jewelry
6127 Havelock
Lincoln 68505
(402) 464-7929
(Buys watches.)

Simon's Jewelry & Loan
  Company
510 S. 16th St.
Omaha 68114
(402) 393-1080
(Buys scrap gold.)

Western Rare Coins &
  Stamps
110 Omaha Mall Westroads
Omaha 68114
(402) 393-1080

(Buys silver and gold.)

NEVADA

(C) Stall
  Box 3885
  Incline Village 89450
  (Wants Nevada souvenir spoons. Send description and price wanted.)

Coins & Gifts
421 E. Fremont
Las Vegas 89101
(702) 385-2777
(Buys gold jewelry.)

Odd Shop Antiques
57 E. Hacienda Road
Las Vegas 89119
(702) 736-2724
(Wants heirloom jewelry.)

NEW HAMPSHIRE

Brentwood Auction Gallery
Rte. 125
Brentwood 03106
(Buys jewelry.)

Hookset Trading Post
Daniel Webster Hwy., N.
Manchester 03104
(603) 627-4969
(Wants gold and silver items.)

Sandi's Antiques
426 Chestnut
Manchester 03101

(603) 624-1069
(Specializing in antique
jewelry.)

Treasure Chest Coins
44 S. Main St.
Manchester 03106
(603) 623-0801
(Buys gold and silver, rings.)

NEW JERSEY

The Antique Place
10 West St.
Englewood 07631
(201) 567-9403
(Buys antique jewelry.)

Garden City Metals
  Corporation
50 Voorhis Lane
Hackensack 07601
(201) 487-0422
(Buys gold, silver, platinum
scrap.)

The Gold Man
183 Main St.
Hackensack 07601
(201) 342-6110
(Buys jewelry and
watches.)

Barrett Jewelers
185 E. Ridgewood Ave.
Ridgewood 07450
(201) 445-3060
(Buys antique watches and
jewelry.)

Easton Jewelers
6719 Atlantic Ave.
Ventnor City 08406
(609) 823-3751
(Buys jewelry and gold.)

NEW YORK

Asian Gallery
24 E. 80th St.
New York 10021
(212) 734-1379
(Buys jade objects.)

Astor Galleries
754 Broadway
New York 10003
(212) 473-1658
(Buys fine silver.)

Dealer's Den Inc.
578 5th Ave.
New York 10020
(212) 575-8180
(Antique jewelry and
precious stones.)

I. Freeman & Son, Inc.
12 E. 52nd St.
New York 10022
(212) 759-6900
(Buys Georgian silver, old
Sheffield and Victorian
plated ware.)

E. P. Gross
1200 Avenue of the
  Americas
New York 10036
(212) 757-6214

(Wants all types of jewelry, antique silver and gold pieces.)

Lenard's Galleries, Ltd.
37 E. 12th St.
New York 10003
(212) 677-7260
(Buys silver pieces.)

Lubin Galleries
72 E. 13th St.
New York 10003
(212) 254-1080
(Buys fine silver.)

Macklowe Gallery
1088 Madison Ave.
New York 10021
(Buys, sells, and appraises authentic antique jewelry.)

Klusner Stanleys & Son, Ltd.
968 Madison Ave.
New York 10021
(212) 249-3505
(Buys estates and antique jewelry.)

NORTH DAKOTA

(C) Collector
Box 2183
Fargo 58102
(Buys old sterling souvenir spoons from North Dakota.)

OHIO

Advance Mercury Sales
3550 W. 140th St.
Cleveland 44111
(216) 251-1990
(Buys scrap silver and gold. Jewelry, flatware, X-ray film, bridgework, eyeglass frames.)

H. L. Morris
Rogers Antiques
248 W. Park Ave.
Mansfield 44902
(Buys old jewelry, pocket watches.)

(C) Horter
495 Harris Road
Richmond Heights 44143
(Wants August Spoon of the Month by Wallace.)

PENNSYLVANIA

Edward G. Wilson
1802 Chestnut St.
Philadelphia 19103
(215) 563-7369
(Buys all kinds of fine antique jewelry, silver, gold, and pewter pieces.)

SOUTH CAROLINA

Amco
P.O. Box 33009
Charleston 24907
(Wants gold, diamonds, silver, platinum, jewelry,

and coins.)

American Metallurgy
Company
P.O. Box 33009
Charleston 29407

(Buys silver and gold scrap
in any form. Shipment held
intact for your approval.)

(C) Suzanne Snow
200 Dellrose Circle
Taylors 29687

(Wants old dining-car
holloware—silverplate.)

TEXAS

Amco Jewelry Company
Houston Citizen Bank Bldg.
1010 Jefferson St.,
Suite 1006
Houston 77002

(Wants antique jewelry.)

VIRGINIA

Marquise Jeweler, Ltd.
130 S. Washington St.
Alexandria 22314

(Buys antique jewelry,
pocket watches.)

WISCONSIN

(C) William Parks
4715 Sheboygan Ave.,
Apt. 303
Madison 20441

(Wants old sterling-silver

Wisconsin cities spoons.)

WYOMING

Cheyenne Trading Post
2115 E. Lincoln Way
Cheyenne 82001
(307) 635-5641

(Gold jewelry.)

Ed's Jewelry
210 Grand Ave.
Laramie 82070
(307) 742-2719

(Buys diamonds and railroad
watches.)

TOYS

(no code indicates dealer)

Dolls

ALABAMA

Claudia's Antiques & Doll
  Hospital
1024 Forrest Ave.
Gadsden 35901
(205) 546-1358
(Buys dolls.)

CALIFORNIA

Ella Mae Russell
2155 Park St.
Concord 94520
(Buys antique dolls.)

Antique Dolls
133 Westward Dr.
Corte Madera 94925
(415) 924-9304
(Buys dolls.)

Betty's Doll Shop & Hospital
7501 Seville
Huntington Park 90255
(213) 585-3456
(Wants French and German
bisque dolls. Repairs.)

Gladys Hollander
5928 Garford St.
Long Beach 90815
(Wants Kewpies and Rose

O'Neill illustrations.)

Millie's Dolls
P.O. Box 8540
Long Beach 90308
(Wants old dolls.)

Kate's Antique Shoppe
3612 W. 3rd St.
Los Angeles 90020
(213) 385-9666
(Specializes in dolls and
toys. Buys.)

Dee Byrnes
16660 Kennedy Road
Los Gatos 95030
(Buys antique dolls.)

Dew Drop In
819 Main St.
Redwood City 94063
(415) 365-2556
(Buys and repairs antique
dolls.)

Wee Doll Shoppe
2621 University
San Diego 92104
(714) 298-6246
(Buys antique dolls.)

Ye Olde Smith Shoppe
3493 University

San Diego 92104
(714) 284-1467
(Buys dolls.)

Fernando's Boutique
1365 Noriega
San Francisco 94122
(415) 731-5394
(Buys new and antique
dolls.)

Phillip for Dolls
165 O'Farrell
San Francisco 94102
(415) 981-0516
(Buys antique dolls.)

Marjorie's Little Bit Shop
169 E. Main St.
San Jacinto 92383
(714) 654-2241
(Buys old dolls.)

Billie Nelson Tyrrell's Dolls
P.O. Box 69556
West Hollywood 90069
(Wants antique dolls.)

COLORADO

Margaret Tarket
1570 G 96 Road
Delta 81416
(Wants dolls.)

Cinderella Antique Shop
631 15th St.
Denver 80202
(303) 825-6442

(Buys old dolls.)

Hart Industries
1788 S. Broadway
Denver 80202
(303) 777-5196
(Miniature specialist, buys
dolls, doll houses, miniature
doll items.)

Yesterday's Dolls
281 S. Pennsylvania
Denver 80209
(303) 744-7248
(Buys old dolls; doll repair.)

S. Ash
5600 E. Oxford
Englewood 80110
(Doll heads wanted.)

CONNECTICUT

The Doll Hospital
196 Whitfield
Guilford 06437
(203) 453-2160
(Antique dolls.)

DELAWARE

The Glass Porch
2201 Philadelphia Pike
Clymont 19703
(302) 798-5261
(Buys dolls and toys.)

Koester Doll Hospital
Shipley Road
Wilmington 19809

(302) 764-4442
(Wants dolls.)

Regina A. Steele, Antique
  Dolls
23 Wheatfield Dr.
Wilmington 19810
(302) 475-5374
(Wants French and German
bisque dolls: also china, wax,
parean, and others.)

FLORIDA

Grandma's Garage
3791 Bird Ave.
Coral Gables 33146
(Buys all kinds of antique
dolls.)

(C) R. H. Stevens
    2131 N.E. 30th St.
    Lighthouse Point 33064
    (Wants paper dolls.)

C. & B. Antique Doll
  Hospital
4900 30th Ave.
St. Petersburg 33705
(813) 343-7830
(Buys old dolls and parts.)

GEORGIA

Lila Benton Antique Dolls
311 Lakemore Dr., N.E.
Atlanta 30342
(404) 252-6817
(Buys antique dolls.)

Beverly Pridgeon
413 Moss Dr.
Columbus 31904
(Antique dolls wanted.)

Temptations-Upstairs-
  Downstairs
230 W. Bay St.
Savannah 31401
(912) 233-5500
(Buys dolls.)

IDAHO

The Victorian Shops
109 N. 8th St.
(208) 344-2541
108 N. 10th St.
(208) 344-2634
Boise 83706
(Buys all types of antique
dolls.)

ILLINOIS

Liberty Farm
Rte. 2, Box 133
Aurora 60504
(Buys old dolls.)

Antique Doll Hospital
3110 W. Irving Park
Chicago 60618
(312) 478-7554
(Buys antique dolls.)

Loretta Boehm
821 W. Lill St.
Chicago 60614
(312) 327-9732

(Buys antique and modern
dolls.)

(C) Patricia Derus
     8 W. Hubbard St.
     Chicago 60610
     (Solid dome babies
     wanted.)

Doll Land
6334 W. Eastwood
Chicago 60630
(Buys dolls.)

Julia Mayes
545 Bradley Court
Decatur 62522
(Bisque shoulder heads
wanted.)

(C) Mrs. R. M. Pinkston
     239 55th St.
     Downers Grove 60515
     (Wants Kewpie dolls.)

La Verne Kowalski
3434 Madison
Lansing 60438
(Wants dolls.)

Grace Ochsner
Doll House
Niota 62358
(Buys dolls.)

Ford's Enchanted Cottage
Lorraine & George Ford
567 S. Greenleaf St.
Waukegan 60085
(312) 623-0653

(Buys antique dolls.)

Elizabeth Coffin
1506 Muirfield
Waukegan 60085
(312) 662-6189
(Wants dolls.)

INDIANA

Windy Acres Doll Hospital
Carolos 47329
(317) 874-3302
(Dolls and doll-house
miniatures wanted.)

Dorothy's Dolls
2707 E. Gum St.
Evansville 47714
(812) 476-1110
(Collector and dealer of
antique dolls. Buys and sells
only via mail.)

Knopps Dolly Shop
2105 W. 300 S.
Marion 46952
(Wants dolls.)

IOWA

Maxine's Limited Editions
6579 University
Des Moines 50311
(515) 276-7204
(Wants Kewpie dolls.)

KANSAS

Mary Cowell Antiques
1213 S. Washington
Wellington 67152
(316) 326-2347
(Buys old dolls.)

Lisa's Antiques
1522 S. Broadway
Wichita 67214
(316) 264-4911
(Wants antique dolls.)

Mini Shoppe Antiques
10821 Hidden Lake
Wichita 67219
(316) 722-5971
(Buys antique dolls.)

KENTUCKY

Mary Ridley
Rte. 1
Gilbertsville 42044
(502) 362-4072
(Buys antique dolls.)

(C) Lois Shearer
2901 Tremont Dr.
Louisville 40205
(502) 459-2108
(Wants celebrity dolls,
antique dolls.)

LOUISIANA

Aunt Jennie's Doll Hospital
641 Caffin Ave.
New Orleans 70117
(504) 949-9021
(Buys old dolls.)

Joel Pearson
4427 Danneel St.
New Orleans 70113
(504) 899-1485
(Wants old dolls.)

MAINE

Red Kettle Antiques
Rte. 1
Searsport 04974
(207) 548-2978
(Wants old dolls and toys.)

MARYLAND

Edna Barney
Rte. 3, Box 74D
Annapolis 21403
(Wants antique dolls.)

Little Old Doll Shop &
   Hospital
5224 Harford Road
Baltimore 21207
(301) 426-2665
(Wants antique dolls.)

H & J Foulke, Inc.,
   Specializing in Antique
   Dolls
8202 Main St.
Ellicott City 21043
(301) 572-4917
(Buys better German,
French, good composition

dolls; all bisque dolls. Cloth
dolls and Madame
Alexander dolls.)

Center Craft Doll House
5505 42nd Ave.
Hyattsville 20781
(301) 277-3051
(Buys antique dolls.)

MASSACHUSETTS

Bette Ann Doll Hospital,
Inc.
Reservation Road
Mattapoisett 02739
(617) 758-6420
(Buys dolls; sells
reproductions, also.)

MICHIGAN

Joyce Doll House
Gene & Joyce Francis
20188 Williamson
Mount Clemens 48043
(Wants old dolls.)

Anne Rankin Antique Dolls
& Related Items
3387 Reese Road
Ortonville 48462
(313) 625-2281
(Wants character dolls,
action Kewpies, miniature
doll houses and furnishings.)

MISSOURI

Carol Ojinemus

P.O. Box 741
Fenton 63026
(314) 842-2264
(Wants old dolls.)

Kimport Dolls (World Wide
Dolls)
Box 495
Independence 64051
(Buys all kinds of antique
dolls.)

Ralph's Antique Dolls
7 Main St.
Parkville 64152
(816) 741-3120
(Buys dolls.)

Blanche's Doll Hospital
6108 Leona
St. Louis 63116
(314) 832-2679
(Buys antique dolls.)

NEVADA

Sandy Rankow
2304 Oquendo Road
Las Vegas 89109
(702) 736-7263
(Buys and sells antique dolls
via mail order only.)

NEW HAMPSHIRE

Yankee Drummer Antiques
428 Chestnut St.
Manchester 03101
(603) 668-6446

(Buys dolls and old toys.)

NEW JERSEY

Bee's Doll Hospital
736 Haddon Ave.
Collingswood 08108
(609) 858-6044
(Buys antique dolls.)

Good Fairy Doll Hospital &
  Museum
205 Walnut Ave.
Cranford 07016
(201) 276-3815
(Wants to buy broken dolls.)

Raggedy Ann Antique Doll
  & Toy Museum
171 Main St.
Flemington 08821
(201) 782-1243
(Buys old dolls and toys.)

The Calico Doll House
Gibbsboro Road
Kirkwood 08043
(Buys antique dolls.)

Fera's Antique Shop
199 Washington St.
Newark 07109
(Buys dolls, toys.)

NEW MEXICO

The Antique Parlor
243 Wyoming Blvd., N.E.
Albuquerque 87123
(505) 266-0171

(Buys dolls and doll-house
miniatures.)

NEW YORK

Helen Fields
Box 114
Cedarhurst 11516
(212) 471-1155
(Wants all kinds of antique
dolls; makes repairs.)

Julie's Dolls
c/o Evelyn Klenosky
75-68 181st St.
Flushing 11366
(212) 591-4797
(Wants antique dolls.)

Evelyn Klenosky Antique
  Dolls
75-68 181st St.
Flushing 11366
(212) 591-4797
(Buys all types of dolls.
Specializes in composition
celebrities, such as Shirley
Temple, as well as Madame
Alexander dolls. Doll
repairing done also.)

Manhattan Doll Hospital &
  Toys
176 9th Ave.
New York 10011
(212) 989-5220
(Buys antique dolls and
toys.)

New York Doll Hospital

787 Lexington Ave.
New York 10021
(212) 838-7527
(Buys antique dolls.)

Maxine Berv
1 Gerard Court
Oceanside 11572
(Wants antique dolls.)

Evelyn Phillips
Loch Lane
Port Chester 10573
(914) 939-4455
(Buys antique dolls.)

V. Diefenthaler
4057 Amboy Road
Staten Island 10308
(Wants antique dolls.)

NORTH CAROLINA

Johnnie Shuford
1401 Crystal Road
Charlotte 28205
(Buys antique dolls.)

Blue Barn Antique Dolls
Box 295
Mount Airy 27030
(Wants all kinds of antique dolls.)

OHIO

Dudies
7755 Kennedy Lane
Cincinnati 45242

(513) 791-1168
(Wants antique dolls. SASE for correspondence.)

Doll Repair Parts, Inc.
9918 Lorain Ave.
Cleveland 44102
(Antique dolls bought and sold. Monthly list of dolls, odds and ends, 50 cents.)

Antique Doll Shop
Helen Brown Cook's
110 E. Fairview Ave.
Dayton 45405
(513) 275-0828
(Wants rare antique dolls.)

Mary Palcombaro
5205 E. 114th St.
Garfield Heights 44125
(Wants antique dolls.)

OKLAHOMA

Edna Kelly
Box 35284
Tulsa 74135
(Antique dolls wanted.)

Mrs. Wadsworth
319 S. 42 West Ave.
Tulsa 84127
(Buys antique dolls.)

OREGON

Irene's
3722 S.E. Main

Portland 97214
(Wants old dolls.)

PENNSYLVANIA

Elizabeth Kennedy
RD 2
Doylestown 18901
(Wants old teddy bears and
rag dolls.)

Ann Lloyd Dolls &
  Miniatures
4302 June Meadow Dr.,
  Rte.4
Doylestown 18901
(Wants all kinds of dolls in
  good condition. No chips,
cracks, broken fingers,
repainting, or other
mutilation. Redressed,
replaced hair and eyes
permissible. Give full
information.)

(C) Sylvia Frassinelli
  460 Youngwood Dr.
  East Stroudsburg 18301
  (Wants musical twirling
  stick dolls.)

Sylvia Brockmon
6333 Wayne Ave.
Philadelphia 19144
(215) 438-4511
(Buys old dolls.)

Fred and Pat Boedewig
1070 Brennan Dr.
Warm 18974

(215) 672-1413
(Wants antique dolls.)

TEXAS

Kay-Len Dolls
667 Westbury Square
Houston 77035
(713) 729-6648 or
(713) 729-1653
(Buys antique dolls.)

Kay's Dolls
P.O. Box 16322
Lubbock 79490
(Wants antique dolls.)

WASHINGTON

Loraine Burdick
5 Court Place
Puyallup 98371
(Wants antique dolls.)

WYOMING

Doll Hospital & Toy Shop
  of Little Friends
2118 E. 12th St.
Cheyenne 82001
(307) 632-6263
(Wants antique dolls and
toys.)

Toys, Trains, and Banks

CALIFORNIA

Washington & Vermont

Train Shop
1583 W. Washington Blvd.
Los Angeles 90007
(213) 735-7948

(Buys antique trains.)

Lee's Train Service
3980 Piedmont Ave.
Oakland 94611
(415) 652-3980

(Buys used trains.)

Hubert B. Whiting
16736 Diego Dr.
San Diego 92128

(Wants tin and mechanical
banks; iron and tin toys,
tobacco tins.)

Madden & Son
243 8th St.
San Francisco 94118
(415) 864-0610

(Buys Lionel trains.)

COLORADO

The Train Shop
1479 Chester St.
Aurora 80010
(303) 366-5115

(Will buy trains, O, HO, N.)

Caboose Hobbies, Inc.
610 15th St.
Denver 80202
(303) 534-3377

(Will buy used trains.)

Downtown Hobbies
1514 California St.
Denver 80202
(303) 222-5356

(Will buy used Lionel
trains.)

CONNECTICUT

Bob McCumber
201 Carriage Dr.
Glastonburg 06033

(Buys mechanical banks.)

Gordon Train Repair
  Service
465 Congress Ave.
New Haven 06519
(203) 787-2121

(Buys trains.)

Toys
Box 367
Short Beach 06405

(Entertainment toys
wanted.)

DISTRICT OF COLUMBIA

(C) George A. Coupe
    520 New Jersey Ave.,N.W.
    Washington 20001
    (202) 638-3006
    (Wants banks and toys.)

FLORIDA

Knuckle Coupler
2917 Greenridge

Jacksonville 32207
(904) 264-6034
(Buys old trains.)

Jack W. Windt
1939 Golf St.
Sarasota 33577
(Wants toy trains and
trolleys before 1942.)

Ted's Hardware & Trains
3616 W. Cypress
Tampa 33607
(813) 879-5221
(Buys old trains.)

Scofield's
P.O. Box 3443
Tequesta 33458
(Buys mechanical banks and
toys.)

GEORGIA

Olde House Antiques
3845 Peachtree Road, N.E.
Atlanta 30319
(404) 261-5115
(Buys old toys and electric
trains.)

ILLINOIS

American Flyer Trains
5450 W. Belmont
Chicago 60641
(312) 736-0451
(Buys trains.)

40 Thieves Hobby Shop
8020 S. Western
Chicago 60620
(312) 778-9748
(Buys trains: Lionel and
American Flyer.)

Weitz Television, Camera &
    Appliance Store
2609 W. North
Chicago 60647
(312) 486-0290
(Buys trains.)

(C) J. R. Mautner
    2948 Arlington
    Highland Park 60035
    (312) 432-4595 (after 7
    P.M. and on weekends)
(Wants old games
[pre-1940], box, board,
or card. Should be
original box, complete
with instructions and in
good condition.
Interested in old
McLoughlin Brothers,
Parker Brothers, and
Milton Bradley games,
circa 1900. (No Pit,
Rook, Flinch, Authors,
or common types.) Also
wants space toys and
games, 1950–70.)

Toys Unlimited
1049 Keystone Ave.
Northbrook 60062
(312) 546-0460
(Buys antique toys and

trains.)

W. W. Tudor
P.O. Box 2053
Oak Park 60303
(Wants mechanical banks.)

Bill's Hobby & Collectors
  Shop
32 Main St.
Park Ridge 60068
(312) 823-4464
(Wants old toy trains,
1900–1960.)

INDIANA

Stephen Steckbeck
200 W. Superior St.
Fort Wayne 46802
(219) 742-5225
(Wants old banks, wood, tin,
iron.)

Scheid Tire Company, Inc.
9100 E. Washington St.
Indianapolis 46229
(317) 899-5355
(Buys used and old trains.)

IOWA

Eccles
902 Summer
Burlington 52601
(Mold for casting lead toys
wanted; also, old toys.)

KANSAS

Jenny's Junkue & Jewels
1443 S. Broadway
Wichita 67218
(316) 262-4382
(Buys old toys of all kinds.)

LOUISIANA

Royal Toy Store
534 Canal St.
New Orleans 70130
(504) 525-0105
(Wants old wind-up toys, tin
toys, dolls, and miniatures.)

MARYLAND

The Collector's Item
209 W. 25th St.
Baltimore 21218
(301) 243-5072
(Buys trains.)

French's, Inc.
304 W. Baltimore St.
Baltimore 21201
(301) 539-7140
(Buys trains.)

A. Windsor Galleries
1013 N. Charles St.
Baltimore 21201
(301) 539-2691
(Buys old toys.)

Pro Custom Hobbies
742 Frederick Road
Catonsville 21228

(Buys old trains.)

MASSACHUSETTS

Agawain Hobbies
300 Main St.
Agawain 01001
(413) 786-7210
(Buys old toy trains.)

The Hoj Poj
2014B Cambridge 02138
(617) 491-7522
(Buys toys and old dolls.)

Ro Charles Supply
    Company
736 Broadway
Everett 02127
(617) 387-8027
(Buys trains.)

MISSOURI

Ive's Train & Hobby Shop
12900 New Halls Ferry Road
St. Louis 63136
(314) 838-3860
(Buys trains.)

MONTANA

Central Hobbies
14th St. & Central
Billings 59102
(406) 259-9004
(Buys old trains.)

NEW JERSEY

S. & S. Coins
Berlin Farmers Market
Berlin 08009
(609) 767-0775
(Buys old trains.)

Rochat's Trains
408 Hwy. 17
Newark 07109
(201) 438-3087
(Buys Lionel trains.)

Lois Train Junction
563 Main Ave.
Passaic 07055
(201) 473-4720
(Buys old electric trains.)

Nostalgia Shop
53 Broadway
Passaic 07055
(201) 778-8841
(Buys trains.)

Matar
650 Pierpont
Rahway 07065
(Wooden puppets wanted.)

Ridgefield Hobby Center
595 Broad Ave.
Ridgefield 07657
(Buys old Lionel trains.)

F. H. Griffith
P.O. Box 323
Sea Girt 08750
(Cast-iron toys wanted.)

Bill's Trains
Box 833
Turnersville 08012
(609) 228-0096

(Buys used HO trains.)

NEW YORK

I. Chandler
Box 931
Middletown 10940

(Toy trains wanted.)

American Hurrah Antiques
316 E. 70th St.
New York 10021
(212) 535-1930

(Buys old toys.)

Chick Darrow Fun Antiques
1174 2nd Ave.
New York 10021
(212) 838-0730

(Buys old toys and comic watches.)

Edwin H. Mosler, Jr.
Suite 600A
401 7th Ave.
New York 10001

(Buys mechanical banks.)

PENNSYLVANIA

David K. Bausch
252 N. 7th St.
Allentown 18102

(Wants old toy cars, trucks, and objects having an automotive theme.)

(C) Harry McKeon
18 Rose Lane
Flourtown 19087
(215) 233-4094

(Lehmann toy collector. Buys.)

(C) Al Sabol
220 Outlook Dr.
Mount Lebanon 15228
(412) 341-0740

(Buys pre-1940 toy cars and trucks.)

Marvin Benson
345 Dixon Blvd.
Uniontown 15401

(Wants American Flyer and Lionel trains, and toy cars, trucks, buses, etc.)

VIRGINIA

(C) Ralph Berman
3524 Largo Lane
Annandale 22003

(Wants still banks.)

Wyatt's Hobby Craft Centers
118 Branch Road, S.E.
Vienna 22180
(703) 938-7441

(Buys old trains.)

GENERAL ANTIQUE DEALERS

ALABAMA

Cobb Lane
1 Cobb Lane
Birmingham 35205
(205) 933-0273

Cobb Lane Flowers
1318 20th S.
Birmingham 35205
(205) 933-8304
(Antique wicker furniture.)

Lacefield's Plantation
  Antiques
3685 Rockhill Road
Birmingham 35223
(205) 956-4990

The Antique Corner
231 N. & Rossclark Circle
Dothan 36301

Gardendale Auction
696 Main St.
Gardendale 35071
(205) 631-6400

Herefordshire Antiques
2908 Crescent Ave.
Homewood 35209
(205) 871-1832

Happy House Oldtiques &
  Gifts
2009 1st Ave., N.
Irondale 35210
(205) 956-3123

Atchinson Antiques
53 S. Warren
Mobile 36602
(205) 432-8423

ALASKA

Anchorage Auction
424 N. Klevin
Anchorage 99504
(907) 272-7734

Heritage House
6405 DeBarr Road
Anchorage 99504
(907) 333-1114

Homer's Inc.
Auke Bay Auction
P.O. Box 1040
Auke Bay 99821
(907) 789-9611

Now and Then Shop
10 Mi. Glacier Hwy.
Juneau 99801
(907) 789-0560

ARIZONA

Sudee's Antiques
809 N. Arizona Ave.
Chandler 85227
(Specialty: copper and
brass.)

Ron Brunk Auction, Inc.

6120 N. 51st Ave.
Glendale 85301
(602) 247-6472

(Specialty: mahogany and
cherry woods.)

The Buggy Stop
3201 E. Bell Road
Phoenix 85032
(602) 971-5030

(Specialty: relics from old
West.)

Fry's Antiques
6821 N. 16th St.
Phoenix 85016
(602) 277-0426

Millie's Antiques
712 N. Central Ave.
Phoenix 85004
(602) 254-5697

Red House Antiques
914 E. Camelback Road
Phoenix 85014
(602) 265-7795

(Specialty: primitives.)

Stuff—Antiques
407 E. Roosevelt
Phoenix 85004
(602) 252-0612

(Specialty: Tiffany Lamps
and stained-glass windows.)

Sylvia's Dolls & Antiques
3602 N. 24th St.
Phoenix 85016
(602) 957-0545

This 'N That
1014 Southern Ave.
Phoenix 85040
(602) 276-3140

Yesteryear Antiques
2811 N. 7th Ave.
Phoenix 85007
(602) 266-1146

(Specialty: American oak.)

Joanna's Antique Boutique
7125 Main St.
Scottsdale 85256

Sitting Indian Trading Post
3945 N. Brown Ave.
Scottsdale 85251
(602) 947-9246

Ye Olde Curiosity Shoppe
7245 1st Ave.
Scottsdale 95256
(602) 947-3062

(Wants old dolls and antique
jewelry.)

Christine's Curiosity Shop &
  Doll Museum
4940 Speedway Blvd.
Tucson 85712
(602) 793-0018

Hobby Hut
4578 E. Broadway
Tucson 85711
(602) 327-0565

(Buys used HO items.)

ARKANSAS

Margaret's Antiques
Hwy. 1675
Batesville 72501

Henson's Antiques
416 Remount Road
North Little Rock 72118
(501) 758-1426

CALIFORNIA

Alameda Marine Traders
1700 Clement Ave.
Alameda 94501
(415) 865-4050
(Specialty: nautical
antiques.)

Freeby's Antiques
2489 Main
Chula Vista 92011
(714) 423-2252

Shirl-Wil Antiques
1385 N. Magnolia
El Cajon 92020
(714) 442-5557
(Specialty: oak and Early
American primitives.)

Nina's Antiques
454 W. Colorado St.
Glendale 91204

Park Antiques
3168 E. Gage
Huntington Park 90040
(213) 589-0811

House of Yesteryear
8037 La Mesa
La Mesa 92041
(714) 466-7007

Richard Yeakel Antiques
1175 S. Coast Hwy.
Laguna Beach 92677
(714) 494-5526
(Specialty: seventeenth- and
eighteenth-century
antiques.)

Antique World
331 1st
Los Altos 94022
(415) 941-6480

ABCO Antiques
133 S. Vermont
Los Angeles 90004
(213) 388-7177

Copper & Things
371 N. Robertson
Los Angeles 90048
(213) 276-8800
(Specialty: country copper.)

The Marco Polo
123 S. Western
Los Angeles 90004
(213) 387-8689
(Specialty: Oriental objects.)

Old Curiosity Shop
Ian Arundel
8629 Melrose
Los Angeles 90069
(213) 652-4285

Portobello Road Antiques
8460 Melrose Ave.
Los Angeles 90069
(213) 653-3858

Daniel Postar
6808 Melrose Ave.
Los Angeles 90038
(213) 939-0834

What Not Shop
8271 Santa Monica Blvd.
Los Angeles 90046
(213) 656-6523

Howard's Furniture
2058 Old Middlefield Way
Mountain View 94040
(415) 968-5970

(Specialty: wardrobes and
sideboards.)

Marie's Antiques & Fine
   Old Furniture
2668 El Camino Real W.
Mountain View 94040
(415) 941-2988

Betty's Antiques
5387 Bancroft Ave.
Oakland 94601
(415) 261-9292

(Specialty: copper and
brass.)

Glenview Antiques
4230 Park Blvd.
Oakland 94610
(415) 482-1420

(Specialty: American oak

furniture.)

Yvettes Antiques
4636 Mission
Pacific Beach 92109
(714) 488-6050

A & A Furniture Co.
4231 Voltaire
San Diego 92107
(714) 222-5071

The Antiquer
4152 Voltaire
San Diego 92107
(714) 224-0107

Aubrey's Antiques
4622 Park
San Diego 92116
(714) 296-6464

Changing Tymes Antiques
2520 Adams
San Diego 92116
(714) 295-9534

Cob Web Antiques
3021 Adams
San Diego 92116
(714) 284-6579

The Connoisseur
3165 Adams
San Diego 92116
(714) 284-1132

Humberston's Antiques
228 W. Washington
San Diego 92103
(714) 298-1522

Lamb Antiques
2834 Adams
San Diego 92116
(714) 283-9505

McDonald's Antiques
3043 Adams
San Diego 92116
(714) 280-3720

Nancy Morris Antiques
320 W. Washington
San Diego 92103
(714) 291-2366
(Specialty: candy-store
antiques.)

The Owl and the Crow
729 W. Washington
San Diego 92103
(714) 296-4468

Showcase Antiques
804 W. Washington
San Diego 92103
(714) 299-1682

Ye Olde Smith Shoppe
3493 University
San Diego 92104
(714) 284-1467

Antique Cupboard
2512 Clement
San Francisco 94121
(415) 668-4841
(Specialty: Victorian
furniture.)

The Antique Traders
4314 California

San Francisco 94118
(415) 668-4444

Antiques by C. W. Moody
  & J. D. Lacey
542 B Mason
San Francisco 94102
(415) 981-6176

Antiques Unlimited
219 Monterey Blvd.
San Francisco 94131
(415) 585-7100

Robert K. Borman Antiques
1869 Union
San Francisco 94123
(415) 922-9411

Busvan Bonded Dealers
Clement & 4th Ave.
San Francisco 94118
(415) 752-5353

Carolyn's Antiques
1725 Taraval
San Francisco 94116
(415) 731-5892

Cinnamon Toast
3585 Sacramento
San Francisco 94118
(415) 921-1676
(Buys exceptional quilts and
American furniture of
1870–1910.)

The Collector
2130 Fillmore
San Francisco 94115
(415) 346-9270

311

1823 Antique
1823 Clement
San Francisco 94121
(415) 387-4311

Harrington Brothers
  Antiques
599 Valencia
San Francisco 94110
(415) 861-7300

Horsefeathers Antiques
3044 Fillmore
San Francisco 94123
(415) 929-9338

J. M. Lang Antiques
361 Sutter St.
San Francisco 94108
(415) 982-2213

Allen Maret
3036 Fillmore
San Francisco 94123
(415) 929-9339
(Specialty: old baskets,
Navajo blankets, Alaskan
items.)

Robert J. Neale
278 Post
San Francisco 94108
(415) 989-0319

Old Stuff Antiques
1728 Divisadero
San Francisco 94115
(415) 931-8860

Old Wagon Wheel Antiques
1125 Clement

San Francisco 94118
(415) 752-2117

Prairie Dog Emporium
3927 Sacramento
San Francisco 94118
(415) 751-4261

Solanne Antiques
2238 Polk
San Francisco 94109
(415) 775-1653

Sylvar Antiques and Fine
  Arts
1216 Polk
San Francisco 94109
(415) 776-0300

Youll's Antiques
1651 Polk
San Francisco 94109
(415) 441-8361

Joan Gray Antiques
1381 E. Valley Road
Santa Barbara 93108
(805) 969-4321

Detour Antiques
12378 S. Saratoga-Sunnyvale
  Road
Saratoga 95070
(415) 257-4010

Shadow Hills Antiques
P.O. Box 911
Tustin 92680
(714) 544-7055

Mignon's Antiques

Box 1384
Yuba City 95991
(916) 743-3568

COLORADO

AAA Auction
995 Sheridan Blvd.
Denver 80214
(303) 234-0110

Antique Trader
2227 E. Colfax Ave.
Denver 80206
(303) 333-9292

Bee's Antiques
4166 Tennyson
Denver 80236
(303) 458-5010

Gateway Antiques
2910 Tejon
Denver 80211
(303) 761-0650

Grandma's Stuff Antiques
5300 W. Mississippi Ave.
Denver 80226
(303) 922-3283

McKinley & Hill Antiques
4340 Harlan
Denver 80212
(303) 424-1102

Turn of Century Antiques
1421 S. Broadway
Denver 80203
(303) 722-8700

CONNECTICUT

The Tontine Emporium,
  Inc.
Settler's House
Rte. 7
Ridgefield 06877

D. & D. Auction Galleries
35 Pearl St.
Enfield 06082
(203) 745-8981

Antique Shop of Elizabeth
  Winsor McIntyre
Riverton (Hitchcocksville)
  06065
(203) 379-0846

Polly Jolly's Antiques
2964 Dixwell Ave.
Hamden 06518
(203) 248-3788

Red Door Shop
Old Saybrook 06475

Littlefield's Antiques
534 Whalley Ave.
New Haven 06511
(203) 933-1062 or (203)
  389-9264

De Lew's Antiques
514 Whalley Ave.
New Haven 06511
(203) 389-4893

The Antique Center
2614 Boston Post Road
Guilford 06437
(203) 453-9922

DELAWARE

George W. Thomas
Middletown 19709
(302) 378-2414

DISTRICT OF COLUMBIA

Arpad Antiques, Inc.
3125 M St., N.W.
Washington 20007
(202) 337-3424

Bonnie & Clyde
1101 Pennsylvania Ave.,S.E.
Washington 20003
(202) 547-3195

Arthur J. Dettmers, Jr.
2200 Wisconsin Ave., N.W.
Washington 20007
(202) 333-4887

Franco Antiques
3269 M St., N.W.
Washington 20007
(202) 337-5335

Georgetown Temptations
3210 O St., N.W.
Washington 20007
(202) 338-2336

Gonzalez Antiques
2601 Connecticut Ave., N.W.
Washington 20008
(202) 234-3336

International Antique
Buyers
2627 Connecticut Ave., N.W.
Washington 20008

(202) 234-4455

Old Antique House
817 Pennsylvania Ave., N.W.
Washington 20004
(202) 628-5699

Rose Brothers Antiques
3317 Connecticut Ave.,N.W.
Washington 20008
(202) 363-3681

C. G. Sloan & Company,
  Inc.
715 13th St., N.W.
Washington 20005
(202) 628-1468
(Auctioneers.)

Adam A. Weschler & Sons
905 E St., N.W.
Washington 20004
(202) 628-1281
(Auctioneers.)

FLORIDA

Little White House Antiques
5025 S. Ridgewood Ave.
Allandale 32023
(904) 767-4040

Mimi's Antiques
1311 S.W. 5th Court
Boca Raton 33432
(305) 392-7795

Sergeant's Elite Antiques
1018 N.E. 28th Ave.
Gainesville 32601
(904) 378-7627

The Auction Barn
8051 W. Beaver St.
Jacksonville 32205
(904) 781-9968

B & R Auctions
605 Edgewood Ave., N.
Jacksonville 32205
(904) 388-8063

Brass Lantern Antiques
4308 Herschel St.
Jacksonville 32205
(904) 387-0038

Johnny Appleseed's
3557 St. Johns Ave.
Jacksonville 32205
(904) 387-1424

Treasure House Antiques
1642 San Marco Blvd.
Jacksonville 32207
(904) 396-0869

AAA Furniture & Auction
190 N. Hwy. 17-92
Longwood 32750
(305) 339-7020

Lockwood's Antiques
1472 Guava Ave.
Melbourne 32935
(305) 254-6261

ABC Antiques
5927 N.E. 2nd Ave.
Miami 33137
(305) 754-6791

Barbara Saks Antiques

2250 Magnolia Dr.
Miami 33181
(305) 891-2623

Stoneage Antiques
3236 N.W.S. River Dr.
Miami 33139
(305) 633-5114

Attic Treasures
14811 W. Dixie Hwy.
North Miami 33161
(305) 947-4780

Alexander's Antiques
1115 Tucker Ave.
Orlando 32807
(305) 273-7220

Auction Exchange
11247 E. Colonial Dr.
Orlando 32807
(305) 277-8213

Dupont Center Auction
U.S. Hwy. 1, S.
St. Augustine 32084
(904) 794-0044

Gene's Used Furniture &
  Antiques
185 San Marco Ave.
St. Augustine 32084
(904) 824-9655

Hilda's Antiques & Curios
173 San Marco Ave.
St. Augustine 32084
(904) 829-6748

Pomar's Antiques

RFD 1, Box 74
St. Augustine 32084
(904) 824-2341

The Lavender Lion
17 Filmore Dr.
Sarasota 33577
(813) 338-3447

Berner's Auction
746 Reed Canal Road
South Daytona 32019
(904) 761-3652

Keene's Korner Kottage
400 S. Orlando Ave.
Winter Park 32789
(305) 644-4461

GEORGIA

American Eagle Antiques,
  Inc.
2181 Peachtree Road, N.E.
Atlanta 30309
(404) 355-4310

Atlanta Antiques Exchange
1185 Howell Mill Road
Atlanta 30318
(404) 351-0727

Colony Galleries
238 14th St., N.E.
Atlanta 30309
(404) 892-2843

Gold's Antiques & Auction
  Gallery
1149 Lee St., S.W.
Atlanta 30310

(404) 753-1493

Hudson Antiques Odds &
  Ends
905 Dill Ave., S.W.
Atlanta 30310
(404) 753-1056

Tom's Treasure House
1288 Oakdale Road, N.E.
Atlanta 30307
(404) 378-7976

The Attic Antiques
3227 Peach Orchard Road
Augusta 30906
(404) 792-1839

Merry's Trash & Treasures
1236 Broad St.
Augusta 30902
(404) 722-3244

Cliff's Antiques
2230 Wynnton Road
Columbus 31906
(404) 322-0208

Old Hub Antiques
Martinez 30907
(404) 863-7142

The Attic Antiques
230 W. Bay
Savannah 31401
(912) 234-4141

Rose M. Fromberg
407 Bull St.
Savannah 31401
(912) 233-8247

Stuff'n Such Antiques
125 W. Congress
Savannah 31401
(912) 232-9736

Temptations—Upstairs—
  Downstairs
230 W. Bay St.
Savannah 31401
(912) 233-5500

Warehouse Antiques
430 Paces Ferry Road
Vinings 30080
(404) 436-4812

HAWAII

Evelyn's Antiques &
  Unusual Gifts
Rm. 216, 1993 S. Kihei Road
Maui 96817
(808) 879-9998

The Treasury
85 Hana Hwy.
Maui 96817
(808) 579-9557

Tinny Fisher's Antique Shop
Mt. View
Hawaii Island 96814
(808) 968-6011

IDAHO

Antique Bargain Barn
2301 Illinois Ave.
Boise 83706
(208) 344-0224

Boise Antique Auction
1501 N. 13th St.
Boise 83702
(208) 342-9533

Bice Antique & Gift Shop
824 Winther Blvd.
Nampa 83651
(208) 466-6232

Trivia To Treasures
Rte. 1, Box 208
Orofino 83544

Star Galleri Antiques
Hwy. 44 & Star Road
Star 83705
(208) 286-7672

ILLINOIS

Williams Antiques
Albion 62806

Antique World
1440 W. Howard
Chicago 60626
(312) 743-1049

Beverly Hills Antiques &
  Collectibles
10605 S. Wood St.
Chicago 60643
(312) 239-0891

Brown Beaver Antiques
6826 N. Sheridan
Chicago 60660
(312) 338-7372

Direct Auctioneers

7232 N. Western
Chicago 60645
(312) 465-3300

Fischer's Antiques
2569 N. Clark St.
Chicago 60614
(312) 525-4999

Victorian House Antiques
806 W. Belmont St.
Chicago 60657
(312) 348-8561

The World's Antique Mart
1006 S. Michigan Ave.
Chicago 60605

Old Toll Gates Antiques
Rte. 5, Box 7X
Milan 61264
(309) 787-2392

Carousel Industries, Inc.
6288 Oakton
Morton Grove 60053
(312) 967-8290

Friendship House Antiques
111 S. Marion
Oak Park 60302
(312) 771-6064

Sentimental Journey
  Antiques
P.O. Box 82
Park Ridge 60068
(312) 698-2669

Rudy's Relics
532 Eden Park

Rantoul 61866
(217) 892-2554

Bocar Antiques
P.O. Box 3663
Springfield 62708
(217) 525-0271

Lord's Enchanted Cottage
567 Greenleaf St.
Waukegan 60085
(312) 623-0653

JRS Antiques, Ltd.
600 Green Bay
Winnetka 60093
(312) 446-0470

Suzanne Antique
  Accessories
384 Green Bay Road
Winnetka 60093
(312) 446-4656

INDIANA

Antiques from Helen Marie
909 Raible Ave.
Anderson 46011
(317) 642-0889

Rustic Relics
110 S. Line
Columbia City 46725
(219) 244-7246

The Wood and Stone
  Antiques
1116 Pearl St.
Columbus 47201
(812) 376-8337

Antiques & Interiors
404 E. Main St.
Delphi 46923
(317) 564-4195

Old World Gifts
3509 Broadway
Fort Wayne 46807
(219) 456-5437

Country Cousin Antiques
110 W. King St.
Garrett 46180
(219) 357-5587

Lois & William Altman
405 Bixler Road
Indianapolis 46227
(317) 787-1479

Cross Trade Winds
1422 W. Washington St.
Indianapolis 46222
(317) 632-9988

Earl's Auction Company
5199 Lafayette Road
Indianapolis 46254
(317) 291-5843

Golden Rule Antiques
9600 E. Washington
Indianapolis 46229
(317) 897-4080

Larry & Cathy Martin
4715 N. Winthrop
Indianapolis 46222
(317) 283-3618

Myers Antiques

8914 Southeastern Ave.
Indianapolis 46239
(317) 862-5012

Selected Antiques
8624 Pendleton Pike
Indianapolis 46226
(317) 898-4330

Things Unlimited, Antique
  Flea Market
24th & Meridian
Indianapolis 46222
(317) 923-0938

Trash & Treasures
2805 E. 10th St.
Indianapolis 46201
(317) 638-5145

VIP Antiques
1367 Sadlier
Indianapolis 46239

Livery Stable Antique Mart
120 Washington St.
Lowell 01853
(219) 696-9395

Emerson & Evelyn
  Niswander
1401 E. Orchard Drive
North Manchester 46962

Charlie's Kloset
P.O. Box 8
West Newton 46183
(317) 856-4172

IOWA

Northern Lite Antiques
317 Main Slater
Des Moines 50314
(515) 685-3032

The Lion's Den Antiques
RR 1
Ogden 50212
(515) 275-4011

Don Williams Antiques
2753 N. Court
Ottumwa 52501
(515) 682-52501

Ben Boone Valley Antiques
211 5th St.
West Des Moines 50309
(515) 279-7309

KANSAS

Betty Jean's Antiques
10941 State Ave.
Kansas City 66111
(913) 721-2233

Maude House
8009 Freeman
Kansas City 66112
(913) 299-6385

Sunflower
Lorraine 67459

M & M Antiques
Rte. 3, Box 62
McPherson 67460
(316) 241-1803

White Eagle Antiques
1215 Franklin St.
Riverside 66605
(316) 262-1514

Murfey Collectibles
P.O. Box 7113
Shawnee Mission 66207
(913) 341-7666

Anderson Antiques
4409 W. 17th St.
Topeka 66604
(913) 272-6454

Antiques Gallery of Topeka
3115 Huntoon
Topeka 66604
(913) 235-5956

The Century House
2100 Maryland
Topeka 66605
(913) 354-1776

Copper Kettle Antiques
1907 W. 10th St.
Topeka 66604
(913) 232-4844

Radenz Red House Antiques
2922 Munson
Topeka 66604
(913) 233-0914

Spencer Antiques-Oddiques
1937 Gage
Topeka 66604
(913) 272-8450

Woodshed Antiques

1903 W. 6th St.
Topeka 66606
(913) 233-3068

Mary Cowell Antiques
1213 S. Washington St.
Wellington 67152
(316) 326-2347

Antiques Plus
2130 N. Market St.
Wichita 67214
(316) 263-1564

Alma & Don Taylor's House
   of Antiques
1401 W. River Blvd.
Wichita 67203
(316) 267-7967

KENTUCKY

Nancy & Winfield Goblart
335 Bacon Court
Harrodsburg 40330

Amberson House Antiques
1622 Bardstown Road
Louisville 40205
(502) 451-9267

Arifactories Antiques
640 Baxter Ave.
Louisville 40204
(502) 583-4014

Auctions Unlimited
331 W. Oak
Louisville 40203
(502) 584-4131

Baize Antiques
620 Market St.
Louisville 40202
(502) 548-5916

Sexton's Antiques
213 E. Market
Louisville 40202
(502) 584-5080

Driftwood Antique Shop
U.S. 627
North Winchester 40391
(606) 744-9464

LOUISIANA

Brass Roots Antiques
3947 Magazine
New Orleans 70115
(504) 891-8989

Chartres Antiques
610 Chartres
New Orleans 70130
(504) 525-7870

Danny's Dungeon
1813 Magazine
New Orleans 70130
(504) 522-3042

Dixon Antiques
641 Royal
New Orleans 70130
(504) 523-6308

Juanita Elfert
633 St. Peter
New Orleans 70116
(504) 525-2964

Golden Age Antiques
3137 Magazine
New Orleans 70115
(504) 891-3201

Frank Kane Antiques
1809 Magazine
New Orleans 70130
(504) 525-7298

Moliere's Antique Shop
612 Chartres
New Orleans 70130
(504) 525-9479

The Queen Flea
3441 Magazine
New Orleans 70115
(504) 891-0481

Sanchez Antiques &
    Auction
1584 Magazine
New Orleans 70130
(504) 524-0281

White Pillars Emporium
8238 Oak St.
New Orleans 70118
(504) 861-7118

Idle Isle Antiques
P.O. Box 258
St. Joseph 71366
(318) 766-3902

MAINE

Antique Galleries
990 Wilson
Bangor 04401

(207) 989-3794

Bell's Antiques
489 Wilson
Bangor 04401
(207) 989-3357

Happy Acres Auction House
687 N. French St.
Bangor 04401
(207) 942-4958

Frank Taylor
400 Wilson
Bangor 04401
(207) 989-5287

Kings Kreations
Denmark 04022
(207) 452-2062

Lois & Kaye Siegel
46 N. Main St., Rte. 1
Ogunquit 04104
(207) 646-9735

The Barn
Gray Road, N.W.
Portland 04102
(207) 892-9776

Gem Antiques
25 Longwood Terr.
Portland 04102

Southwest Harbor Antiques
    Gallery
Clark Point Road
Southwest Harbor 04679
(207) 244-3162

MARYLAND

Art Mart Galleries
861 N. Howard St.
Baltimore 21201
(301) 669-8669

Ken's Antiques
710 N. Howard St.
Baltimore 21201
(301) 669-1127

Second Hand Rose, Ltd.
5748 Falls Road
Baltimore 21209
(301) 433-3077

Thayres Antiques
881 N. Howard St.
Baltimore 21201
(301) 728-7109

Antiques by Wallace, Inc.
4912 Cordell Ave.
Bethesda 20014

Walter Reed Antique Shop
8118 Woodmont Ave.
Bethesda 20015
(301) 652-2727

Mendelsohn Galleries
6826 Wisconsin Ave.
Chevy Chase 20015
(301) 656-2766

Beltway Antique Exchange
5810 Kirby Road
Clinton 20735
(301) 297-5814

Country Trader

11319 York Road
Cockeysville 21030
(301) 667-1060

Colonel James' Auction
  Galleries
4926 Wisconsin Ave., N.W.
Washington, D.C.
Also at: 9210 Baltimore Blvd.
College Park 20016
(301) 345-6363

Oland Antiques
RFD 1, Box 162
Frederick 21701

Crazy Al's Nostalgia Shop
Prince Georges Plaza
Hyattsville 20785
(301) 559-8262

Old Mill Antiques
6522 Sligo Pkwy.
Hyattsville 20782
(301) 422-2400

Kensington Art & Antiques
Box 423
Kensington 20795
(301) 949-2041

Montgomery's Antiques &
  Collectibles
2080 University Blvd., E.
Langley Park 20783
(301) 431-0313

Arlen Gue
6830 Olney-Laytonsville
  Road
Laytonsville 20760

323

(301) 926-0856

Yesteryear Farms (Antique
  Village)
7420 Hawkins Creamery
  Road
Laytonsville 20760
(301) 948-3979

Gaslight Antiques of Silver
  Springs
9311 Ocala St.
Silver Spring 20901

MASSACHUSETTS

Brimfield Antiques
Main St.
Brimfield 01010
(413) 245-3350

Ben Gerber & Son
1285 Belmont
Brockton 02401
(617) 586-2547

Washington Antiques
8 Cypress St.
Brookline 02147
(617) 566-9474

The Old House
Buzzards Bay 02532

Collector's Den
2020 Massachusetts Ave.
Cambridge 02138
(617) 776-6293

The Brown Jug
Main St. at Jarves

Sandwich, Cape Cod 02563

Windsong Antiques
John & Cassandra Baylis
243 Bank St.
Harwich, Cape Cod 02645
(617) 432-1994

Ox Bow Antiques
20 Germania St.
Jamaica Plains 02130
(617) 524-1269

Adirondack Antique Barn
345 West St.
Ludlow 01056
(413) 583-4430

Brookside Antiques
24 N. Water St.
New Bedford 02740
(617) 993-4944

Norm's Little Red Barn
380 Worthington
Springfield 01103
(413) 733-3334

Richmond Brothers
1562 Main St.
Springfield 01103
(413) 734-3191

The Blue Lady Antiques
283 Linden St.
Wellesley 02181
(617) 237-3442

MICHIGAN

Village Gate Antiques

407 N. 5th Ave.
Ann Arbor 48104
(313) 995-3335

Maze Pottinger Antiques
726 N. Woodward Ave.
Birmingham 48011

Plantation Galleries
6400 Davison Road
Davison 48423
(313) 743-5258

Jon Nielsen
22450 Park
Dearborn 48124
(313) 274-1660

DuMouchelle Art Galleries
409 E. Jefferson
Detroit 48226
(313) 963-6255

Diana Peters
3217 McClure St.
Flint 48506
(313) 743-0284

Robert L. Tedhams &
  Associates
1522 Garland St.
Flint 48503

Washington Street Antiques
110 Washington St.
Grand Haven 49417
(616) 842-9340

Lydia's Antiques
P.O. Box 141
Lathrup Village 48076

(313) 557-5104

J and J Antiques
18025 Division Dr.
Marshall 49068
(616) 781-5581

At the Sign of the Blue Pear
P.O. Box 209
New Buffalo 49117
(616) 469-2894

Longton Hall Galleries
117 Howard St.
Petoskey 49409
(616) 347-9672

Stable 'N House Antiques
1500 18½-Mile Road
Tekonsha 49092
(517) 767-4791

MINNESOTA

The Trinket Boy
P.O. Box 125
Champlin 55316
(612) 421-7586

Hansen's Antiques
6945 Park Ave.
Minneapolis 55423
(612) 869-5774

Temple's Antiques
6721 Portland Ave., S.
Minneapolis 55423

MISSOURI

Billy G. Hughes

30 Park St.
Farmington 63640
(314) 756-3176

The Pavilion Galleries
Rte. 2, Box 147K
Joplin 64801

Brookside Antiques
6219 Oak St.
Kansas City 64113
(816) 444-4774

Husted's Antiques
915 N. Osteopathy Ave.
Kirksville 63501
(816) 665-2392

Carter's Antiques
Rte. 3
Memphis 63555
(816) 883-5548

Joy Luke Antiques
P.O. Box 153
Novinger 63559
(816) 488-6666

Irene McMinn
8811 E. 61st St.
Raytown 64133
(816) 356-2181

Nichols Antique Buyer
5 Antique Court
St. Louis 63117
(314) 296-5561

Village Antiques
1215 S. Big Bend Blvd.
St. Louis 63117

(314) 645-7921

Ye Olde Shoppe
826 Louwen Dr.
St. Louis 63124
(314) 997-7885 (after 6 P.M.)

Park Central Flea Market
431 Boonville
Springfield 65803
(417) 866-9629

Elvira Rickmers
309 Academy
Wentzville 63385
(314) 327-4275

MISSISSIPPI

The Homeplace, Inc.
Hwy. 8, E.
Forest 39074
(601) 469-1761

MONTANA

Big Sky Antiques
2929 8th Ave., N.
Billings 59101
(406) 259-1298

Lefler Antiques
1404 Main St.
Billings 59101
(406) 252-1198

Antique Shop
108 S. Montana St.
Butte 59701
(406) 792-9008

Copper City Antiques
16 N. Montana St.
Butte 59701
(406) 723-8371

Merrie Antiques
2612 2nd Ave., S.
Great Falls 59405
(406) 452-4420

Al's Sales & Antique
    Furniture
343 W. Front St.
Missoula 59801
(406) 549-0822

The Woodshed
106 N. Main St.
Twin Bridges 59754
(406) 684-5559

NEBRASKA

Coach House Antiques, Inc.
135 N. 26th St.
Lincoln 68503
(402) 475-0429

Jo-em's Nook
2710 Vine St.
Lincoln 68503
(402) 477-2993

Payne & Son Furniture &
    Antiques
6036 Havelock St.
Lincoln 68507
(402) 467-1220

Raggedy Ann's Antique
    Shop

1527 N. Cotner Blvd.
Lincoln 68505
(402) 464-0456

Amity, Inc.
1214 Howard St.
Omaha 68102
(402) 345-7522

Beauty & Beast Antiques
5011 Leavenworth
Omaha 68106
(402) 551-6155

Cedar Island Antiques
8010 Cedar Is. Road
Omaha 68147
(402) 731-2511

Franx Antiques & Art
3124 Harney
Omaha 68131
(402) 345-5266

Frosted Lion Antique Shop
2204 S. 13th St.
Omaha 68108
(402) 342-4711

Ginger Jar Antiques
8604 N. 30th St.
Omaha 68112
(402) 455-2529

McMillan's Old Market
    Antiques
509 S. 11th St.
Omaha 68102
(402) 342-8418

Moore's of Omaha

327

5220 Ames Ave.
Omaha 68104
(402) 453-5230

Morris Antiques
5830 Maple St.
Omaha 68104
(402) 558-9700

Omaha Antique & Job
   Plating Co.
846 S. 24th St.
Omaha 68105
(402) 341-3193

Papio Flea Market
132 N. Washington St.
Papillion 68046
(402) 339-1484

NEVADA

Village Antiques
5947 Boulder Hwy.
East Las Vegas 89112
(702) 451-5258

Attic Antiques
1243 Las Vegas Blvd., S.
Las Vegas 89104
(702) 382-7760

Auld Country Corner
1626 E. Charleston Blvd.
Las Vegas 89104
(702) 382-3716

Buzz & Dave's Old
   Memories Antiques
1431 E. Charleston Blvd.
Las Vegas 89104

(702) 384-2400

Dell's Antiques & Gifts
1422 E. Clark St.
Las Vegas 89101
(702) 384-3234

Don's Den of Antiquity
1701 E. Charleston Blvd.
Las Vegas 89104
(702) 384-9053

Downtown Antiques
417 Carson St.
Las Vegas 89101
(702) 382-8885

House of Antiques
1334 Las Vegas Blvd.
Las Vegas 89104

Margie La Sorella
1800 Kassabian Ave.
Las Vegas 89104
(702) 731-6875

Lee's Antiques
1647 E. Charleston Blvd.
Las Vegas 89104
(702) 384-7848

C. G. Monson Antiques
509 S. 6th St.
Las Vegas 89101
(702) 384-6212

NEW HAMPSHIRE

Wilson's Antiques
2 Main St.
Goffstown 03045

(603) 497-4488

Ronald Bourgeault
Hampton 03842
(603) 926-8222

Lindentree Antiques
71 Depot Road
Hollis 03049
(603) 465-2542

Hookset Trading Post
Daniel Webster Hwy., N.
Manchester 03104
(603) 627-4969

Burlwood Antiques
Rte. 3
Meredith 03253
(603) 279-6387

Herbert Dyer Antiques
153 Atlantic Ave.
North Hampton 03256
(603) 964-5532

Leo R. Dupius
3 Boynton's Lane
Seabrook 03874
(603) 474-9970

Dow's Corner Shop
Rte. 171
Tuftonboro 03811
(603) 539-4790

NEW JERSEY

Abel's Antique Shop
1833 Boardwalk
Atlantic City 08401

(609) 344-6826

David Bauman Antiques
1506 Pacific Ave.
Atlantic City 08401
(609) 344-1242

Princeton Antiques
2917 Atlantic Ave.
Atlantic City 08401
(609) 344-1943

Kern's Antiques
1244 Heartwood Dr.
Cherry Hill 08003
(609) 428-6151

Trent Antique Shop
Main St.
Crosswicks 08515
(609) 298-9090

Bedlam Brass Beds &
    Antiques
19-21 Fairlawn Ave.
Fair Lawn 07410
(201) 796-7200

Antiques & Temptations
136 Main St.
Fort Lee 07024
(201) 944-1692

A Antiques, Inc.
110 Anderson St.
Hackensack 07601
(201) 342-7282

Riverview Antique Shop
1 Old New Bridge Road
New Milford 07646

(201) 836-6655

House of Treasures
U.S. Hwy. 1
Princeton 08540
(609) 452-1234

Herb & Alice's Antiques
U.S. Hwy. 130
Robbinsville 08691
(609) 259-3384

Antique Evelyn
132 S. Orange Ave.
South Orange 07103
(201) 762-7700

Beverly Antiques
2516 Pennington Road
Trenton 08638
(609) 737-0073

The Antique Gallery
35 Hadden Ave.
Westmont 08006

NEW MEXICO

Antiques Direct
2026 Central Ave., S.W.
Albuquerque 87104
(505) 842-1222

Cannon's Antiques
6215 Montgomery Blvd.,
    N.E.
Albuquerque 87109
(505) 881-0960

Hill Top Shop
Hwy. 66, S.E.

Albuquerque 87112
(505) 296-2880

Hansen Galleries
923 Paseo De Peralta
Santa Fe 87501
(505) 983-2336

Don J. Madtson Antiques
806 Old Santa Fe Trail
Santa Fe 97501
(505) 982-4102

Crespin Antiques of Taos
N. Pueblo Road
P.O. Box 357
Taos 87571

NEW YORK

Century House Antiques
Box 802
Alfred 14802
(607) 587-3322

Exquisite Antiques, Ltd.
2938 Merrick Road
Bellmore 11710
(516) 781-7305 or
(516) 432-2104

Mountain Ash Antiques
Box 54
Depew 14043
(716) 683-2188

Axtell Antiques
1 River St.
Deposit 13754
(607) 467-2353

Brickwood Antiques
RD 1
Gloversville 12078
(518) 725-0230 (after 6 P.M.)

The Carrousel
Box 736
Huntington 11743
(516) 423-1757

Kew Gardens Galleries
P.O. Box 255
Kew Gardens 11415
(212) 846-2563

Farmstead Antiques
Marian K. Peduzzi
Kinderhook 12106

Tuthill Cut Glass Company
   Museum & Stepping
   Stone Inn Antiques
Road 3
Middletown 10940
(914) 361-3211

The Woodshed
479 California Ave.
Middletown 10940

The Wicker's Antiques
Millbrook 12545
(914) 677-3906

Rusey Art & Antiques
P.O. Box 456
Millwood 10546
(914) 941-0920

Red Shutter Antiques
621 W. Green St.

Olean 14760
(716) 372-7599

The Antiques Center of
   America
415 E. 53rd St.
New York 10022
(212) 486-0941

Aubusson Chrystian
160A E. 55th St.
New York 10022
(212) 755-2432

Gem Antiques
415 E. 53rd St.
New York 10022

Hartman Auction Studios,
   Inc.
425 E. 53rd St.
New York 10022
(212) 371-1234

Keyman's Antique Shop
1026 2nd Ave.
New York 10022
(212) 355-6756

Lenard's Galleries, Ltd.
37 E. 12th St.
New York 10003
(212) 677-7260

Macklowe Gallery
1088 Madison Ave.
New York 10028
(212) 288-1124

The Manhattan Galleries
201 E. 80th St.

New York 10021
(212) 744-2844

York Antiques
46 E. 11th St.
New York 10003
(212) 893-7588

Lyon's Den
P.O. Box 565
Riverhead, L.I. 11901

The Glass Corner
P.O. Box 7130
Rochester 14616
(716) 225-2387

Cara's Corner Antiques
18 Sheridan Road
Scarsdale 10583

The Cobbler's Bench
P.O. Box 661
Smithtown 11787
(516) 979-7984

Village Antiques
7780 N. Main St.
Springwater 14560

The Olive Branch Antiques
Box 542
West Shokan 12494

NORTH CAROLINA

The Nostalgia Store
103 Cherry St.
Black Mountain 28711
(704) 669-6093

Morton's
133 W. Franklin St.
Chapel Hill 27514
(919) 967-5089

Mandarin Antiques
812 W. Pine St.
Farmville 27828

Byerly's Antique Shop
4311 Wiley Davis Road
Greensboro 27407
(919) 229-6510

Bernadette's Antiques
Hillsborough House of
    Antiques
Daniel Boone Complex
Hillsborough 27278
(919) 383-2033

Ezzard's Antique Shop
220 Church St.
Hillsborough 27278

Griffin's Antiques
220 Church St.
Hillsborough 27278

Edith Medlin Antiques
2747 North Blvd.
Raleigh 27604
(919) 876-6920

Mulberry Antiques
313 George St.
New Bern 28560

OHIO

Barnett's Antiques

11954 E. Gypsy Lane Road
Bowling Green 43402
(419) 352-5194

Cape Cod Antiques
7265 Far Hills Ave.
Centerville 45459
(513) 433-1585

Mar-Lae Antiques
P.O. Box 518
Chesapeake 45619
(614) 867-8966 (after 1 P.M.)

Mt. Washington Antiques
2204 Beechmont Ave.
Cincinnati 45230
(513) 231-8358

Grover Antiques
22450 Byron Road
Cleveland 44122
(216) 751-2444

Paul Brown Antiques
3866 Woodbridge
Cleveland Heights 44121
(216) 381-0034

Vel's Place
195 W. Schreyer
Columbus 43214
(614) 263-8460

The Post House
P.O. Box 456
Crestline 44827
(419) 683-1207

Brookhaven Antiques
3700 Grand Ave.

Middletown 45042

Hitching Ring Antiques
Box 56
North Bloomfield 44450
(216) 685-4764

Moran's Antiques
Box 181
Sycamore 44882

Mona Dennis Antiques
P.O. Box 2633
Toledo 43606
(419) 536-2994

OKLAHOMA

Trade Mart
600 S. 2nd St.
Ponca City 74601
(405) 765-9169

Sharp's 1860 Antiques
1860 E. 15th St.
Tulsa 74104
(918) 939-1121

PENNSYLVANIA

Wallace's Antiques
320 W. King St.
Rte. 30
Abbottstown 17122
(717) 259-7021

Black Angus Antiques
Mall, Rte. 222
Adamstown 19501
(215) 484-4655

Jackson's Antiques
701 E. 3rd St.
Route 11
Bloomsburg 17113
(717) 784-6470

Brandywine House Antiques
U.S. Rte. 1
Chaddsford 19317
(215) 388-6060

Bradley House Antiques
121 Witter Ave.
Connellsville 15425
(412) 628-2623

Fred A. Reed
374 Maple Ave.
Doylestown 18901
(215) 348-5829

Dynan Antiques
(Pocono Mountains)
125 Centre St.
East Stroudsburg 18301
(717) 421-4537

Benny's Antique Shop
100 N. 67th St.
Harrisburg 17111

Silver Spring Antiques &
  Flea Market
U.S. Rte. 11
Harrisburg 17111
(717) 766-7215

Kutztown Gallery of
  Antiques
19 E. Main St.
Kutztown 19530

(215) 683-8089

The Pewter Cupboard
Rte. 202
Lahaska 18931
(215) 794-7820

Kocevars Antiques
907 Lancaster Road
Manheim 17545
(717) 665-2981

Ross's Antiques
Apple Valley Village
Rte. 6
Milford 18337

H & R Sandor, Inc.
P.O. Box 207
New Hope 18938
(215) 862-9181

Joseph Davidson Antiques
924 Pine St.
Philadelphia 19107
(215) 563-8115

Edward G. Wilson
1902 Chestnut St.
Philadelphia 19103
(215) 563-7369

ABA Antiques
3524 5th Ave.
Pittsburgh 15232

Martha Brown
3524 5th Ave.
Pittsburgh 15232
(412) 681-6055

Bill Feeny Antiques
Rector 15677
(412) 593-2102

Gray Cottage Antiques
529 N. Keel Ridge Road
Sharon 16146
(412) 347-1184

Richard Wright Antiques
807 Schuylkill Road,
Rte. 724
Spring City 19475
(215) 948-9696 or (215)
   933-3072 (nights)

Cedar Hollow Country Store
Yellow Springs Road
Malvern
Valley Forge 19355
(215) 647-2648

Mack & Nicholson
1781 Lenape Road
West Chester 19380
(215) 793-1312

H. M. Cargan Antiques
P.O. Box 186
Yardley 19067
(215) 736-2153

C. L. Prickett Antiques
Bucks County
Stony Hill Road
Yardley 19067
(215) 493-4284

RHODE ISLAND

Hawthorn Cottage

Main St. (Rte. 138)
Hope Valley 02832
(401) 539-2914

SOUTH CAROLINA

Elizabeth Austin Antiques,
   Inc.
165 King St.
Charleston 29401
(803) 722-8227

One Thousand Gervais
1000 Gervais St.
Columbia 29201

TENNESSEE

Clements Antiques, Inc.
7022 Dayton Pike
Chattanooga 37343

Morton's Antiques
377 Parkway
Gatlinburg 37738
(615) 436-5504

Ault Antiques
1414 Watauga St.
Kingsport 37664
(615) 245-5378

Allison Antiques
4005 Franklin Road
Nashville 37204
(605) 383-6039

TEXAS

Tye Boll Weevil
Hwy. 6

Calvert 77837
(713) 364-2835

The Collectors House of
  Antiques
3900 Montrose Blvd.
Houston 77006
(713) 526-6296

Hazel M. Rawls Antiques
2117 Monterrey
Orange 77630
(713) 886-2554

Coles Antique Village
1021 N. Main St.
Pearland 77581
(713) 485-2277

Annie Lee Myers
Rte. 2, Box 540
Tyler 75701

VERMONT

Ebenhart Antiques
169 Cherry St.
Burlington 05251
(802) 863-3734

Coach House Antiques
Box 815
Manchester Center 05255
(802) 362-1436

VIRGINIA

A Thieves Market
7704 Richmond Hwy.
Alexandria 22306
(703) 360-4200

Hart's Antiques
7704 Richmond Hwy.
Alexandria 22306
(703) 360-9699

Perennial Antiques
2600 Commonwealth Ave.
Alexandria 22303

The Black Cocker
911 N. Quincy St.
Arlington 22203
(703) 527-9673

Collectors Corner
3200 Wilson Blvd.
Arlington 22201
(703) 527-9654

Cupboard Antique Shop
2645 N. Pershing Dr.
Arlington 22201
(703) 527-2894

Old Trunk, Inc.
3325 Wilson Blvd.
Arlington 22201
(703) 528-0400

Sandwing Antiques
1235 N. Irving St.
Arlington 22201
(703) 528-9229

The Balogh Gallery
1 Village Green Circle
Boar's Head Complex
Charlottesville 22901

Cannon Ridge Antiques
12716 Lee Hwy.

Fairfax 22039
(703) 830-2478

Daube's Old Brick House
923 W. Broad St.
Falls Church 23324
(703) 534-2120

Martin & Hare Antiques
706 S. Washington St.
Falls Church 23320
(703) 533-9278

Dean Wilson Antiques
Box 102
Fort Defiance 24437
(703) 885-4292

N'Atiques
Natalie F. Dynes
P.O. Box 7240
Roanoke 24019
(703) 563-1280

Petticoat Lane
Rte. 2, Box 2011
Virginia Beach 23456

Barn Village
Drawer B
White Post 22663

Swan Tavern Antiques
104 Main St.
Yorktown 23690
(804) 887-5078

WASHINGTON

That Log Cabin Place
U.S. Hwy. 2

General Delivery
Gold Bar 98251

Alley Antiques
Glena & R. J. Horn
8432 7th Ave., S.W.
Seattle 98106
(206) 763-8972

WEST VIRGINIA

John C. Newcomer
1141 Washington St.
Harper's Ferry 25425
(304) 535-6902

WISCONSIN

White River House
400 W. Chestnut St.
Burlington 53105
(414) 763-8042

Christophersen's
B-334, W. Fillmore
Eau Claire 54701
(715) 835-9886

Ellen Hannisch
4926 N. 40th St.
Milwaukee 53209
(414) 463-6738

Mineral Point Antique Shop
159 High St.
Mineral Point 53565
(608) 987-3617

Attic Antiques
4101 E. 2nd St.
Superior 54880

(715) 398-7051

Bluebeard Antiques
1911 Wisconsin Ave.
Superior 54880
(715) 394-7065

WYOMING

The Cottage
512 E. 25th St.
Cheyenne 82001

Holmes Auction House
3411 E. Pershing Blvd.
Cheyenne 82001
(307) 632-8813

Paces Antiques
4 miles N. of Hillsdale
Cheyenne 82001

Index

Academy of Comic Art, 73

Advertiques, 29–32, 94, 96
  dealers and collectors listed, 127–130

Advertising buttons, 31

Advertising cards, 31

American Book-Prices Current, 43

Anthony, Susan B., 37–38

Antiquarian Booksellers Association of America, 44

Antique Cameras (Smith), 58

Antique shows, 20–21

Antiques:
  advertising rates, 123–124
  fakes, 5–6
  general dealers listed, 307–338
  publications, 123–124
  shipping, 22–25
  value guides, 125–126

Antiques for Amateurs on a Shoestring Budget (Brunner), 7, 8

Appraisals, 12
  art, 35
  glass, 85, 86

Art, 33–41
  appraisals, 35
  collectors listed, 133–134
  dealers listed, 131–133

Auctions, 18–20

Autographs, 42, 43, 47, 48–49
  Civil War, 49

Avon bottles, 52, 53–54

Banks, toy, 109
  dealers and collectors listed, 301–306

Baseball cards, 8, 32

Batelle, Phyllis, 8

Batman comics, 9, 71

Bayonets, 76

Beatles memorabilia, 9, 88–89

Bee Hive china, 82

Beer advertising, collectibles, 31–32

Bibles, 45

Bicentennial memorabilia, 13, 87

Bingham, George Caleb, 39

Bitters bottles, 54–55

Blacksmith tools, 62

Blue Willow china, 84

Book Collector's Handbook of Values, The (Bradley), 43
Book fairs, 46–47
Books, 42–50
  Americana, 46
  bindings, 44
  comic, 8, 9
  condition of, 44–45
  first edition, 43, 48
  illustrations, 44, 45
  out of print, 42, 47
    dealers listed, 135–189
  rare, 43, 44, 46
    dealers listed, 135–189
  specialty, dealers and collectors, 190–195
Bottles:
  Avon, 52, 53–54
  bitters, 54–55
  blown, 51, 52
  Coca-Cola collectibles, 29
  collectors listed, 196–202
  colored, 52
  cork stoppers, 53
  dealers listed, 202–203
  historical, 55
  medicine, 14
  milk, 54
  original labels, 52
  patent date, 53
  perfume, 14
Bowls, wooden, 61–62
Brasher, Rex, 40
Bubble gum cards, 32
Bulletin of the National Association of Watch and Clock Collectors of America, 57
Bush, Mrs. L. E., 5
Butter churns, 62

Buttons, 74–75
  advertising, 31
  political, 88

Calendars, 97, 98
California Perfume, collectibles, 53
Cameras, 58–59
  collectors and dealers listed, 208
Campbell Kids, 96
  paper dolls, 8, 31
Candles, 117
Candy tins, 14
Captain America comics, 71
Captain Marvel comics, 71
Carder, Fredrick, 81
Cards, greeting, 96–97
Cartoon art, 73
Catalogue sales, 19
Catalogues, collectible, 71, 72
  dealers and collectors listed, 226–231
Ceramics, 119
Chandeliers, 61
Chapman, John Gadsby, 40
China, 10–11, 78, 82–86
  appraisals, 85, 86
  collectors listed, 239–247
  dealers listed, 247–253
  Dresden, 82
  hand-painting and decals, 82–83
  Haviland, 11
  Limoges, 11
  marks, 10
Chippendale antiques, 3–5
Churns, butter, 62
Cigarette cards, 32
Cigarette tins, 30

Civil War memorabilia,
74–75, 76
autographs, 49
Classified ads, 12, 15–16
Clocks, 56–58
dealers listed, 204–205
European, 57
Clothing, vintage, 63–66
markets listed, 266–268
Coca-Cola collectibles,
29–30
Coffee tins, 30
Coins, 67–70
cleaning, 68
dealers listed, 212–221
Comic books, 8, 9, 71, 72–73
dealers and collectors
listed, 226–231
Consignment, selling on, 18,
65
Contemporary Art Glass
(Grover), 81–82
Cookie tins, 14
Corning glass, 81
Counterfeiting, antique, 5–6
Craft shows, 20–21
Crafts, 113–120
marketing, 119–120
sewing, 114–117, 120
collectors and dealers
listed, 274–275
shops selling on
consignment listed,
275–277
*Curious History of Musical
Boxes,* (Mosoriak), 91
Currency, U.S., 67–70
Currier and Ives Prints
(Cunningham), 34
Currier and Ives prints,
33–34

Davis, Jefferson, autographs,
49
Declaration of
Independence, 50
Depression glass, 80
Diamonds, 104
Doll furniture, 107
Dolls:
character, 108
comic strip and movie
idol, 108–109
dealers and collectors
listed, 293–301
Shirley Temple, 8, 12, 109
Dough boards, 61–62
Drayton, Grace Weiderseim,
31, 96
Dresden china, 82

Embroidery, 115
Encyclopedias, 44
Engravings, 44
Exploration accounts, 46, 49

Fake antiques, 5–6
Fans, 30
Fashion prints, 35
Firearms, 74–76
collectors listed, 237–238
dealers listed, 232–237
mailing, 75–76
Fireplace collectibles, 62
Flapper clothes, 63
Flash Gordon comics, 71
Flasks, 51, 52, 55
collectors listed, 196–202
dealers listed, 202–203
Flea markets, 20
Folk art, 34–35
Folk festivals, 113–114
Forks, wooden, 62

Fountain pens, 105–106
Franklin stoves, 13
Furniture-making, 118

Garage sales, 12, 17–18
  and Internal Revenue
    Service, 17
Gems, 103–104
Glass, 6, 78–82, 86
  American, 11
  appraisals, 85, 86
  blown, 81–82
  collectors listed, 239–247
  dating, 14
  dealers listed, 247–253
  Depression, 80
  marketing, 85–86
  reproduction, 14
  Sandwich, 79–80
  shipping, 25
  "sick" glass, 10
  signatures, 81
  wire-insulators, 79
Glass of Fredrick Carder,
    The (Gardner), 81
Glossary of Packaging
    Terms, The, 25
Godey's Lady's Book, 35
Gold, 99, 100, 101, 103
  buyers listed, 278–292
  marks, 3, 99, 100
Gold in Your Attic
    (Bradley), 43, 46
Grant, Ulysses S.,
    autograph, 49
Guns, 74, 75, 76
  collectors listed, 237–238
  dealers listed, 232–237

Haviland china, 11
Heisey Collectors of

America, 80
Heisey glass, 80
Hildesley, Christopher
    Hugh, 85
Hobby Protection Act, 88
House of Kirk, 101

Insulators, glass, 79
  collectors listed, 196–202
  dealers listed, 202–203

Jackson, Stonewall,
    autographs, 49
Jade, 104
Jars, 51, 52
  collectors listed, 196–202
  dealers listed, 202–203
Jewelry, 99, 105
  buyers listed, 278–292
  handcrafted, 120
Jugs, 54
"Junque," 9

Karat marks, 3
Kewpie clubs, 95–96
Kewpie collectibles, 95–96,
    108
King Kong collectibles, 13
Knives, 74, 76–77
  collectors listed, 237–238
  dealers listed, 232–237

Lamps, 59, 60–61
  bridge, 60
  collectors listed, 206
  dealers listed, 205–206
  Tiffany, 78–79
Leather crafts, 117–118
Lee, Robert E., signatures,
    49
Leigh, William Robinson, 40

Letters, collectible, 46, 47, 48, 49
Libbey glass, 80–81
Limoges china, 11
Lincoln, Abraham, signatures, 49

Macramé, 116
Magazines, 46, 71, 72
  dealers and collectors listed, 221–231
Mail order, selling by, 22–25
Mailing, of antiques, 22–25
Manuscripts, 46, 49–50
Maps, 42, 46, 49
Marks:
  china, 10
  glass, 14
  gold, 3, 99, 100
  silver, 99, 100, 101
"Married" pieces, 6
  lamps, 61
Matchbook covers, 11, 31
Memorabilia, 87–89
  Bicentennial, 13, 87
  collectors listed, 254–258
  dealers listed, 254
Mickey Mouse collectibles, 109
Military collectibles, 74–76
  collectors listed, 237–238
  dealers listed, 232–237
Milk bottles, 54
Mirrors:
  Chippendale, 5
  shipping of, 25
Monster, 72
Montgomery Ward and Co., 72
Museum of American Folk Art, 35

Music boxes, 90–92
  dealers and collectors listed, 259–265
Musical collectibles, 90–93
  dealers and collectors listed, 259–265
Musical instruments, 92–93
  dealers and collectors listed, 259–265
Muskets, 74

National Geographic, 72
Needlepoint, 115
Nutting, Wallace, 35–36

Oddities, dealers and collectors listed, 209–211
Old Bottle Magazine, 55
Onassis, Jacqueline Kennedy, 65–66
O'Neill, Rose, 31, 95, 96

Packaging, of antiques, 24–25
Packaging for Mailing, 25
Paddles, wooden, 62
Paintings, oil, 33–37, 41
  shipping of, 25
Pamphlets, 42, 47
Paper collectibles, 94–98
  collectors listed, 270–273
  dealers listed, 269–270
Paper dolls, 8, 31, 94, 96
  collectors listed, 270–273
  dealers listed, 269–270
Patent dates, 10
Pearls, 104–105
Pennies, 69
Pens, 105–106
Pepsi-Cola collectibles, 30

Pewter, 102
  buyers listed, 278–292
Photographs, 33, 36, 40–41
Pistols, 74, 75, 76
Playboy, 72
Political memorabilia, 87–88,
  89
Porcelain, 82
Postcards, 11, 94, 95, 96, 97
  collectors listed, 270–273
  dealers listed, 269–270
Posters, 94
Pottery, 119
Primitives, 61–62
  dealers listed, 206–208
Prints, art, 33–34, 40, 41
Professional Numismatic
  Guild, 69

Quilts, 115–116

Raccoon coats, 63
*Record of American Uniform
  and Historical
  Buttons* (Albert), 75
Records, 7, 90
  dealers and collectors
  listed, 259–265
Revere, Paul, 107
Revolvers, 75, 76
Rifles, 74, 75, 76
Rookwood art pottery, 83
Rummage sales, 16

Samplers, 115
Sandwich glass, 79–80
Sandwich Glass Company,
  80
Saturday Evening Post, 72
Schielkopf, George, 34
Sculpture, 39–40

Sears, Roebuck and Co.,
  catalogue, 72
Secondhand shops, 18
Sewing crafts, 114–117, 120
  collectors and dealers
  listed, 274–275
Shaker primitives, 61
Shipping, of antiques, 22–25
Shirley Temple
  memorabilia, 32, 89
  dolls, 12, 109
  paper dolls, 8
Silver, 99, 100, 101, 103
  buyers listed, 278–292
  coins, 68
  marks, 99, 100, 101
Soft-drink collectibles, 29–30
Sotheby Parke Bernet, Inc.,
  85, 86
Spider-Man comics, 71
Spoons, wooden, 62
Stamps, 69–70
  dealers listed, 212–225
Steeple clocks, 56
Steuben glass, 81
Stiegel glass, 52
Stones, precious, 103–104
Stoves, 13
Stuart, Jeb, autograph, 49
Superman comics, 71
Swords, 74

Tea sets, children's, 107
Telephones, 59–60
  dealers listed, 209
  wall models, 60
Temple, Shirley. *See* Shirley
  Temple memorabilia
Tiffany antiques, 59, 78–79
Tin containers, 14, 30
Tin soldiers, 9

Tobacco tins, 30
Toys, 107–109
  dealers and collectors
    listed, 301–306
Trade cards, 8, 32
Trains, electric, 109
  dealers and collectors
    listed, 301–306
Trays, beer and soft drink,
    29, 30, 31–32
Turner, Thomas, 84
Typewriters, dealers listed,
    209

Uniforms, 74, 75

Valentines, 94, 95, 97
  collectors listed, 270–273
  dealers listed, 269–270
Victorian antiques, 6

Washington, George,
    autographs, 48
Watches, 57–58, 103
Watercolor paintings, 33, 35,
    36
Weapons, 74–77

collectors listed, 237–238
  dealers listed, 232–237
Wedgwood, Josiah, 83
Wedgwood pottery, 83
*Western World Avon
    Collectors Newsletter,*
    53
Whiskey flasks, 51, 52
Whistler, James McNeill, 36
White House Vinegar book,
    54
White House Vinegar
    bottles, 54
Whittling, 118
Who's Who in American Art,
    35
Who's Who in English Art,
    35
Wire-insulators, glass, 79
Woodcarvings, 118
Woodward Foundation
    Collection of
    Contemporary
    American Art, 38
World Wars I and II,
    collectibles, 74, 76

Yard sales, 17–18